The Black Librarian in America

The Black Librarian in America

Reflections, Resistance, and Reawakening

Edited by Shauntee Burns-Simpson, Nichelle M. Hayes, Ana Ndumu, and Shaundra Walker
Foreword by Carla D. Hayden

ROWMAN & LITTLEFIELD
Lanham • Boulder • New York • London

Published by Rowman & Littlefield
An imprint of The Rowman & Littlefield Publishing Group, Inc.
4501 Forbes Boulevard, Suite 200, Lanham, Maryland 20706
www.rowman.com

86-90 Paul Street, London EC2A 4NE

Copyright © 2022 by The Rowman & Littlefield Publishing Group, Inc.

All rights reserved. No part of this book may be reproduced in any form or by any electronic or mechanical means, including information storage and retrieval systems, without written permission from the publisher, except by a reviewer who may quote passages in a review.

British Library Cataloguing in Publication Information Available

Library of Congress Cataloging-in-Publication Data

Names: Burns-Simpson, Shauntee, editor. | Hayes, Nichelle M., editor. | Ndumu, Ana, editor. | Walker, Shaundra, editor. | Hayden, Carla Diane, 1952- writer of foreword.
Title: The Black librarian in America : reflections, resistance, and reawakening / edited by Shauntee Burns-Simpson, Nichelle M. Hayes, Ana Ndumu, and Shaundra Walker ; foreword by Carla D. Hayden.
Description: Lanham : Rowman & Littlefield Publishers, [2021] | Includes bibliographical references and index. | Summary: "This book will contribute to the discourse on ways of increasing anti-racism, empowerment, and representation in the LIS field and beyond. It continues in the civil rights legacy of African American librarian pioneers including Dr. E.J. Josey, Dr. Virginia Lacy Jones, Dr. Carla Hayden, and Dr. Eliza Atkins Gleason"— Provided by publisher.
Identifiers: LCCN 2021034087 (print) | LCCN 2021034088 (ebook) | ISBN 9781538152669 (cloth) | ISBN 9781538152676 (paperback) | ISBN 9781538152683 (epub)
Subjects: LCSH: African American librarians. | African Americans and libraries.
Classification: LCC Z682.4.A37 B575 2021 (print) | LCC Z682.4.A37 (ebook) | DDC 020.89/96073—dc23
LC record available at https://lccn.loc.gov/2021034087
LC ebook record available at https://lccn.loc.gov/2021034088

∞™ The paper used in this publication meets the minimum requirements of American National Standard for Information Sciences—Permanence of Paper for Printed Library Materials, ANSI/NISO Z39.48-1992.

Contents

About BCALA		ix
Foreword by Dr. Carla D. Hayden, Fourteenth Librarian of Congress		xi
Introduction by Editors		1

Part I: A Rich Heritage: Black Librarian History

Chapter 1	Libraries and the Color Line: Du Bois and the Matter of Representation—Rhonda Evans	9
Chapter 2	Wearing Many Hats: A Conversation with Robert Wedgeworth—Ana Ndumu	25
Chapter 3	Disadvantaged by (Financial) Design: The Disappearing Act of HBCU Library Science Programs—Aisha Johnson	39
Chapter 4	A Hidden Figure: Adella Hunt Logan, Tuskegee Institute's First Librarian—Shaundra Walker	53

Part II: Celebrating Collective and Individual Identity

Chapter 5	"I'm Rooting for Everybody Black": A Labor of Love—Jina DuVernay	67
Chapter 6	Assumed Identity: Realities of Afro-Caribbean Librarians—Twanna Hodge, Kelsa Bartley, and Kenya Flash	73
Chapter 7	The Western Librarian: Community and Collective Individualism—James Allen Davis Jr.	91
Chapter 8	Margins of the Margins of the Margins: On Being Black with Disabilities and/or Neurodivergence in Libraries and Archives—Kai Alexis Smith	103
Chapter 9	Uhuru Celebration of Individual and Collective Healing and Empowerment: Five Lessons from an Activist Librarian-Author-Griot—Roland Barksdale-Hall	123

Part III: Black Librarians across Settings

Chapter 10	Building Community through Digital Innovation: @BlackLibrarians and WOC+Lib—Shannon Bland and LaQuanda Onyemeh	141
Chapter 11	Empowerment through Access: Fostering Youth STEM Engagement with Culturally Reflective Library Services—Teresa A. Quick, Cheryl R. Small, and Amalia E. Butler	153
Chapter 12	Leading in Health Sciences Librarianship: Perspectives from Black Library Leaders—Bethany McGowan and Jahala Simuel	173
Chapter 13	The HBCU Librarians' Experience: Doing More with Your Time and Talent for Less Treasure—Jamillah Scott-Branch, Vernice Riddick Faison, and Danielle Colbert-Lewis	187

Chapter 14	Leading While Black: Are We Up for the Challenge?—Deloice Holliday and Michele Fenton	197

Part IV: Moving Forward: Antiracism, Activism, and Allyship

Chapter 15	Passing the Torch: The Tradition of Mentorship among Black Librarians —Satia M. Orange and Tracie D. Hall	211
Chapter 16	Rethinking Black MLIS Student Recruitment: A Call to Action—Vivian Bordeaux and Jahala Simuel	221
Chapter 17	Post-2020 Public Libraries: The Urgency for Community Dialogue and Healing—Taliah Abdullah, Hadiya Evans, Regina Renee Ward	233
Chapter 18	Thoughts on Sustaining the Academic Library —Angiah L. Davis and Michelle E. Jones	243
Chapter 19	Expanding the Black Archival Imagination: Digital Content Creators and the Movement to Liberate Black Narratives from Institutional Violence—keondra bills freemyn	251
	Afterword by Julius C. Jefferson Jr.	263
	Index	267
	About the Editors and Contributors	275

About BCALA

Established in 1970, the Black Caucus of the American Library Association (BCALA), was formed to serve as an advocate for the development, promotion, and improvement of library services and resources to the nation's African American community and to provide leadership for the recruitment and professional development of African American librarians.

As far back as the 1930s, a small number of Black librarians would gather in hotel rooms at ALA Conferences about the injustice they experienced at work and the lack of leadership opportunities for them. Under the suggestion of Effie Lee Morris, Black librarians met at the 1968 annual conference to discuss their concerns about not having a voice in the ALA. At a meeting in 1969, it was decided by several Black librarians that ALA was not serving the needs of Black library professionals, and the Black Caucus was formed to address those concerns. The following year, E. J. Josey, a member of the ALA Nominating Committee, wanted to find qualified Black candidates and socially responsible white candidates to run for Council in the 1971 election. Josey sent out letters inviting all African American librarians to attend the 1970 midwinter meeting to discuss a candidate they would support. In 1970 BCALA was founded at the ALA midwinter meeting by Effie x ~ About BCALA

Lee Morris, Dr. E. J. Josey, Thomas E. Alford Sr., and a few others. Dr. Josey was elected the first chairperson of BCALA. In 1992, BCALA became formally affiliated with ALA. One of the organization's most significant endeavors is the annual scholarship named after E. J. Josey. The scholarship offers financial assistance to African Americans to pursue a graduate-level library and information science degree. That same year also marked the first National Conference of African American Librarians (NCAAL). The conference is held every five years and brings together librarians from all over the country. In 2020, BCALA celebrates fifty years of service to librarians and the Black diaspora.

Foreword

Carla D. Hayden, Fourteenth Librarian of Congress

"No matter what accomplishments you make, somebody helps you."

—Althea Gibson, tennis champion

It is truly an honor to be a part of a book that is in celebration of the fiftieth anniversary of the founding of the Black Caucus American Library Association and the first publication of *The Black Librarian in America*. This volume is notable for so many reasons and has a special personal and professional resonance for me. It is the first time that a work about Black librarianship has been edited entirely by women. It brings the issues facing Black librarians identified a half a century ago into the context of current events, with special emphasis on the challenges that remain and must be addressed in the future. It is also an opportunity to reflect on the influences and people who were part of my own journey to become the first woman and African American to become Librarian of Congress—Black librarians in whose footsteps I followed and who always provided inspiration and support. They are part of the legacy of Black librarians in this country who provided the road map, helped thousands to chart their own journeys, and definitely made sure that their communities were respected and served.

The first edition of *The Black Librarian in America* was seminal for a new library associate in 1973, inspired by the words of Dr. E. J. Josey, Virginia Lacey Jones, Vivian Hewitt, James Welbourne, and A. P. Marshall, whose daughter Satia Orange had a significant impact at the American Library Association. As a new youth librarian, I was especially inspired by the legacies of Vivian Harsh, Charlemae Rollins, Augusta Baker, Henrietta Smith, Spencer Shaw, and Binnie Tate.

The influences and inspiration continued with the next edition, twenty years later in 1994, *The Black Librarian in America Revisited*. By that time, I had graduated from library school where Eliza Gleason, who was celebrated in both volumes, became the first African American to receive a PhD in library science. In addition, I was blessed to share professional experiences with contributors Alexander Boyd, Wendall Wray, Charles Brown, Lou Helen Sanders, Margaret Collins, Ella Gaines Yates, Clara Stanton Jones, and Lisa Biblo, whose mother Mary is legendary in ALA. I came to know Andrew Venable, Jean Curtis, Anna Curry, Hardy Franklin, Maurice Wheeler, and Lucille Thomas, who was a model of strength and excellence.

And so, with this edition, we renew E. J. Josey's observation in 1970 that hundreds of "Black librarians, including those deceased and retired, have been faithful to the highest ideals of the profession." My career was enhanced, propelled, and shaped by Annie Lee Carroll, Dorothy Evans, Deborah Taylor, Vivian Fisher, Theresa Edmonds, Martha Ruff, Kathleen Bethel, and Andrew Jackson. It is particularly fitting to have a tribute in this volume to Robert Wedgeworth, who was the first to be the executive leader at ALA. The perseverance and contributions of Black librarians will continue to pave the way for the next generations dedicated to service for their communities. I am sincerely grateful for their legacy.

Introduction

Shauntee Burns-Simpson, Nichelle M. Hayes,
Ana Ndumu, and Shaundra Walker

This book began with the goal of commemorating the fiftieth anniversary of the Black Caucus of the American Library Association (BCALA) along with the first publication of *The Black Librarian in America*. As if to remind us of both how far Black/African American librarians have come yet how little US society has changed, 2020 would bring with it virtually no cause for celebration. Instead, the year of crisis forced the world into solemnness and contention. Blacks/African Americans fought multiple perils: a merciless virus, police-led murders of innocent Blacks, emboldened white supremacists, and political and voter suppression. To be sure, none of these injustices, nor the resultant uprisings, were new. In fact, these conditions existed when the Black Caucus of the American Library Association was founded in 1970. Many of the chapters in the first iteration of *The Black Librarian in America* addressed racial inequality within and beyond the library and information science (LIS) field. Sadly, the constancy and potency of anti-Black racism has not changed. Despite notable professional gains, as witnessed through the inclusion of Blacks/African Americans in the highest echelons of library leadership, these milestones remain the exceptions rather than the norm among Black librarians not for want of professional capacity or dynamism but on account of bureaucratic or systemic icing out.

It is for this reason that we shifted this work to represent both memory and ambition. Rather than framing it as a badge of honor for arriving at fifty years, we hoped to capture how Black librarians have navigated structural disempowerment. We sought to be attentive to Black librarians' many achievements while also being mindful to not ignore the shortcomings and variance among us. It became important to expand this edition's coverage by including various intersections of Black/African American identity along with greater diversity of thought. As Black Caucus of ALA leaders, we fully know that there is room for improvement. It is our belief, for example, that Black women leaders need better support mechanisms. There were no women presidents in the first decade of the organization's history and, out of twenty-seven past BCALA presidents, only ten women filled the role. Not only does this volume represent the first *Black Librarian in America* volume to be exclusively edited by women, but it includes contributions from notable women library leaders such as Librarian of Congress Carla Hayden, ALA Executive Director, Tracie D. Hall, former director of ALA's Office of Diversity, Outreach and Literacy Services (ODLOS) Satia Orange, among several others.

A theme arose from our initial motivations and convictions: "Reflections, Resistance, Reawakening." We welcomed varied insight, that is, historical works that situate Black librarianship within long-standing societal and professional norms and critical-analytical pieces that probe our assumptions of both librarianship and Blackness, along with insight on the way forward. We received strong responses to some topics, while others, like the call for speculative and LGBTQ perspectives, went nearly unanswered. We expect that future iterations of *The Black Librarian in America* will fare better when it comes to deepening representation and imagining Black librarian futures. Still, we are optimistic that the book will demonstrate how Black librarians come out of and contribute to a remarkable but unfinished story. We are complex and soulful, perceptive and persistent. Racial oppression will never define us.

The Black Librarian in America: Reflections, Resistance, and Reawakening comprises four sections that took shape during a tectonic period in our country's history. Months of trauma prompted seemingly performative social justice statements and promises. We took earnest care in placing a boundary between this volume and the many posturing declarations from libraries, universities, government, the media, and other public institutions. Instead, we strove for an earnest, meaningful, and unified voice made up of both well-known and emerging thinkers from across the field.

The book leads with the section A Rich Heritage: Black Librarian History, which lays a firm foundation for the remainder of the book, as it explores various aspects of the Black librarianship experience. Rhonda Evans opens the section with chapter 1, a revelation of how the struggle for equal access to libraries has been an underexplored topic in larger discussions of the Black freedom struggle. Her case study highlights W. E. B. DuBois's work in partnership with other Black leaders to support Black women librarians working within the New York Public Library. The second chapter of this section features Ana Ndumu's interview with Robert Wedgeworth, the first Black executive director of the American Library Association. Their dialogue provides a rare glimpse into the life of a living Black librarian legend. Chapter 3 transitions the discussion to a different angle by revealing the struggles Blacks faced when seeking education for librarianship. The current problem of a lack of diversity within the profession is firmly anchored within the the challenge of gaining lack of access to library education programs. Aisha Johnson shines a light on the contributions of LIS education programs at Historically Black Colleges and Universities, suggesting that these institutions have the potential to once again significantly influence the number of Black librarians in America. In chapter 4, Shaundra Walker introduces two little-known activist-librarians, Adella Hunt Logan and Ruby Stutts Lyells. Logan's work on behalf of Black women as a part of the suffragist movement is well known; her brief but consequential role as the first librarian at Tuskegee Institute receives much-needed attention here. Similarly and relatedly, the life and career of Ruby Stutts Lyells, Mississippi's first professionally trained African American librarian, gains long overdue exposure.

Jina DuVernay opens the second section, Celebrating Collective and Individual Identity, with a poignant thesis on the ethic of care that characterizes Black librarianship, particularly when serving our own community. In chapter 5, DuVernay acknowledges a shared Black experience is such that Black librarians assume the role of advocates and intermediaries for their communities; this additional labor often goes uncompensated and unrecognized. It is born of a commitment to Black humanity. Yet, we are reminded of the variance among the Black population and especially Black librarianship in chapter 6. In "Assumed Identity: Realities of Afro-Caribbean Librarians," Kenya Flash, Twanna Hodge, and Kelsa Bartley discuss how librarians of Afro-Caribbean descent are subsumed within the African American narrative. They question "who actually counts as Black," as they put it. Through survey research and personal reflections, they underscore how racial identity is constructed and employed to exclude Black librarians with familial ties beyond the United States. Their chapter challenges us to probe assumptions of Blackness and belonging. In chapter 7, James Allen Davis Jr. describes the experiences of Black librarians in the American West. He draws similarities between the Tulsa, Oklahoma, massacre and the pioneering work of Black librarians in the neighboring state of Colorado, specifically the contributions of Black librarians to library service in the city of Denver. We also hear from Kai Alexis Smith, who provides yet another significant perspective in chapter 8. Smith centers Blacks/African Americans who live with visible or invisible disabilities. Kai writes in "Margins of the Margins of the Margins: On Being Black with Disabilities and/or Neurodivergence in Libraries and Archives" that Black/African American librarians have also contributed to the disability rights movement. However, there remains tremendous work to dismantle ableist and elitist structures within the field. Anti-oppression work must extend to making the library profession accessible through disability justice. And, quite aptly, the section Celebrating Collective and Individual Identity is bookended with "Uhuru Celebration of Individual and Collective Healing and Empowerment," in which Roland Barksdale-Hall urges us to remember that the differences among us as Black librarians must not deter us from fashioning a more hopeful Black existence. In chapter 9, Barksdale-Hall draws on the Swahili concept of "uhuru," meaning freedom, to present four lessons for healing and transformation as a profession and a community.

 The third section of the book shifts to exploring Black Librarians across Settings. In chapter 10, Shannon Bland and LaQuanda Onyemeh detail their commitment to creating Black librarian cybercultures. Their chapter on "Building Community through Digital Innovation" walks us through the inspiration, processes, challenges, and triumphs of designing @BlackLibrarians Network and WOC+Lib (Women of Color in Librarianship), two paradigm-shifting spaces that fuse professional development, social networking, and cultural celebration. In chapter 11, Amalia E. Butler, Cheryl Small, and Teresa A. Quick champion Black youth engagement through STEM education in "Empowerment through Access: Fostering Youth STEM Engagement with Culturally Reflective Library Services." They emphasize the role of school and youth librarians in transforming and improving STEM education for youth of color. Though they warn that STEM is not a cure-all for societal and workforce challenges, their message emphasizes that STEM participation among Blacks can improve medical, science, and technological advances on behalf of people of color particularly since medicine, science, and technology are often weaponized to inflict racial inequality. Chapter 12 continues with STEM, this time turning to health sciences librarianship, another sector in which Black librarians remain few in number. Bethany McGowan and Jahala Simuel present findings and recommendations from their study of the perspectives of Black/African American health sciences librarians. Their evidence-based suggestions are applicable to other library settings. Next, in chapter 13, Danielle Colbert-Lewis, Jamillah Scott-Branch, and Vernice Reddick Faison describe the realities of providing stellar service with limited financial and institution support, specifically at HBCUs. Finally, section III concludes with a call to action from Deloice Holliday and Michele Fenton, who in chapter 14 make a compelling case for leadership training and development for Black librarians. The library status quo will not improve, they argue, until librarians of color hold decision-making positions. Their chapter is vividly entitled "Leading While Black: Are You Up for the Challenge?"

The final section of the book, Moving Forward: Antiracism, Antiracism Activism, and Allyship, looks toward the future. In chapter 15, Tracie D. Hall and Satia Orange encourage mentorship by reflecting on their mentoring relationship as well as their experiences being mentored by other giants within the profession. Considering that this volume follows in the footsteps of other books in the *Black Librarian in America* series, theirs is a fitting tribute. Jahala Simuel and Vivian

Bordeaux follow in chapter 16 by speaking directly to Black LIS students and stakeholders interested in recruiting them to the profession, suggesting that social media can play an important role in increasing the number of Black librarians. They share the results of a pilot survey administered to Black LIS students that explored their career paths and motivations for entering the profession. In chapter 17, Taliah Abdullah, Hadiya Evans, and Regina Renee Ward discuss the promise and potential of the public library to address present challenges through public programming. Concrete suggestions are provided for promoting both community dialogue and healing as well as internal (library) healing and support among Black library workers. Relatedly, in chapter 18, Michelle Jones and Angiah Davis reflect on the present moment, considering lessons learned in the midst of a global pandemic and nationwide racial reckoning. In addition to making suggestions for improvement in academic libraries, they offer personal reflections from years of experience in the profession. Finally, in chapter 19, keondra bills freemyn focuses on Black digital content creators, situating their work squarely within the long tradition of Black memory collectors who have come before them, such as Arturo Schomburg and Jesse E. Moreland. By highlighting the work of projects such as The Free Black Women's Library, Black Archives, and Black Women Radicals, freemyn amplifies the potential for independent memory workers to bridge the divide between institutional archives and the Black community and suggests ways that both can work collaboratively to promote Black narratives.

Through their collective work, Black/African American librarians continue to improve the conditions of Black and otherwise minoritized people. It is this mandate that we set out to convey in *The Black Librarian in America: Reflections, Resistance, and Reawakening*. Certainly, there are many ways by which Black librarianship can be enhanced, and our hope is that this volume both energizes current library workers and inspires others to seize the opportunity to pursue librarianship.

PART I

A RICH HERITAGE: BLACK LIBRARIAN HISTORY

CHAPTER ONE

Libraries and the Color Line

DuBois and the Matter of Representation

Rhonda Evans

A close examination of scholarship on the history of the African American struggle for freedom and equality, specifically concerning the eras of Jim Crow and the civil rights movement, demonstrates that activism in libraries is often excluded from the narrative.[1] The rationale for the absence of this piece of history is an important discussion within itself due to the failure to recognize American libraries' tenuous racial history.[2] However, the consequences of not studying the efforts of African Americans to gain equal access to and employment by public libraries are that it allows for the assumption that this issue was not a priority to the Black community and it thus supports the sanitized version of American library history.

The truth, as seen through more recent scholarship, is that libraries have always been a part of the freedom struggle for African Americans.[3] Furthermore, this cause was taken up by some of the most notable leaders of the African American community. A prime example is W.E.B. Du Bois, specifically, the account of his work with other Black leaders of the early twentieth century to protect and promote Black women librarians at the New York Public Library.

Du Bois's Lifelong Affinity for Libraries

In a draft of a speech to be given at the Schomburg Library in 1957,[4] Du Bois explained the love he held for libraries from a young age to the significant role that libraries played in his scholarship.

> During the next half century, I worked in some of the greatest collections of books in the world. I sat long hours in the British Museum. I had a card to the great National Library in Paris. I worked in the largest library in the world, the Marx-Lenin Library of Moscow. I used libraries in Japan and the West Indies, and those in most of the great American universities. As a teacher I helped to open and arrange libraries in Wilberforce and Atlanta universities, where my own library of Africa and the Negro problems became of importance.[5]

It is therefore no great surprise that included among his many social justice causes was access to libraries and to the library profession. As early as 1902, while a professor at Atlanta University, Du Bois was an outspoken critic of the segregated Carnegie public library branch in Atlanta. Du Bois described the events in the *Bulletin of Atlanta University*:

> And so in behalf of these 36,000 Negroes my companions and I called upon the Trustees of the Library on this opening day, for we had heard that black folk were to have no part in this "free public library," and we thought it well to ask why.... Every argument which can be adduced to show the need of libraries for whites applies with redoubled force to the Negroes.[6]

Also, in 1906, not long after the Louisville Public Library for Colored People opened in Louisville, Kentucky,[7] a telegraph was sent to Du Bois requesting his thoughts on the library.[8] In his reply Du Bois stated, "*while I should prefer a library open to all cultures regardless of color* [emphasis added], I am nevertheless very glad to see what Louisville is doing."[9] Du Bois throughout his life was openly concerned with the integration of public libraries.[10] Perhaps the most significant demonstration of Du Bois's passion for equitable library services and careers was his involvement in the issues that arose with the early integration of the New York Public Library, specifically the 135th Street Branch.[11]

The 135th Street Branch

The New York Public Library was officially established in 1895,[12] and the 135th Street Branch opened to the public in 1905.[13] In the early twentieth century, Harlem's population was predominantly Jewish,[14] but as African Americans began to migrate North to escape the Jim Crow South and an increase in the immigrant population pushed Black residents farther north,[15] the Black population of Harlem increased from 5 percent in 1905 to 95 percent by 1925.[16] As Harlem began to experience a cultural movement of literature, art, music, theater, dance, and fashion, the community desired access to more resources documenting the Black experience from their local library, which also included a desire to interact with more Black library staff.[17] In 1920, the Urban League brought these concerns to the head librarian of the 135th Street Branch,[18] Ernestine Rose. Rose, who already had a long history curating library materials and services for immigrant communities, agreed with the Urban League that there should be a Black librarian on staff as well as more Black assistants.[19] In 1920, the first Black librarian, Catherine Latimer, was hired at the New York Public Library's 135th Street Branch; three years later, the second Black librarian, Regina Anderson Andrews, was also hired by Rose,[20] and Nella Larsen, one of the most celebrated authors of the Harlem Renaissance, served as the Children's Librarian at the branch from 1923 to 1926.[21]

The 135th Street Branch can be considered the library of the Harlem Renaissance. Names commonly associated with the Harlem Renaissance all had some form of involvement with the branch.[22] One only needs to review the Schomburg Center archives and collections to repeatedly see names such as Alain Locke, Countee Cullen, Augusta Savage, Aaron Douglas, Zora Neale Hurston, James Weldon Johnson, and of course Nella Larsen and W.E.B. Du Bois. Theater, art, and music were created and performed at the branch, and writers made constant use of the librarians' services and the library's resources.[23] Much has been written about Ernestine Rose's involvement in the integration of the New York Public Library as well as her other work concerning library services to Black communities.[24] However, Rose was not always viewed in the same glowing light, specifically by Black members of the library profession.[25] Although the branch she managed did employ the first Black librarians within the New York Public Library system, equal treatment, especially in terms of promotion and pay, became significant concerns of the Black librarians during this period in the library's history.

Prior to her career at the New York Public Library, Catherine Latimer studied library science at Howard University and then spent a year as an assistant librarian at Tuskegee Institute before returning to New York, where she had spent most of her youth.[26] During her early years at the 135th Street Branch, Latimer worked closely with the community, including many artists and writers we associate with the Harlem Renaissance.[27] In "1924 Latimer and Rose, with the assistance of famed bibliophile, Arturo Schomburg, and other prominent African Americans, worked on creating a 'reference collection of books on the Negro.'"[28] In 1925 that collection became the Division of Negro History, Literature and Prints, and Latimer was placed in charge of this division with a promotion to head reference librarian (Grade 3).[29] The following year, the library purchased Arturo Schomburg's massive collection of books, pamphlets, manuscripts, and art.[30] As head librarian of the Division of Negro History, Literature and Prints, it was Latimer's task to integrate this collection into the division.[31]

Du Bois also had a personal relationship with Latimer, as she was the daughter of two of his classmates from Fisk University, and her mother, Minta B. Allen, was a fierce advocate for social causes in her own right.[32] However, by the early 1930s, independent of Latimer, Du Bois had already developed a significant relationship with the New York Public Library, specifically, those employed at the 135th Street Branch. Rose personally reached out to Du Bois for his assistance, for example, to help develop the "Negroid Department" of the 135th Street Branch.[33] Also, prior to his intervention concerning Latimer, Du Bois was already working on behalf of Black constituents and librarians at the New York Public Library.[34]

It is also important to note that, unlike many public library systems at the time, the New York Public Library did not have an official policy excluding African Americans from library buildings or denying them library services.[35] However, despite not having a documented policy against access by Black New Yorkers, it was perceived that Black people were not welcome in many library branches.[36] Du Bois even claimed in a 1930 letter to the Civil Service Commissioner of New York that "for a long time no Negroes were admitted at all at the library branches even in colored districts, paid just as little attention as possible to the colored constituency."[37] There also appeared to be some resistance by the library administration to hiring Black staff and Black librarians.[38] This quickly became an issue of importance in predominantly Black parts of the city.

Case Study: Du Bois; the NAACP; and the Division of Negro Literature, History and Prints

In 1931, the New York Public Library hired Arturo Schomburg as the head curator of the collection in the Division of Negro Literature, History and Prints.[39] As part of the reorganization of the division, Rose planned to demote Latimer to a fieldworker in the library's new Adult Education Program.[40] In addition, plans were made to hire a "white, recent library school graduate, to catalog Schomburg's collection."[41] The demotion and hiring of a new librarian, especially a white librarian, to work with Schomburg's collection was, to say the least, a shock to Latimer.[42] The argument made by Rose (and later by Franklin Hopper, the chief of the Circulation Department) was that Latimer lacked the qualifications and skills to work with the rare items in Schomburg's collection.[43] Latimer stated in her defense that she had already been doing this work for five years and in addition had completed cataloging courses at Columbia University.[44]

Du Bois, who was made aware of Latimer's situation, intervened on her behalf. Familiar with Latimer as a family friend, but also in her capacity as a librarian, he believed the basis for her demotion was made in bad faith.[45] Du Bois was also aware that the argument regarding "qualified" Black library staff was frequently used as a defense by the library administration as to why there were so few Black librarians working within the system.[46] This argument was made weaker by the fact that current and previous Black New York Public Library employees, whom Du Bois corresponded with, noticed that white librarians and assistants were being hired instead of Black women with more education and experience. Du Bois spoke frankly to the library, "There is no reason except prejudice and jealousy which prevents the New York Public

Library from having in its system a reasonable number of intelligent and well-trained colored people." In addition, Du Bois pointed out that "[t]oday, there are only four colored persons in service and we learned with regret and astonishment that Mrs. Latimer is liable to be displaced from her position in charge of the Negro Division."[47] Du Bois also previously noted that in 1922 "Myra Logan and Lucille Spence have both applied at the library and been refused. Lucille Spence was a Phi Beta Kappa student and a new teacher."[48]

Du Bois closely followed the work of the Chicago Public Library, whose Black population had also significantly increased as a result of the Great Migration, and he kept up correspondence with some of its Black staff.[49] In a letter to Hopper he explained:

> In the city of Chicago, with a Negro population less than ours, although perhaps proportionately a little larger, there are thirty-six colored librarians in the service of the city, including three Branch Librarians, and numerous First Assistants. . . . Why should there be this extraordinary difference in these two cities if it does not arise from the fact that there is clear color discrimination in the library service of New York?[50]

It was also no coincidence that almost all of the library's Black employees worked only in neighborhoods with predominantly Black populations. In an earlier letter Du Bois sent to the library administration, he illustrated this point by explaining, "whereas there are forty-two branches in the New York system where white librarians may be appointed, apparently there are only one or two where the color line permits a colored assistant."[51] A survey conducted prior to this incident in 1922 appears to support Du Bois's claims that, although the library administration emphatically stated they wished to hire more Black staff,[52] it was not in fact a true part of the mission of the library. The survey, "Work with the Negroes Round Table," referencing the 135th Street Branch, explained that the integration of the library was an experiment.[53] It can be surmised that the initial hiring of Latimer was not considered a first step into full integration of the library but merely an experiment in a neighborhood already predominantly Black.

Not only were Black librarians not being hired in non-Black neighborhoods, Du Bois was concerned that library branches outside of the Black communities were not welcoming to Black patrons. As more

African Americans made their way to New York, Du Bois believed that the library resisted increasing services or staff to serve them: "the number of employees have not increased with the colored population . . . while promotion in library work has been increasingly difficult."[54]

After a year of correspondence and meetings, this specific incident was resolved in Latimer's favor. The decision was made that she remain in her role as the reference librarian for the Division of Negro History, Literature and Prints and Schomburg would serve as curator.[55] However, the greater lesson from this account is observing the effort and time Du Bois, the NAACP, and the Harlem community put into supporting services for the Black community and increasing Black staff members at the New York Public Library.[56]

Du Bois, the NAACP, and the New York Public Library

In a letter to the library administration in 1930, Du Bois and leaders of the Harlem community made clear that their advocacy was not just for Latimer but also on behalf of the constituents and all qualified African Americans who work for and apply for work at the library:

> The undersigned have been increasingly alarmed during the last few years at the relations of the New York Public Library to the colored population of New York City. For years the Library ignored the Negroes, even in the districts where they predominated. They were not made welcome and no literature was arranged to meet their wants or needs.[57]

It quickly became apparent that what was taking place at the New York Public Library concerning Black staff and patronage was an issue of top importance to other leaders of the Black community. Walter White, then acting secretary of the NAACP, refused to speak at an event organized by Rose in protest of the treatment of Black librarians, specifically Regina Andrews.[58] As the situation with Latimer continued, Du Bois began to reach out to notable members of the community, one of the first being legendary clergyman William Lloyd Imes. Imes immediately acknowledged that there was a "growing concern about the attitude and growing lack of respect for community opinion at our 135th street Branch Library."[59]

In addition to White and Imes, other notable leaders such as the writer George Schuyler; the Reverends Adam Clayton Powell Sr. and Jr.; the surgeon Louis T. Wright; board members from the NAACP and the YMCA; and other clergymen from across New York all expressed their concerns about the library. A letter with their signatures and others from the community states, "It would be shameful if a general movement for the betterment of colored people were turned into a method of demoting without cause their best representative in the library system."[60] In addition, the group requested that "a sincere effort be made to encourage the entrance of a reasonable number of well-trained young colored women to enter the library service and that no discrimination against them be permitted in the library system."[61]

Conclusion

The case study presented here is only one example of the fact that, in addition to schools, businesses, transportation, and public spaces, equal access to visit and be employed in libraries was an important part of the African American struggle for equality. Libraries provided free access to books, programming, space, and knowledgeable librarians, and therefore leaders of the Black community understood the importance of this institution in improving Black lives. Libraries have acquired over time the reputation as places of inclusivity. This falsity can partly be attributed to the fact that most works documenting African American history overlook the efforts concerning libraries by prominent members of the Black community, such as Du Bois, and organizations, such as the NAACP. To date there have been important works published on this topic but not nearly enough when compared to works published on other causes of the struggle for Black equality. The hope is that this case will encourage more scholarship on the valuable work and efforts to make the library profession and library services accessible to the Black community.

Notes

1. Aisha Johnson-Jones, *The African American Struggle for Library Equality: The Untold Story of the Julius Rosenwald Fund Library Program* (Rowman & Littlefield, 2019).

2. American Library Association, "ALA Takes Responsibility for Past Racism, Pledges a More Equitable Association" [Press release], June 26, 2020, http://www.ala.org/news/press-releases/2020/06/ala-takes-responsibility-past-racism-pledges-more-equitable-association.

3. Cheryl Knott, *Not Free, Not for All: Public Libraries in the Age of Jim Crow* (University of Massachusetts Press, 2016); Mike Selby, *Freedom Libraries: The Untold Story of Libraries for African Americans in the South* (Rowman & Littlefield, 2019); Shirley A. Wiegand and Wayne A. Wiegand, *The Desegregation of Public Libraries in the Jim Crow South: Civil Rights and Local Activism* (Louisiana State University Press, 2018).

4. W.E.B. Du Bois, "At the Schomburg Library, May 7, 1957," W.E.B. Du Bois Papers (MS 312), Special Collections and University Archives, University of Massachusetts Amherst Libraries, https://credo.library.umass.edu/view/full/mums312-b205-i044.

5. Ibid., 4–5.

6. W.E.B. Du Bois, "The Opening of the Library," *Bulletin of Atlanta University*, 1902.

7. William Yust, "The Louisville Library for Colored People," *Louisville Courier Journal*, 1906.

8. Louisville Free Public Library. "Letter from Louisville Free Public Library to W.E.B. Du Bois, April 17, 1906." W.E.B. Du Bois Papers (MS 312). Special Collections and University Archives, University of Massachusetts Amherst Libraries. http://credo.library.umass.edu/view/full/mums312-b003-i209.

9. W.E.B Du Bois, "Letter from W.E.B. Du Bois to Louisville Free Public Library, April 24, 1906," W.E.B. Du Bois Papers (MS 312), Special Collections and University Archives, University of Massachusetts Amherst.

10. Marjorie Kemp, "Letter from Marjorie Kemp to W.E.B. Du Bois, ca. April 1931," W.E.B. Du Bois Papers (MS 312), Special Collections and University Archives, University of Massachusetts Amherst Libraries, 1931, http://credo.library.umass.edu/view/full/mums312-b059-i091; Nellie M. Towns, "Letter from Nellie M. Towns to W.E.B. Du Bois, 1956," W.E.B. Du Bois Papers (MS 312), Special Collections and University Archives, University of Massachusetts Amherst Libraries, http://credo.library.umass.edu/view/full/mums312-b146-i030.

11. W.E.B. Du Bois, "Letter from W.E.B. Du Bois to the New York Public Library, February 18, 1930." W.E.B. Du Bois Papers (MS 312), Special Collections and University Archives, University of Massachusetts Amherst Libraries, 1930a, http://credo.library.umass.edu/view/full/mums312-b055-i475.

12. "History of the New York Public Library," New York Public Library System, https://www.nypl.org/help/about-nypl/history.

13. N. R. Jeter and D. Lachatanere, *Guide to the 135th Street Branch Records*, 135th Street Branch Records, Sc MG 219, Schomburg Center for Research in Black Culture, Manuscripts, Archives and Rare Books Division, New York Public Library, 2005.

14. Jonathan Gill, *Harlem: The Four-Hundred-Year History from Dutch Village to Capital of Black America* (Grove/Atlantic, 2011).

15. Marcy S. Sacks, *Before Harlem: The Black Experience in New York City before World War I* (University of Pennsylvania Press, 2006).

16. L. A. Walton, "Library Is Barometer of Race's Growth in N.Y.," *Pittsburgh Courier*, August 15, 1925.

17. Knott, *Not Free, Not for All*.

18. Ibid.

19. Celeste Tibbets, *Ernestine Rose and the Origins of the Schomburg Center*, New York Public Library, Astor, Lenox and Tilden Foundations, 1989; Rose's 1921 *Library Journal* article, "Serving New York's Black City," is a telling insight into Rose's understanding of New York's "Black city" and the need to have Black librarians on staff.

20. Bob Sink, "Catherine Bosley Allen Latimer (1896–1948)," *NYPL Librarians*, October 27, 2015, http://nypl-librarians.blogspot.com/2015/10/catherine-bosley-allen-latimer-1896-1948.html.

21. George Hutchinson, *In Search of Nella Larsen: A Biography of the Color Line* (Belknap Press of Harvard University Press, 2006); Nella Larsen is documented at the library as Nella Imes. Part of Larsen's career at the New York Public Library was spent at the Seward Park Branch.

22. Knott, *Not Free, Not for All*; the 135th Street Branch was officially renamed the Schomburg Center for Research in Black Culture in 1972. In the same year, the Schomburg Center also became one of the New York Public Library's four research libraries.

23. "Harlem Opens Theater School to Train Youth for Professional Stage; Will Develop Playwrights," *Pittsburgh Courier*, March 22, 1924, 9.

24. Tibbets, *Ernestine Rose and the Origins of the Schomburg Center*.

25. Morris Lewis, "Letter from Morris Lewis to Robert W. Bagnall, April 7, 1923," W.E.B. Du Bois Papers (MS 312), Special Collections and University Archives, University of Massachusetts Amherst Libraries, 1923, http://credo.library.umass.edu/view/full/mums312-b022-i237; Rose even chaired the Negro Round Table of the American Library Association, although many of her views were controversial among the Black members. See Knott, *Not Free, Not for All*.

26. Rhonda Evans, "Catherine Latimer: The New York Public Library's First Black Librarian," New York Public Library, March 20, 2020, https://

www.nypl.org/blog/2020/03/19/new-york-public-library-first-black-librarian-catherine-latimer.

27. "Schomburg Center for Research in Black Culture Records," Schomburg Center for Research in Black Culture, Manuscripts, Archives and Rare Books Division, New York Public Library, http://archives.nypl.org/scm/20769.

28. "Four Colored Girls Chosen by New York Public Library," *New York Age*, August 7, 1920, 1.

29. Bob Sink, "Regina M. Anderson Andrews (1901–1993)," *NYPL Librarians*, May 21, 2011, http://nypl-librarians.blogspot.com/2011/05/regina-m-anderson-andrews-1901-1993.html.

30. "Rare Library Brought to Harlem," *New York Amsterdam News*, January 19, 1927, 8.

31. Sink, "Regina M. Anderson."

32. Du Bois, "At the Schomburg Library."

33. Earnestine Rose, "Letter from New York Public Library 135th Street Branch to W.E.B. Du Bois, March 6, 1924," W.E.B. Du Bois Papers (MS 312), Special Collections and University Archives, University of Massachusetts Amherst Libraries, http://credo.library.umass.edu/view/full/mums312-b026-i019.

34. W.E.B. Du Bois, "Letter from W.E.B. Du Bois to Ferdinand Q. Morton, February 18, 1930," W.E.B. Du Bois Papers (MS 312), Special Collections and University Archives, University of Massachusetts Amherst Libraries, http://credo.library.umass.edu/view/full/mums312-b055-i465; Du Bois, "Letter to New York Public Library, February 18, 1930," 1930a.

35. Knott, *Not Free, Not for All*.

36. W.E.B. Du Bois, "Notes from Meeting with Franklin Hopper, ca. December 23, 1929," W.E.B. Du Bois Papers (MS 312), Special Collections and University Archives, University of Massachusetts Amherst Libraries, http://credo.library.umass.edu/view/full/mums312-b050-i161.

37. Du Bois, "Letter from W.E.B. Du Bois to Ferdinand Q. Morton, February 18, 1930," 1930b, 1.

38. W.E.B. Du Bois, "Letter from W.E.B. Du Bois to the New York Public Library, March 1, 1930," W.E.B. Du Bois Papers (MS 312), Special Collections and University Archives, University of Massachusetts Amherst Libraries, 1930c, http://credo.library.umass.edu/view/full/mums312-b055-i481.

39. Knott, *Not Free, Not for All*.

40. Ibid.

41. Sink, "Regina M. Anderson."

42. W.E.B. Du Bois, "Memorandum from W.E.B. Du Bois to New York Public Library, December 22, 1931," W.E.B. Du Bois Papers (MS 312), Special

Collections and University Archives, University of Massachusetts Amherst Libraries, http://credo.library.umass.edu/view/full/mums312-b060-i169.

43. Ernestine Rose, "Letter from Ernestine Rose to New York Public Library (excerpt), ca. 1931," W.E.B. Du Bois Papers (MS 312), Special Collections and University Archives, University of Massachusetts Amherst Libraries, http://credo.library.umass.edu/view/full/mums312-b060-i173; Franklin Hopper would later become the director of the New York Public Library.

44. Ibid.; this excerpt is cataloged as a letter from Ernestine Rose; however, there is no signature and actually appears to have been written by Catherine Latimer.

45. Du Bois, "Memorandum from W.E.B. Du Bois to New York Public Library, December 22, 1931."

46. Franklin Hopper, "Letter from the New York Public Library to W.E.B. Du Bois, February 26, 1930," W.E.B. Du Bois Papers (MS 312), Special Collections and University Archives, University of Massachusetts Amherst Libraries, http://credo.library.umass.edu/view/full/mums312-b055-i477; Hopper and Rose both adamantly expressed that race had nothing to do with the lack of Black librarians and they wanted to hire more but qualifications were the barrier. Later, they also claimed that financial constraints due to the Great Depression were also to blame.

47. Du Bois, "Letter to New York Public Library," 1930b, 2–3.

48. "Library Discrimination, ca. 1922," W.E.B. Du Bois Papers (MS 312), Special Collections and University Archives, University of Massachusetts Amherst Libraries, http://credo.library.umass.edu/view/full/mums312-b157-i378.

49. Kemp, "Letter from Marjorie Kemp to W.E.B. Du Bois, ca. April 1931."

50. Du Bois, "Letter to New York Public Library," 1930c, 1.

51. Ibid.

52. Hopper, "Letter from the New York Public Library to W.E.B. Du Bois, February 26, 1930."

53. Knott, *Not Free, Not for All*.

54. Du Bois, "Memorandum from W.E.B. Du Bois to New York Public Library, December 22, 1931."

55. W.E.B. Du Bois, "Memorandum of Interview between W.E.B. Du Bois and New York Public Library, January 13, 1932," W.E.B. Du Bois Papers (MS 312), Special Collections and University Archives, University of Massachusetts Amherst Libraries, http://credo.library.umass.edu/view/full/mums312-b063-i291.

56. "Deny Library's Staff Will Be Jim Crow One," *New York Amsterdam News*, October 16, 1937; these claims continued long after the incident with Latimer was resolved. Claims were made that the library would not give Afri-

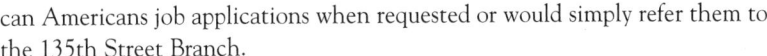

can Americans job applications when requested or would simply refer them to the 135th Street Branch.
57. Du Bois, "Memo between DuBois and NYPL," 1932, 1.
58. Walter White, "Letter from Walter White to Ernestine Rose, February 20, 1930," W.E.B. Du Bois Papers (MS 312), Special Collections and University Archives, University of Massachusetts Amherst Libraries, http://credo.library.umass.edu/view/full/mums312-b055-i178.
59. William Lloyd Imes, "Letter from Nella Imes to W.E.B. Du Bois, December 5, 1931," W.E.B. Du Bois Papers (MS 312), Special Collections and University Archives, University of Massachusetts Amherst Libraries, http://credo.library.umass.edu/view/full/mums312-b058-i456.
60. Du Bois, "Memo between DuBois and NYPL," 1932, 3.
61. Ibid.

Bibliography

American Library Association. "ALA Takes Responsibility for Past Racism, Pledges a More Equitable Association" [Press release]. June 26, 2020. http://www.ala.org/news/press-releases/2020/06/ala-takes-responsibility-past-racism-pledges-more-equitable-association.

Du Bois, W.E.B. "The Opening of the Library." *Bulletin of Atlanta University* 127 (1902): 4.

———. "Letter from W.E.B. Du Bois to Louisville Free Public Library, April 24, 1906." W.E.B. Du Bois Papers (MS 312). Special Collections and University Archives, University of Massachusetts Amherst Libraries, 1906. http://credo.library.umass.edu/view/full/mums312-b003-i210.

———. "Notes from Meeting with Franklin Hopper, ca. December 23, 1929." W.E.B. Du Bois Papers (MS 312). Special Collections and University Archives, University of Massachusetts Amherst Libraries, 1929. http://credo.library.umass.edu/view/full/mums312-b050-i161.

———. "Letter from W.E.B. Du Bois to the New York Public Library, February 18, 1930." W.E.B. Du Bois Papers (MS 312). Special Collections and University Archives, University of Massachusetts Amherst Libraries, 1930a. http://credo.library.umass.edu/view/full/mums312-b055-i475.

———. "Letter from W.E.B. Du Bois to Ferdinand Q. Morton, February 18, 1930." W.E.B. Du Bois Papers (MS 312). Special Collections and University Archives, University of Massachusetts Amherst Libraries, 1930b. http://credo.library.umass.edu/view/full/mums312-b055-i465.

———. "Letter from W.E.B. Du Bois to the New York Public Library, March 1, 1930." W.E.B. Du Bois Papers (MS 312). Special Collections and University Archives, University of Massachusetts Amherst Libraries, 1930c. http://credo.library.umass.edu/view/full/mums312-b055-i481.

———. "Memorandum from W.E.B. Du Bois to New York Public Library, December 22, 1931." W.E.B. Du Bois Papers (MS 312). Special Collections and University Archives, University of Massachusetts Amherst Libraries, 1931. http://credo.library.umass.edu/view/full/mums312-b060-i169.

———. "Memorandum of Interview between W.E.B. Du Bois and New York Public Library, January 13, 1932." W.E.B. Du Bois Papers (MS 312). Special Collections and University Archives, University of Massachusetts Amherst Libraries, 1932. http://credo.library.umass.edu/view/full/mums312-b063-i291.

———. "At the Schomburg Library, May 7, 1957." W.E.B. Du Bois Papers (MS 312). Special Collections and University Archives, University of Massachusetts Amherst Libraries, 1957. https://credo.library.umass.edu/view/full/mums312-b205-i044.

Evans, Rhonda. "Catherine Latimer: The New York Public Library's First Black Librarian." New York Public Library. March 20, 2020. https://www.nypl.org/blog/2020/03/19/new-york-public-library-first-black-librarian-catherine-latimer.

Gill, Jonathan. *Harlem: The Four-Hundred-Year History from Dutch Village to Capital of Black America*. Grove/Atlantic, 2011.

Hopper, Franklin. "Letter from the New York Public Library to W.E.B. Du Bois, February 26, 1930." W.E.B. Du Bois Papers (MS 312). Special Collections and University Archives, University of Massachusetts Amherst Libraries, 1930. http://credo.library.umass.edu/view/full/mums312-b055-i477.

Hutchinson, George. *In Search of Nella Larsen: A Biography of the Color Line*. Belknap Press of Harvard University Press, 2006.

William Lloyd, Nella. "Letter from Nella Imes to W.E.B. Du Bois, December 5, 1931." W.E.B. Du Bois Papers (MS 312). Special Collections and University Archives, University of Massachusetts Amherst Libraries, 1931. http://credo.library.umass.edu/view/full/mums312-b058-i456.

Jeter, N. R., and D. Lachatanere. *Guide to the 135th Street Branch Records*. 135th Street Branch Records, Sc MG 219, Schomburg Center for Research in Black Culture, Manuscripts, Archives and Rare Books Division, New York Public Library, 2005.

Johnson-Jones, Aisha. *The African American Struggle for Library Equality: The Untold Story of the Julius Rosenwald Fund Library Program*. Rowman & Littlefield, 2019.

Kemp, Marjorie. "Letter from Marjorie Kemp to W.E.B. Du Bois, ca. April 1931." W.E.B. Du Bois Papers (MS 312). Special Collections and University Archives, University of Massachusetts Amherst Libraries, 1931. http://credo.library.umass.edu/view/full/mums312-b059-i091.

Knott, Cheryl. *Not Free, Not for All: Public Libraries in the Age of Jim Crow.* University of Massachusetts Press, 2016.

Lewis, Morris. "Letter from Morris Lewis to Robert W. Bagnall, April 7, 1923." W.E.B. Du Bois Papers (MS 312). Special Collections and University Archives, University of Massachusetts Amherst Libraries, 1923. http://credo.library.umass.edu/view/full/mums312-b022-i237.

"Library Discrimination, ca. 1922." W.E.B. Du Bois Papers (MS 312). Special Collections and University Archives, University of Massachusetts Amherst Libraries. http://credo.library.umass.edu/view/full/mums312-b157-i378.

Louisville Free Public Library. "Letter from Louisville Free Public Library to W.E.B. Du Bois, April 17, 1906." W.E.B. Du Bois Papers (MS 312). Special Collections and University Archives, University of Massachusetts Amherst Libraries. http://credo.library.umass.edu/view/full/mums312-b003-i209.

New York Age. "Four Colored Girls Chosen by New York Public Library." August 7, 1920, 1.

New York Amsterdam News. "Deny Library's Staff Will Be Jim Crow One." October 16, 1937.

New York Amsterdam News. "Rare Library Brought to Harlem." January 19, 1927, 8.

New York Public Library System. "History of the New York Public Library." https://www.nypl.org/help/about-nypl/history.

New York Times. "Minta Bosley Trotman." May 4, 1949, 29.

Pittsburgh Courier. "Harlem Opens Theater School to Train Youth for Professional Stage; Will Develop Playwrights." March 22, 1924, 9.

Rose, Earnestine. "Letter from New York Public Library 135th Street Branch to W.E.B. Du Bois, March 6, 1924." W.E.B. Du Bois Papers (MS 312). Special Collections and University Archives, University of Massachusetts Amherst Libraries, 1924. http://credo.library.umass.edu/view/full/mums312-b026-i019.

———. "Letter from Ernestine Rose to New York Public Library (excerpt), ca. 1931." W.E.B. Du Bois Papers (MS 312). Special Collections and University Archives, University of Massachusetts Amherst Libraries. http://credo.library.umass.edu/view/full/mums312-b060-i173.

Sacks, Marcy S. *Before Harlem: The Black Experience in New York City before World War I.* University of Pennsylvania Press, 2006.

"Schomburg Center for Research in Black Culture Records," Schomburg Center for Research in Black Culture, Manuscripts, Archives and Rare Books Division, New York Public Library. http://archives.nypl.org/scm/20769.

Selby, Mike. *Freedom Libraries: The Untold Story of Libraries for African Americans in the South.* Rowman & Littlefield, 2019.

Sink, Bob. "Catherine Bosley Allen Latimer (1896–1948)." *NYPL Librarians.* October 27, 2015. http://nypl-librarians.blogspot.com/2015/10/catherine-bosley-allen-latimer-1896-1948.html.

———. "Regina M. Anderson Andrews (1901–1993)." *NYPL Librarians.* May 21, 2011. http://nypl-librarians.blogspot.com/2011/05/regina-m-anderson-andrews-1901-1993.html.

Tibbets, Celeste. *Ernestine Rose and the Origins of the Schomburg Center.* New York Public Library. Astor, Lenox and Tilden Foundations, 1989.

Towns, Nellie M. "Letter from Nellie M. Towns to W.E.B. Du Bois, 1956." W.E.B. Du Bois Papers (MS 312). Special Collections and University Archives, University of Massachusetts Amherst Libraries. http://credo.library.umass.edu/view/full/mums312-b146-i030.

Walton, L. A. "Library Is Barometer of Race's Growth in N.Y." *Pittsburgh Courier.* August 15, 1925.

White, Walter F. "Letter from Walter White to Ernestine Rose, February 20, 1930." W.E.B. Du Bois Papers (MS 312). Special Collections and University Archives, University of Massachusetts Amherst Libraries. http://credo.library.umass.edu/view/full/mums312-b055-i178.

Wiegand, Shirley A., and Wayne A. Wiegand. *The Desegregation of Public Libraries in the Jim Crow South: Civil Rights and Local Activism.* Louisiana State University Press, 2018.

Yust, William. "The Louisville Library for Colored People." *Louisville Courier Journal.* April 8, 1906.

CHAPTER TWO

Wearing Many Hats

A Conversation with Dr. Robert Wedgeworth

Ana Ndumu

In 1972, just two years after the Black Caucus of the American Library Association's founding and forty-five years after the inaugural Negro Library Conference convening, Dr. Robert Wedgeworth became the first African American to be appointed to the role of American Library Association executive director. It would be another four years until Dr. Clara Stanton Jones became the association's first African American president and twelve years to Dr. E. J. Josey's service as the first African American male ALA president.

Wedgeworth's transformative leadership came at a critical point in library history. The two decades after the civil rights movement triggered tremendous social, fiscal, and technical challenges throughout the field, which necessitated both preservation and progression of library practice. His achievements are well documented: Wedgeworth oversaw changes that culminated in a net of twenty-two thousand ALA members; the successful National Library Week campaign; an increase in ALA property and real estate valuation; and a healthier, balanced organizational budget of more than $10 million in net equity. These milestones were no small feat given that Wedgeworth assumed the position of ALA executive director in the midst of pressure brought on by the introduction of computing technologies to library operations; strained relationships with Southern state library associations that were reluctant to integrate libraries; and financial challenges of a growing, complex organization. Under these circumstances, Wedgeworth ignited change throughout the library and information science field, beginning with his tenure as ALA executive director from 1972 to 1985; then dean of the historic Columbia University School of Library Science from 1985 to 1992; followed by university librarian at the University of Illinois Urbana–Champaign from 1993 to 1999; and, finally, president and CEO of ProLiteracy Worldwide, the largest international nongovernmental adult literacy training organization. In between those posts, Wedgeworth served two terms as president of the International Federation of Library Associations (IFLA). In his forty-year career, Wedgeworth authored and edited more than one hundred publications and received numerous awards, including the ALA Lippincott and Melvil Dewey awards from ALA; the Medal of Honor, the highest award given by the International Council of Archives; and, most recently, ALA's Honorary Life Membership. A graduate of Wabash College, the University of Illinois MLIS program, and Rutgers University's PhD in Information Studies program, Wedgeworth remains celebrated as a library pioneer among not only African Americans but librarians around the world.

I set out to explore how an African American male from the Midwest would go on to lead in a profession where there are few like him. According to the latest available US data, African American males comprise 0.67 percent of the US LIS field[1] and just 135 of 2,842 reported MLIS students in 2019.[2] Few Black or African American males hold positions as library directors or association presidents. Currently, there are only two African American males serving as a LIS program dean or director.

The goal of this chapter is to learn from Dr. Wedgeworth's multifaceted library career. What follows is a series of questions and answers that reflect our conversation on the state of librarianship and the special place that Black/African American librarians occupy within it. As fate would have it, Dr. Wedgeworth penned a chapter in the original *Black Librarians in America* book published in 1970. Over fifty years later, he again lent his voice to this important series.

Dr. Ndumu: It's a delight to converse with you today, Dr. Wedgeworth. You earned your MLS in 1961, during the civil rights movement. Nine years later, the Black Caucus of ALA was born out of this period of collective action and fight for racial equality. Please reflect on how you initially came to the library profession and your early experiences during and after receiving your MLS at Illinois.

Dr. Wedgeworth: When I got my MLS at the University of Illinois, the civil rights movement was just beginning. When I started my first job, I was the first African American librarian to ever work at the Kansas City [Missouri] Public Library. From the time I left high school, having attended racially segregated elementary schools and high school and on to an all-white college, it was all in a world where almost everything African Americans did was pioneering. So that's the environment. And when I joined the ALA in 1962 shortly after I got my MLS, the ALA appointed me to work at the Seattle World's Fair. That's when I became active in the ALA. It was just a few years later that the Social Responsibilities Roundtable was established. And that was a broader movement that the emergence of Black librarianship benefited from because there was already a sizable percentage of the ALA membership that was receptive to the ideas that were being espoused in favor of Black librarianship. That's the general background in which my career started.

Dr. Ndumu: To what extent did this decade influence your professional journey?

Dr. Wedgeworth: Well, at the Seattle World's Fair, I was introduced to the possibilities of applying computers to library problems. So I was really focused on advancing my professional career through additional skills that I had acquired, and that was really my primary motivation. I became one of the first librarians to actually apply computers to library problems. When I went on to work at Brown University in 1963, I developed the first fund accounting system for a major research library. I was really focused on my profession and developing my knowledge and skills of librarianship, including international librarianship. But I realized at that time that librarians didn't have difficulties understanding how to apply computers to library problems. What I realized was that there wasn't enough focus on giving librarians a clear understanding of the theory of librarianship and problem solving in general.

Dr. Ndumu: That's quite insightful. Do you think that that problem of a lack of theory of librarianship was ever addressed? Has the gap closed, in your perspective?

Dr. Wedgeworth: Not completely. I think events sort of overtook us because what happened was the introduction of computers to the library field overwhelmed almost everything else. And so people really didn't want to focus on theory; they really wanted to focus on applications. But my training at Rutgers—as in my doctoral study—was very helpful to me as far as understanding what was going on but also helpful later on in terms of strengthening my ability to engage in problem solving. It was during that period when I was at Rutgers that I became actively involved in Black librarianship.

Dr. Ndumu: To clarify, did you become involved in BCALA after it was formed or were you a part of its establishment?

Dr. Wedgeworth: I was a part of its establishment. Those of us who were involved in the beginning find it difficult to remember a lot of the things that happened because there were so many things happening at once. The summer before I began my PhD program at Rutgers, I received a Council on Library Resources Fellowship to study the Western European book trade. So, when I left the US to do that study, things were relatively calm within the ALA, even though there were rumblings of social dissatisfaction. I missed the 1969 conference in New Jersey. And when I came back to the US after that research study and I went to the meeting in 1970, there were all these new faces that I'd never seen before, who were actively agitating for change in the ALA. There was like a sea of change. All of this had happened at the New Jersey conference, which almost fell apart, and then continued with the Detroit conference that followed it.

What happened was a confluence of several different movements. Number one, we were still in the middle of the Vietnam War. There were lots of antiwar protesters who were active in ALA. The Social Responsibilities Roundtable was agitating for change to get librarians to recognize that it had broader responsibilities than just the technical understanding of librarianship. You also had the strengthening of Black librarianship where African Americans were actively asserting their interests and need for more prominent leadership roles within the ALA. All of these things are happening at the same time. So that came to a head in Detroit in 1971. And that was also at the time when they began the initial search for a new ALA executive director.

Under normal circumstances, I wouldn't have been even considered. They had sent out this broad letter asking for nominations, and I got one and threw it in the trash. It was something that was way above my pay grade at the time. But that initial search failed because there was so much turmoil in ALA. What was overriding all of these movements was that you had a new generation coming to power within the association. When they searched again for a new director, my name came up as a nominee. I decided that I would at least explore what they wanted to talk about because I had been studying the ALA and had written that article for E. J.'s book on how Black librarians should actively seek leadership roles within the ALA, using the Black Caucus as a platform where you can get leadership training and then project that into the broader association. That was the thesis.

Then I was called for an interview by the Executive Board of ALA to ask me what I thought about what was happening in the association and what they needed. What I came to understand very quickly was that the leaders of the association really didn't have a good idea of what was going on in the ranks because these movements were really being propelled by the ranks of librarianship, not by the leadership. And the leadership was, in general, a little perplexed by all of this because they couldn't understand these different movements coming together at the same time.

Dr. Ndumu: Becoming ALA executive director was quite serendipitous for you.

Dr. Wedgeworth: Yes, I just happened to be at the right place at the right time and had the right background. I had very strong training in fundamental librarianship. Then, I had a very strong research orientation. I had been introduced to a lot of the leaders very early in my career thanks to my director at the Kansas City Public Library when I first came into the field. When I went to my first ALA conference, he introduced me to a lot of the leaders in the field. At the time, the publishers would host these big cocktail receptions. The only people invited were the leaders in the association. And if you were a junior member, the only way you got into one of those receptions was if one of those leaders brought you into it. So, by the time I was interviewed, to ask my opinion about what was going on in the association, I knew most of those leaders from having been introduced to them very early in my career. Although I didn't have a big name in the association, they all knew me or of me.

Dr. Ndumu: This is a great segue into the next question: Needless to say, your career has really spanned a lot of boundaries from being a library director, library school dean, ALA executive director, and more. What role would you say was the most challenging? Which was the most rewarding?

Dr. Wedgeworth: Clearly, the thirteen years I spent as ALA executive director were, I would say, the most rewarding and really laid the basis for what happened later. I don't know that I have shared this with anyone, but at the time I was interviewed (I'm not talking about that first interview where they were just asking my opinion but, later, when I formally became a candidate for the executive director position) I had a formal interview with the ALA Executive Board. It just so happened that at the time there were three African American members of the ALA Executive Board. There was A. P. Marshall, who had run for president but hadn't won. He was second vice president of the association and, therefore, on the executive board. That position was later eliminated. Then, there was Virginia Lacey Jones, the dean at the Atlanta library school. And, finally, there was Carrie Robinson, coordinator, School Libraries, Alabama Department of Education. There had never before been three African Americans on the executive board. Many years later, when A. P. Marshall was on his deathbed, he told his wife that he wanted to talk to me because he had been one of my early mentors. He had been the director at Lincoln University in Jefferson City, Missouri, one of the HBCUs.

Well, when I got word that he wanted to talk to me, I called right away. We just had a really good time reminiscing. But at the end of that conversation, I said "A. P., I have one question to ask you." And he said, "Well, what is it?" And I said, "Well, when the ALA Executive Board interviewed me for the executive director position, what role did the three African American members of the board have in supporting my candidacy?" And he had a real hearty belly laugh; that was one of his great characteristics. He gave out with this big, big belly laugh. And he said, "You know, Bob, it was interesting. We didn't have to do anything." He said, "Most of those members already knew you and knew of your career from when you first started out. So we just sat back and let them talk about you and simply supported what our colleagues had to say." And I said, "Well, I always wondered about that because I couldn't figure it out. I wondered what role you all had played."

I thought that was interesting, the way he shared what actually happened. The significance of that was that I came into that position with very broad support among the leadership of the ALA, white and Black. That really was very important for me because this was, of course, the most important position I'd ever held and the most responsibility I'd ever held. I needed that support in the initial years. The ALA afforded me significant experience in handling large amounts of money that was not committed to staff or collections, and handling a sizable staff which I have not had before. So that was important. Secondly, it gave me exposure in dealing with issues at the national level, especially issues related to the Congress and the federal agencies. For example, I made an initial decision when I went to the ALA that I really wasn't going to try to get involved in the copyright issue. It turned out that I wasn't able to avoid it. I was thrust right in the middle of the discussions between the publishers and librarians about the revision of the copyright law and actively participated in resolving those issues that resulted in the Copyright Revision Act of 1976.

The other issue was that I had come into international librarianship from the book side because I had been actively involved in buying books internationally from my early career. When I got to Brown, I had this multimillion-dollar budget for buying materials from all over the world. I actively pursued that. And I actually made several trips to Europe to meet with our major booksellers who supplied books to the Brown University Libraries. When I got to the ALA, I had to be involved more actively in international work. But for the first time, I was involved in international librarianship, as distinct from the international book trade. The fact that those booksellers knew me helped me in introducing myself to the international library leadership. More importantly, there were a few individuals like Leo Weins, who was the president of the H. W. Wilson Company, and Robert Vosper, the director at UCLA's library, who was a vice president of IFLA. People were amused to see an African American ALA leader when I went to my first IFLA conference. All of their colleagues from primarily the

European countries kept coming to Weins and Vosper asking, "Is he really the leader of the US delegation?" They chuckled to themselves and said, "Yes, Bob Wedgeworth is the leader of the US delegation." So my colleagues were very important in pushing me forth into the international library community.

Dr. Ndumu: I wonder in what ways some of your other roles were challenging. Were there hardships?

Dr. Wedgeworth: Let me tell you a little bit about the challenges. When I was appointed the ALA executive director, which was in the spring of 1972, I met with a hometown friend, an officer in one of the major New York banks. And I called him and told him that I had this new job. And I had a multimillion-dollar endowment. I'd never dealt with an endowment. I wondered if there was somebody in his company who could help me. And he said, "Let me get back to you." He called me a few days later and said, "We set up a one-day seminar for you at our bank. Come in and the vice president for trusts will lead the seminar for you." I went into New York and participated in this one-day seminar. There were just three of us: my friend, the vice president for trusts, and myself. I had sent him three years of ALA's financial records and financial accounts. And what he told me was I didn't have financial problems; ALA had control problems. He said for an organization of its size, it generates substantial revenues. The problem is it didn't control those revenues. In other words, they were overspending their revenue. He said, "The two things you have to do when you go to the ALA is, one, you have to get control of the budget and, two, you have to get control over the size of the staff." So that helped me meet one of the major changes going in because I followed his advice and gained control over those things very early.

The other challenge that I had was legal. That is, we had a very good legal counselor who had a very strong tendency toward secrecy. ALA got into a lot of trouble with its membership because they would ask my predecessor and the chief financial officer questions about the association. And the legal advice that they received was not to reveal too much to the members. After I was at ALA for a couple of years, the firm that my legal counsel worked for broke up, and he moved with one of the partners to a new firm. Rather than just following him, I decided to open up the issue and invite several firms to bid for the ALA's business.

We ended up moving to another major firm that was more consistent with ALA's values. The process of making that move made me much more knowledgeable about the legal issues that affected the profession and the ALA specifically because I had to be able to articulate them for the different firms that were contending to be a legal adviser. So that was another challenge that I was able to meet.

I think what may have been most important was my experience in coming up through the profession through the Social Responsibilities Roundtable and the Black Caucus. It taught me that the rank and file, the people in the field, were really important. Therefore, the first year of my tenure at ALA, I spent a lot of time going to the state conferences, talking to people in the grass roots, getting to understand what was happening in the different sections of the country, and what was happening at the institutional level of librarianship. I think that was really helpful to me long term in my career because I always maintained a very strong focus on what the people out in the field were experiencing rather than getting caught up in what was happening in Washington and what was happening at ALA headquarters. So those were the major challenges that I had to face.

Dr. Ndumu: It sounds like a bottom-up approach.

Dr. Wedgeworth: Yes, and that was because I understood that change really starts at the bottom.

Dr. Ndumu: Following in that thread, what advice would you offer to those who want to transition into new areas of the library profession? For example, what sort of factors did you take into consideration when weighing professional opportunities, especially those involving leadership positions?

Dr. Wedgeworth: Well, I didn't really have much of an opportunity because I never actually sought other jobs. The jobs came to me, and then I had to evaluate how they would benefit me, my family, and my career. I would say that the first thing that people who have ambitions for leadership need to do is you have to really develop your fundamental understanding of the field. You really need to sharpen your knowledge and your skills of librarianship, regardless of what sector of the field you come from. Many of those skills are transferable: public librarians can go into special librarianship or academic librarianship, or an academic librarian can go into public librarianship. But what is really important is that you understand the fundamentals of librarianship.

So that's the thing that I would say: first learn your trade. Then, the second thing is don't just try to move; ensure that you gain experience. You see, by the time that I was considered for more senior positions, I had had over ten years in the field. Even though I had been offered opportunities to be a head librarian here and there during the course of those ten years, I resisted that because I felt that I had more to learn. My advice is try not to make your moves too quickly. Take advantage of every position that you hold in order to learn as much as you possibly can.

Dr. Ndumu: Let me segue into another topic. The 1992 closing of the Columbia University School of Library Science was a major shock to the field. Can you describe your experience as the last dean of that program?

Dr. Wedgeworth: Columbia had tried to close the library school before they invited me to be the dean. The trustees had said, "No, this is a school that has performed well throughout its history. We should invest in the school instead of trying to close it." So the president and the provost approached me to be the dean, and I turned them down. Initially, I said no. I didn't think they were serious, but they came back again and made lots of statements that indicated that they were serious about investing in the program. They were interested in revitalizing the program. So I went there, with the understanding that they couldn't give me any more money; I would have to build the school from within. I agreed. Now, what you need to understand is that higher education was under tremendous pressure to reduce its costs, especially the research institutions. And what tended to happen during that period in the late 1980s was that large academic programs survived. Small, professional programs didn't survive because they didn't have large alumni groups to support them. If you look through that period at what programs closed, they were almost always small professional schools and small academic programs, history of science, for example, or dentistry.

With that background, I went to Columbia. The small faculty in our program worked to really think through what we wanted students to know that would carry them through a career that might last forty or fifty years. We reorganized the curriculum. I brought in one of the real stars in bibliographic control from the University of Chicago. We developed specialties in our programs. The most important thing is that we followed the Canadian schools' example. We instituted a two-year program. We got through the first year of the first cohort when the university stepped in and said, "We're going to review the program." Now, clearly, they saw that if I got the second cohort of that first class in that not only would the school be on a firm foundation, but I would have additional resources that would allow me to recruit, say, a star faculty member from another part of the field. So they intervened, and I was a little puzzled by this. At that time, the director of the New York Public Library, who had formerly been the president of Georgetown University, called me down to his office. And he said, "Bob, I'm going to tell you something that you need to know, but I don't think anybody else will tell you." He said, "The president already has the votes in his hip pocket to close your school." And he said, "I'm not trying to tell you what to do. I just think you need to be aware of what you're up against." Now, clearly, what the president had done was that, after the trustees had turned him down when he wanted to close the school originally, he had just waited until the trustees had changed and came back to the same agenda. And that was what happened and how they ended up getting a vote to close the library school. I talked to the tenured faculty, and I asked them what they wanted to do. They said, "We've been through this before, but we're not going to fight the way we did before, just let them vote us up or down." We've never told that story for any publication anywhere, but I thought I would share it with you.

Dr. Ndumu: Would you say, then, that this was an agenda?

Dr. Wedgeworth: Yes, it seems that there was an agenda, and they needed to find evidence to support this trend. The treasurer of the university said that my school was one of the most improved schools financially of all the professional schools at the university. Well, anyway, those were the circumstances under which this occurred. As I said, you'd also need to see it in the broader picture of higher education at that time. Small professional and academic programs were under fire too; many of them were closed not because of quality but just because they were small.

Dr. Ndumu: It seems, then, that library schools are vulnerable in a way that other programs are not and they were forced to self-preserve.

Dr. Wedgeworth: If you look at the schools that have thrived under these circumstances, they're mostly the programs in public universities that have added an undergraduate program, or they have expanded in other ways to enlarge themselves. They've merged with other departments. Those are the ones that have done the best job of surviving.

It didn't help that the University of Chicago's program had closed before Columbia. And the people at Columbia paid attention to that. But I think that Emory and others, the other thing was that most of these closures were concentrated in private universities. Alright, what the private universities did during that time was they slimmed down their profile so that they put most of their emphasis on the traditional academic programs and their law, business, and medical schools.

Dr. Ndumu: Hence, your dissertation topic on the iSchool movement, correct?

Dr. Wedgeworth: Yes, I studied the difference between the iSchools and the LIS programs, out of which most of them emerged. It wasn't the quality of the faculty. It wasn't the quality of students. It wasn't an emphasis on information science. The administrators in higher education really didn't understand the future impact of the information fields. They thought they would just disappear.

Dr. Ndumu: Excellent point, and this is so much bigger than the US version of librarianship, which leads me to my next question. I'm curious about your thoughts on and experiences with international librarianship. Of course, you've served as president of IFLA, and your family established the Wedgeworth International Fellowship in library leadership at the Mortensen Center. My final question is, how can we continue to promote a more global perspective of the LIS field, particularly Black librarianship?

Dr. Wedgeworth: I think, for one, we need to be more familiar with what's happening in institutions around the world. One of the things that I am proud of was that I was very much instrumental and a part of making IFLA a global organization. In my early years, IFLA was primarily a European and North American organization, with some attention to countries like Australia, New Zealand, and Japan. But it was primarily a European and North American organization. What happened was, in 1994, we made the decision to take the IFLA annual conference to Havana, Cuba, which was under the US embargo. Communication was difficult with Cuba, and they didn't have very much in the way of computer technology in Cuba. And so we had to figure out how we would organize this conference, when we couldn't even do normal mail and email with Cuba.

What we did was we got an American company to create an electronic interface with Cuba so that people from other countries could submit the programs for the annual conference and submit papers that could be put up on the web so that other people could see them before the conference. And for the first time, people who were not in attendance could see what was going on at the annual conference. That was a one-time event. But on the basis of that experience with Cuba, we established what became the default listserv, which meant that librarians in other parts of the world could communicate directly with IFLA. Now, what happened? When we went to Cuba, there were not even one hundred countries that had the ability to communicate electronically beyond their library communities. Between the time we met in Cuba and the time we met in Istanbul, Turkey, the next year, over one hundred countries had obtained the ability to communicate directly and electronically. It was at that point that IFLA became more of a global institution.

Because librarians could communicate with each other, they could share expertise with each other, they could share bibliographic information with each other electronically, which they had not been able to do on a large scale, except for a few countries like the ones in Europe or North America or Australia, Japan, New Zealand. But now it was available to the institutions in Africa and other parts of Asia and South America in ways that it had never been available. I think communication was the key to our field becoming more global.

This communication also enables us to know more about the conditions that apply locally. Now, I did a study for the Carnegie Corporation back in 2000. Carnegie, in his will, required that the foundation devote a certain percentage of its annual revenues to supporting libraries in the former British colonies in Africa. But the foundation had gotten away from that commitment. And then the new president of the foundation, who had been the president of the New York Public Library, Vartan Gregorian, asked me and one of his staff members to do a survey of sub-Saharan African countries that were formerly British Commonwealth countries, to see what they needed to do to reestablish Carnegie's support for libraries in that part of the world. And that's what we did; we were on the ground. Now what? Foundations, like the Bill and Melinda Gates Foundation, found out the hard way when they announced in the 1990s and early 2000s that they were going to do all these things with African libraries. Well, what they didn't understand was that, in many of these communities, they don't have electrical power most hours of the day. So they can't create and run computers the way we run them here in the US. They don't even have electric lights in most of the schools. So the schools operate in daylight. That was at that time. So what we need to develop is a broader understanding of the terms and conditions under which librarians serve in different parts of the world. We got a glimpse of this in 1984 when we had an IFLA conference in Nairobi, Kenya, and African librarians showed up who had never been at any IFLA conference before because IFLA was usually held in Europe. Looking forward, as you were suggesting in your question, we need to use our ability to communicate with these various library communities in order to enrich our understanding of the varying circumstances under which librarians serve. We have to have a deeper understanding of the local conditions under which libraries operate in order to be able to operate more effectively on an international basis.

Notes

1. "2017 ALA Demographic Study" https://www.ala.org/tools/sites/ala.org.tools/files/content/Draft%20of%20Member%20Demographics%20Survey%2001-11-2017.pdf

2. "2019 ALISE Statistical Report" https://www.ala.org/tools/sites/ala.org.tools/files/content/Draft%20of%20Member%20Demographics%20Survey%2001-11-2017.pdf

Bibliography

American Library Association. "2017 ALA Demographic Study." January 11, 2017. Accessed January 10, 2021 https://www.ala.org/tools/sites/ala.org.tools/files/content/Draft%20of%20Member% 20Demographics%20Survey%2001-11-2017.pdf.

Association for LIS Education. "2019 ALISE Statistical Report." Accessed January 10, 2021 https://www.ala.org/tools/sites/ ala.org.tools/files/content/Draft%20of%20Member%20Demographics%20Survey%2001-11-2017.pdf.

CHAPTER THREE

Disadvantaged by (Financial) Design

The Disappearing Act of HBCU Library Science Programs

Aisha Johnson, PhD

This chapter explores the connection between library training for African Americans, Historically Black Colleges and Universities (HBCUs), and the centrality of funding. The goal is to demonstrate how the availability of private and public funding is a decisive factor in the sustenance of pathways for African American librarians. The parallels between financial support, HBCU library science programs, and the growth of African American librarianship are insightful for decision-makers.

HBCUs were established in the nineteenth century to support African American students' educational efforts while also preserving cultural history. However, the schools often lacked funding to maintain adequate resources. One of those essential resources was the institution's library. Until relatively recently, many HBCU libraries lacked a trained librarian, appropriate facilities, modern equipment, and suitable collections to accommodate learners. This posed a rightful concern, as most HBCU libraries also served the local African American community to advance educational and cultural upliftment. Often, any access to literature, education, and desegregated public facilities, including libraries, was relegated to Black colleges. A 1945 study documented that of the 7,100 public libraries in the United States only 802 were in the South, of which only 121 rendered nearly nonexistent library services to Blacks.[1] There was also little in the way of training for prospective African American librarians.

In response, Hampton Institute's Library Science School for African American librarians was established through the American Library Association's and philanthropic support. Soon after, corporate philanthropist Julius Rosenwald agreed to grant experimental aid to five Negro teacher-training colleges, none of which possessed an adequate library.[2] Rosenwald also funded a year of study at Hampton Institute's Library School so that each college would have a trained librarian. Through Rosenwald's funding program, forty-three HBCU libraries were able to provide access to adequate learning material to their faculty, staff, students, and neighboring communities, contributing to many generations of lifelong learners. Many of the libraries are still standing on prestigious campuses. A few institutions also received funding to develop library science programs, including Hampton Institute and Atlanta University.[3]

This overlooked history raises questions regarding the survival of HBCU libraries and the disappearance of the library science programs. Though there have been a number of studies on HBCU libraries and library schools, the story of HBCU library science programs is still unappreciated among library and information science (LIS) and HBCU scholars. Library science education at HBCUs sought to certify, train, and formally educate Black/African American librarians for school, college, and public libraries. Today, there is one HBCU with a LIS program; indeed, it stands strong.

Historical Funding of HBCU Library Science Programs

The development of Black institutions was intentionally hindered as a result of racial discrimination built on the belief that Black institutions and organizations needed to lag behind those of whites. Further, given that the entire Southern region was developmentally and economically suppressed, HBCUs were all the more disadvantaged. Equally inaccessible was library education for African Americans, and Blacks were excluded from Columbia University's Library Economy program, which was founded in 1887 in upper Manhattan, with its bustling and growing Harlem-based African American literary community. This racist exclusion was the same with the Southern Library School established in 1905 and was funded by the Carnegie Corporation from 1914 to 1925. It later became the Carnegie Library School of Atlanta. It was funded by the Carnegie Corporation from 1914 to 1925 to train white librarians for the Carnegie Library of Atlanta, a library that excluded Blacks from the beginning.[4]

It was not until 1900 when Edward Christopher Williams, an African American, would earn a degree as a librarian from New York State Library School.[5] Interestingly, researchers have been unable to locate records documenting publicly supported, freely accessible, or nonsubscription library services to Blacks in the South before 1900. This fact is certainly not to say that Blacks were not interested in literacy or learning, but accessing reading materials was scarce. The growth of African American higher education coincided with that of the Julius Rosenwald Fund's goal of extending opportunities to increase literacy among African Americans through access to libraries, literature, and education.

On the contrary, African Americans knew that literacy and education were essential to Black empowerment and that what we now consider information literacy—that is, locating resources and applying information—is the primary pathway to opportunities. Like much of the growth in African American education, literacy was a grassroots effort that community groups and members, including African American educators and literary societies, sought to contribute. Though abolition, racial uplift, and self-improvement were vital to women's clubs' agendas, literary activism helped establish a Black literary tradition, born in activism and the struggle against racial inequality.[6] The upliftment of the Black culture has been an agenda item for Black institutions, including HBCUs.

Institutes and meetings validated the need for trained professionals, particularly as the demand for access to literature increased. Among the conferences was the 1929 summer institutes for teacher-librarians in Virginia and North Carolina and a meeting among the policy committee of the Southeastern Library Association, with small sums of those in attendance being select Southern African American librarians from the National Institute for Library Field Agents in Wisconsin.[7] Another example is that of the Library Institute for Negro Librarians: Morehouse/Spelman Summer School, held between June 14 and July 25, 1930. Notably, the Julius Rosenwald Fund allocated $10,000 for conducting a summer institute (1930) for thirty-five African American librarians at Atlanta University. The Rosenwald Fund also provided financial support for the Conference of Negro Librarians held November 20–23, 1930, at Fisk University under the direction of Head Librarian Louis Shores.[8] Training of Black librarians continued with the Negro Teacher-Librarian Training Program (1936–1939), primarily funded by the General Education Board, which was held at four HBCU campuses with participants representing sixteen Southern states.[9] The four campuses were Atlanta University (now Clark Atlanta University), Fisk University, Hampton Normal and Agricultural Institute (now Hampton University), and Prairie View Normal and Industrial College (now Prairie View A&M University). With a mission to "improve conditions in the Negro public schools," program participants completed the twelve-credit-hour program and returned to schools better trained. This training program provided an opportunity to impact the students, schools, and communities.[10]

Nonetheless, HBCUs were the center for the training of Black librarians, both formal and informal, for quite some time. After several debates between the American Library Association (ALA) and the Julius Rosenwald Fund, the Hampton Institute Library School was established in 1925 with additional financial support from the Carnegie Corporation, General Education Board, and the Rosenwald Fund. The approach was two pronged: first, qualified and committed teachers would matriculate through library school, and, second, suitable library facilities and literary collections were made available at HBCU institutions, which boosted their propensity toward accreditation.[11] Hampton was selected from the list of four HBCUs: Fisk, Howard, Tuskegee, and Hampton. The Hampton program did not occur without skepticism, and the location seemed to be the center of concern for Southern librarianship development, more specifically Black librarianship.[12] Hampton's program operated under sanction from its inception and was primarily controlled by the ALA.

Thus, Hampton Institute answered the call to produce Black librarians, 183 librarians to be exact.[13] The Carnegie Corporation's ten-year program in library service to professionally train librarians heavily supported the Hampton program. Hampton submitted three requests for continued funding, supported by the ALA, which were all rejected. The Carnegie Corporation had two major concerns: (1) It did not feel that the institution paid its fair share to maintain the library school, contributing "just over 9% of the total $157,054.41 total of expenditures," and (2) it believed that Florence Curtis, the white director of the Library School, was the sole reason for its success and, as she approached retirement, the corporation did not believe the school should continue.[14] The Carnegie Corporation decided to finance a library school for African Americans at Atlanta University after its second rejection to Hampton for continued financial support.[15] The white custodial underpinnings are therefore apparent, and the Hampton Institute library science program closed its doors in 1939.

As the profession and Black America attempted to grapple with the closing of Hampton's Library School in 1939, another HBCU library science program was founded at Atlanta University (now Clark Atlanta University) in 1941. It was then that the library field witnessed a surge in Black librarianship. Amidst this Black excellence, Atlanta University (like many HBCUs) operated underfunded. Remarkably, it continued to thrive during financial difficulty, producing more than 2,600 graduates from the School of Library Science between 1941 and 2005.[16] Unfortunately, for several complex and ambiguous reasons, the School of Library Science officially closed its doors in 2005, leaving its alumni, Black librarianship, the LIS community, and the majority African American metropolis of Atlanta baffled. The Clark Atlanta University administration's official explanation cited financial reasons, though not all accept those reasons.[17] While several LIS community members and alumni feel indifferent, it is critical to document the many conversations they had concerning the program's reopening and the American Library Association's support. The school's impact on Black librarianship is undeniable, and there remains interest in reestablishing this landmark program. Alas, much more is needed beyond conversations, conferences, and roundtables.

Today, Black librarianship at HBCUs stands on North Carolina College's shoulders (now North Carolina Central University, or NCCU) School of Library and Information Science, one of five HBCUs that received funding from the Rosenwald Fund Library Program.[18] In addition to contributions from the Rosenwald Fund, NCCU also received appropriations from the North Carolina General Assembly (ca. 1938) at $550,000 for a library to accommodate 800 readers and 200,000 volumes and to house the library school.[19] Established in 1941, the library school has made significant contributions toward increasing African American inclusion in the library and information science profession. NCCU's SLIS program has graduated nearly 3,000 students.[20] The program shows no signs of slowing down but, rather, continuous efforts to recruit and retain faculty and students of color. North Carolina Central University has innovated its Archives and Records Management program to attract more students to the arena and amplify African American cultural heritage.

HBCU Convergence and Funding around Archival Studies and Cultural Heritage

In the vein of archival and history record keeping, it is also important to acknowledge the need to develop cultural heritage programs with concentrations in archives, records management, historic preservation, and cultural heritage at HBCUs. These institutions are founded on the need for cultural preservation and should reflect marginalized community members who work in archives, preservation, and cultural heritage. Among the key groups working toward preserving America's complete narrative are the Archives and Archivists of Color, Latin American and Caribbean Cultural Heritage Archives, and Women Archivists of the Society of American Archivists. Also, large organizations are taking leadership roles, such as the National Trust for Historic Preservation. Recently, the organization created the HBCU Cultural Heritage Stewardship Initiative to "empower HBCUs with the resources to protect, preserve and leverage their historic campuses, buildings, and landscapes, ensuring these academic institutions and symbols of African American pride are preserved to inspire and educate future generations."[21]

Notwithstanding, when it comes to funding and supporting HBCU libraries, perhaps no group compares to the HBCU Library Alliance. This monumental organization represents the 105 HBCU institutions across twenty-one states with a mission to "transform and strengthen its membership by developing leaders, preserving collections and planning for the future."[22] In its more than twenty-year history, the HBCU Library Alliance has amassed hundreds of thousands of dollars in funding from organizations such as the Andrew W. Mellon Foundation. Most recently, the HBCU Library Alliance in partnership with the Council on Library and Information Resources was awarded a $75,000 planning grant for *Creating Access to HBCU Library Alliance Archives: Needs, Capacity, and Technical Planning* to identify common barriers and shared visions for creating access to historical collections held by libraries at HBCUs.[23] The Alliance also received a $365,000 grant from the National Endowment for the Humanities (NEH) to "strengthen stewardship of special collections documenting the African American experience."[24]

Without question, the Black Caucus of the American Library Association has also mobilized on behalf of African American librarians and the communities that they serve. BCALA represents a historic legacy and for more than fifty years has uplifted Black librarian activists. This group provided a blueprint in its mission to "advocate for the development, promotion, and improvement of library services and resources to the nation's African American community; and provides leadership for the recruitment and professional development of African American librarians."[25] BCALA has recently received two high-profile grants from the Institute of Museum and Library Services: the $100,000 Black History Month programming grant to conduct a comprehensive literature review and produce a taxonomy and framework on Black History Month programming, along with the $100,000 Breaking Barriers Grant to establish a national, virtual student organization for Black/African American MLIS students. The project will also establish an HBCU Recruitment Action Kit to foster partnerships between predominantly white (PWI) LIS programs and neighboring HBCU institutions. Finally, in 2021 the organization pursued a $176,000 grant from the Council of Library and Information Resources (CLIR) through the Digitizing Hidden Collections program to curate and digitize the BCALA archives and Dr. E. J. Josey collection.

HBCU Library Schools, National Policy, and Federal Funding

As noted above with the example of BCALA's receipt of an IMLS grant, the recruitment of African Americans and other librarians of color has also been shaped by early federal policy. Reed[26] highlights the critical role of Title XI of the National Defense Education Act (NDEA) of 1958. Resultantly, twenty-six NDEA Institutes for School Library Personnel were supported in 1965, thirty-two in 1966, and eighteen in 1967.

Title XI was followed by the Title II-B of the Higher Education Act of 1965, which provided funding for professional staff development. This legislation authorized "grants to institutions of higher education to assist them in training persons in librarianship . . . [in order to] substantially further the objective of increasing the opportunities throughout the Nation for training in librarianship."[27] Later in the 1970s, the program made a significant contribution to the education of Black librarians with the development of fellowships for library school attendance and funding to support minority outreach programs at various library schools.[28] Once the federal government mandated Title II-B funds used for equalizing opportunities for minorities, library schools then began to show a commitment to the recruitment of minorities.[29] These legislative efforts recognized the role that libraries play in society and the life of the users; they were instrumental in providing funding for HBCU library schools.

The Institute of Museum and Library Services is now the primary funding source for libraries, and African American librarians—indeed, librarians of color—have benefited from the various IMLS opportunities. For example, the Emmett Till Memorial Project culminated in a traveling exhibit and location-based historical experience through a smartphone application. The application enables Emmett Till Interpretive Center visitors to explore historical and contemporary photos, narration, digital access to archival documents, social media check-ins, and historical documentary footage at each site.[30] The project was funded through a $76,672 IMLS grant through the Museums Grants for African American History and Culture program.

Call to Action

Strengthening Black/African American librarianship requires capital, commitment, and robust backing, as demonstrated throughout this chapter. This piece was motivated by a desire to see the resurrection of HBCU-based library science programs along with the fortification of pathways between HBCUs and PWI MLIS programs. Critical factors include (1) funding structures and opportunities; (2) university systems' compliance with funding regulations that force institutional competition, especially in light of the proven punitive effects of desegregation on HBCUs; and (3) the urgency of funding to increase recruitment and retention of LIS students and faculty of color to MLIS programs.

The LIS field has explored the histories of a select few HBCUs with library science programs, including Hampton Institute, Clark Atlanta University, and North Carolina Central University. We must continue to study and conduct research focused on the recruitment, retention, curriculum, support, and funding of these and other HBCUs that housed library science programs. Doing so will help inform and plan the profession's actions to successfully move forward.[31]

For the richness of scholarship and highlighting of matters during an era when not enough is known about the development of HBCU libraries and Black librarianship, nor the need for culture keepers, the work calls for diversity in representation. This includes accurate representation for librarians, information scientists, archivists, and others who work to serve society's literacy needs and preserve diverse groups' cultural heritage. Our professional organizations, including the American Library Association, Association for Library and Information Science Education, Black Caucus of the American Library Association, Society of American Archivists, the HBCU Library Alliance, must lead the charge. Equally important are nonacademicians who value HBCUs' history and their libraries, information literacy, and importance of representation.

Keeping all discussed in mind, as a profession and society, we indeed understand that an accurate representation of the people we serve is key to inspiring the next generation of librarians and culture keepers. It is a call for action to our survival as a vital and relevant resource.

Notes

1. Carole Taylor, "Contributions of Black Academic Libraries in Providing Services to the Black Community," PhD diss. (University of Michigan, 1981).
2. Aisha Johnson-Jones, *The African American Struggle for Library Equality: The Untold Story of Rosenwald Library Program*. (Rowman & Littlefield, 2019).
3. Fisk University, John and Aurelia E. Franklin Library, Special Collections, Julius Rosenwald Fund Archives, boxes 258–259.
4. Johnson-Jones, *The African American Struggle for Library Equality*.
5. Ibid.
6. Michelle Garfield, "The Pen Is Ours to Wield: Black Literary Society Women in 1830s Philadelphia," PhD diss. (University of Michigan, 2002).
7. Fisk University, John and Aurelia E. Franklin Library, Special Collections, S. L. Smith Collection, box 8, folder 7.
8. Ibid., folder 8.
9. Tommie D. Barker, *Libraries of the South: A Report on Development 1930–1935* (Chicago: American Library Association, 1936); Allison Sutton, "Bridging the Gap in Early Library Education History for African Americans: The Negro Teacher-Librarian Training Program (1936–1939)," *Journal of Negro Education* (2005): 138–150.
10. Sutton, "Bridging the Gap."
11. Johnson-Jones, *The African American Struggle for Library Equality*.
12. O. Lee Shifflett, "The American Library Association's Quest for a Black Library School," *Journal of Education for Library and Information Science* 32 (1994): 68–72.
13. Ana Ndumu, "Shifts: How Changes in the U.S. Black Population Impact Racial Inclusion and Representation in LIS Education," *Journal for Education in Library and Information Science* 62, no. 2 (2021).
14. Arthur C. Gunn, "Early Training for Black Librarians in the U.S.: A History of the Hampton Institute Library School and the Establishment of the Atlanta University School of Library Service," PhD diss. (University of Michigan, 1986, 84).
15. Gunn, "Early Training for Black Librarians in the U.S."
16. Ana Ndumu and Renate Chancellor, "DuMont, 35 Years Later: HBCUs, LIS Education, and Institutional Discrimination," *Journal of Education for Library and Information Science* 62, no. 2 (2021).
17. Risa L. Mulligan, "The Closing of the Clark Atlanta University School of Library & Information Studies," Master's thesis (University of North Carolina at Chapel Hill, 2006).
18. Johnson-Jones, *The African American Struggle for Library Equality*.

19. Ibid.
20. Ndumu and Chancellor, "Du Mont 35 Years Later."
21. "HBCU Cultural Heritage Stewardship Initiative," National Trust for Historic Preservation, April 14, 2021, https://savingplaces.org/hbcus#.YHj0ZOlKj65.
22. "HBCU Library Alliance Mission and Vision," HBCU Library Alliance, April 15, 2021, https://www.google.com/url?q=https://www.clir.org/2020/11/hbcu-library-alliance-andclir-receive-grant/&sa=D&source=editors&ust=1618543191027000&usg=AOvVaw13CtKwimlnhJ0oJ_erEjKq.
23. "HBCU Library Alliance and CLIR Receive Grant to Study Feasibility for Large-Scale Survey of HBCU Archives," Council on Library and Information Resources, November 20, 2020, https://www.clir.org/2020/11/hbcu-library-alliance-and-clir-receive-grant/.
24. "HBCU Library Alliance Mission and Vision."
25. "BCALA Mission," Black Caucus of the American Library Association, April 15, 2021, https://www.bcala.org/about-bcala#:~:text=BCALA%20Mission,development%20of%20African%20American%20librarians.
26. Sarah R. Reed, "Federally Funded Training for Librarianship," *Library Trends* 24, no. 1 (1975): 85–100.
27. Reed, "Federally Funded Training," 88–89.
28. Shaundra Walker, "Critical Race Theory and the Recruitment, Retention and Promotion of a Librarian of Color: A Counterstory." In *Where Are All the Librarians of Color? The Experiences of People of Color in Academia*, edited by Rebecca Hankins and Miguel Juarez, 135–160. Sacramento: Library Juice Press, 2015.
29. Reed, "Federally Funded Training," 88–89; DeLoach, "Title II-B," 81; Walker, "Critical Race Theory," 39.
30. Institute of Museum and Library Service, "Remembering Emmitt Till: From Chicago to Mississippi, Connecting Visitors to Location-Based History," February 2021, https://www.imls.gov/grant-spotlights/remembering-emmett-till-chicago-mississippi-connecting-visitors-location-based.
31. Ana Ndumu and Tina Rollins, "Envisioning Reciprocal and Sustainable HBCU-LIS Pipeline Partnerships," *Information and Learning Sciences* 121, no. 3/4 (2020): 155–174.

Bibliography

Primary Resources

Fisk University, John and Aurelia E. Franklin Library, Special Collections, Julius Rosenwald Fund Archives.

Fisk University, John and Aurelia E. Franklin Library, Special Collections, S. L. Smith Collection.

Secondary Resources

Barker, Tommie D. *Libraries of the South: A Report on Development 1930–1935.* Chicago: American Library Association, 1936.

Black Caucus of the American Library Association. "BCALA Mission." April 15, 2021. https://www.bcala.org/about-bcala#:~:text=BCALA%20Mission, development%20of%20African%20American%20librarians.

Council on Library and Information Resources. "HBCU Library Alliance and CLIR Receive Grant to Study Feasibility for Large-Scale Survey of HBCU Archives." November 20, 2020. https://www.clir.org/2020/11/hbcu-library-alliance-and-clir-receive-grant/.

DeLoach, Marva. "The Higher Education Act of 1965, Title II-B: The Fellowships/Traineeships for Training in Library and Information Science Program: Its Impact on Minority Recruitment in Library and Information Science Education." PhD diss. (University of Pittsburgh, 1980).

Garfield, Michelle N. "The Pen Is Ours to Wield: Black Literary Society Women in 1830s Philadelphia." PhD diss. (University of Michigan, 2002).

Gunn, Arthur C. "Early Training for Black Librarians in the U.S.: A History of the Hampton Institute Library School and the Establishment of the Atlanta University School of Library Service." PhD diss. (University of Michigan, 1986).

HBCU Library Alliance. "HBCU Library Alliance Mission and Vision." April 15, 2021. https://www.google.com/url?q=https://www.clir.org/2020/11/hbcu-library-alliance-andclir-receive-grant/&sa=D&source=editors&ust=1618543191027000&usg=AOvVaw13CtKwimlnhJ0oJ_erEjKq.

Institute of Museum and Library Service. "Remembering Emmitt Till: From Chicago to Mississippi, Connecting Visitors to Location-Based History." February 2021, https://www.imls.gov/grant-spotlights/remembering-emmett-till-chicago-mississippi-connecting-visitors-location-based.

Johnson-Jones, Aisha. *The African American Struggle for Library Equality: The Untold Story of Rosenwald Library Program.* Lanham, MD: Rowman & Littlefield, 2019.

Mulligan, Risa L. "The Closing of the Clark Atlanta University School of Library & Information Studies." Master's thesis (University of North Carolina at Chapel Hill, 2006).

National Trust for Historic Preservation. "HBCU Cultural Heritage Stewardship Initiative." April 14, 2021. https://savingplaces.org/hbcus#.YHj0ZOlKj65.

Ndumu, Ana. "Shifts: How Changes in the U.S. Black Population Impact Racial Inclusion and Representation in LIS Education." *Journal for Education in Library and Information Science* 62, no. 2 (2021).

Ndumu, Ana, and Renate Chancellor. "DuMont, 35 Years Later: HBCUs, LIS Education, and Institutional Discrimination." *Journal of Education for Library and Information Science* 62, no. 2 (2021).

Ndumu, Ana, and Tina Rollins. "Envisioning Reciprocal and Sustainable HBCU-LIS Pipeline Partnerships." *Information and Learning Sciences* 121, no. 3/4 (2020): 155–174.

Reed, Sarah R. "Federally Funded Training for Librarianship." *Library Trends* 24, no.1 (1975): 85–100.

Shiflett, O. Lee. "The American Library Association's Quest for a Black Library School." *Journal of Education for Library and Information Science* 32 (1994): 68–72.

Sutton, Allison M. "Bridging the Gap in Early Library Education History for African Americans: The Negro Teacher-Librarian Training Program (1936–1939)." *Journal of Negro Education* (2005): 138–150.

Taylor, Carole R. "Contributions of Black Academic Libraries in Providing Services to the Black Community." PhD diss. (University of Michigan, 1981).

Walker, Shaundra. "Critical Race Theory and the Recruitment, Retention and Promotion of a Librarian of Color: A Counterstory." In *Where Are All the Librarians of Color? The Experiences of People of Color in Academia*, edited by Rebecca Hankins and Miguel Juarez, 135–160. Sacramento: Library Juice Press, 2015.

CHAPTER FOUR

A Hidden Figure

Adella Hunt Logan, Tuskegee Institute's First Librarian

Shaundra Walker

Recent scholarship has shone a light on the experiences of Black women librarians such as Audre Lorde (Pollock & Haley 2018), Nella Larsen (Hochman 2018), Belle da Costa Green (Ardizzone 2007), and Regina Andrews Anderson (Whitmire 2014). As Pollock and Haley (2018) make clear, "Black women have always been integral to first, literacy movements of the 1800s and later librarianship. It also became clear that literacy, social justice activism, and literary cultural production have always intersected for middle class, educated Black women." One place where this can be observed is within the profession of librarianship" (15). One name that is absent from the canon of noteworthy Black women librarians is Adella Hunt Logan. This chapter will explore the degree to which the collection and dissemination of information and social justice activism intersected within her life and work.

Adella Hunt Logan

The February 1916 issue of the NAACP's *Crisis* magazine reported the death of Adella Hunt Logan as follows: "Mrs. Warren Logan, wife of treasurer of Tuskegee Institute, is dead. She was a woman of energy and influence and the mother of an interesting family" ("Personal" 1916, 167).

Mrs. Warren Logan, born Adella Hunt (1863–1915), was a librarian, educator, reformer, and suffragist. Her unique life spanned the Civil War into the nadir of the Black experience in America. She was a contemporary and associate of leaders and scholars as diverse as Susan B. Anthony, George Washington Carver, Mary Church Terrell, Booker T. Washington, and W.E.B. DuBois.

Logan was born near Sparta, Hancock County, Georgia, the daughter of a free woman of color, Mariah "Cherokee Lilly" Hunt, and a white planter and former Confederate soldier, Henry Alexander Hunt Sr. Nineteenth-century Hancock County was a peculiar locale in terms of race relations (Alexander 2021). As Schultz (1999, 2006) and Alexander (1991) have noted, the rural Black Belt County was the type of place where wealthy white men could live openly with their common-law Black wives and children, unpunished by the opinions of common white people. A well-known case is that of Hancock County's Amanda America Dixon, at one time the wealthiest Black woman in America. Dixon, the product of her wealthy planter father's rape of her enslaved thirteen-year-old mother, inherited the bulk of her father David Dickson's estate at his 1885 death.[1] Although the will was contested by David Dickson's white family, a Georgia Supreme Court judge ruled that Dickson rightly inherited the estate. Before meeting a premature death in 1893, Dixon would go on to marry Nathan Toomer, the father of Harlem Renaissance author Jean Toomer (Leslie 1995).[2]

Although her family was not as wealthy as the Dicksons, Logan's lineage was similar, as she was the granddaughter of Susan Hunt, also a mixed-race woman, and Judge Nathan Sayre. A legislator and lawyer, Sayre lived openly with Susan and their children in a palatial Sparta estate called Pomegranate Hall (Alexander 1991). Logan's ambiguous racial status allowed her at times to straddle two worlds. The proximity that she gained to whiteness through her father provided her and her seven siblings certain opportunities and privileges, such as discussions about politics with her white father, but, at the same time, her mother's racially mixed background limited her access to schooling and the vote. Remarking on her origins, Logan stated, "I was not born a slave, nor in a log cabin" (Culp 1902, 198). Such was the complicated and contradictory world in which Adella Hunt Logan lived and operated.

Figure 4.1. Mrs. Warren Logan, 1902. African American Women on Race, published in 1902.

Logan was privileged to receive a primary education, attending Bass Academy in Sparta, a school for Black children that was started by the Freedmen's Bureau and supported by the American Missionary Association. At age sixteen, she earned a scholarship to attend Atlanta University, an institution that was pivotal in preparing Black women to become teachers. There, she took the normal curriculum in preparation for her future career as an educator. Upon graduating in 1881, she assumed a position as a teacher in the southwest Georgia town of Albany. In 1883, she turned down an opportunity to teach at her alma mater, preferring instead to join the all-Black faculty at Booker T. Washington's prodigy, Tuskegee Institute (Smith & Zepeda 2009, Sanders 2021).

Logan's career at Tuskegee, both her formal work and the relationships she would develop with various leaders with whom she crossed paths, would prove to be pivotal to her development as an activist. Over the span of her career, she assumed several positions at the institution, including serving as an instructor of English and social sciences, interim lady principal, and debate team coach. She was well respected within and outside of Tuskegee. A review of Black newspapers during the 1880s and 1890s reveals that Logan was a frequent speaker at educational conferences related to Black education. In 1903, the *Bulletin of Atlanta University* reported that she was awarded an honorary master's degree by her alma mater, Atlanta University, "for conspicuous success as a teacher and helper in the work of the Tuskegee Normal and Industrial Institute" (Annual Meeting 1903, 1).

Logan's Life at Tuskegee Institute

While working at Tuskegee, the former Adella Hunt met and married Warren Logan (1888), the institution's treasurer and one of Washington's trusted generals and a fellow graduate of Hampton Institute. Like his wife, Logan was of mixed-race heritage, although his white father's identity provided him no financial or social benefits (Alexander 2021).

By virtue of their positions, the Logans had proximity to both Booker T. Washington and his spouses, first Olivia Davidson Washington and later Margaret Murray Washington. As Tuskegee grew and Washington gained notoriety for his work at the institution, such proximity allowed them to cross paths with several notable and influential figures.

For example, Logan became acquainted with W.E.B. Du Bois after meeting him during one of his visits to Tuskegee's campus, an encounter that would lead to a lifelong relationship. One can imagine that they may have discussed conditions in Albany, Georgia, where Logan once worked and where Du Bois would conduct his famed sociology study. When George Washington Carver arrived at the Tuskegee campus, recruited by Washington himself, he became a friend of her family; her children referred to him as "Uncle Fess" (Alexander 2021, 154–56). In her later years, Logan would mentor Bess Bolden Walcott, who was recruited to Tuskegee by Washington, to catalog his personal library. Walcott would go on to serve as curator of the school's George Washington Carver Museum (Williams 2021).

Logan met Susan B. Anthony through her relationship with Margaret Murray Washington. They would bond through their mutual, yet diverging, opinions on women's suffrage. When Logan was suggested to speak at a National American Woman Suffrage Association (N-AWSA) conference, Anthony responded as follows: "I cannot have speak for us a woman who has even a ten-thousandth portion of African blood who would be an inferior orator in matter or manner, because it would so mitigate against our cause. . . . Let your Miss Logan wait till she is more cultivated, better educated, and better prepared and can do our mission and her own race the greatest credit." Despite her reticence to make space on her platform for a Black woman, the two women maintained contact. Logan was a lifetime member of N-AWSA. Among the books in Logan's personal library was a copy of Anthony's four-volume set, *The History of Women Suffrage*, inscribed as follows: "because of my admiration of you and your work" (Alexander 1995, 88).

Libraries at Historically Black Colleges

To appreciate the significance of Logan's accomplishments related to libraries, it is important to contextualize them within the larger framework of library access for African Americans. To be clear, free-standing libraries at Historically Black Colleges and Universities such as Tuskegee Institute were virtually nonexistent at the time that Logan assumed the role of librarian at Tuskegee. Despite this fact, Booker T. Washington understood the importance of reading and libraries, especially for a disenfranchised population of formerly enslaved men and women. Said Washington in one of his Sunday-evening talks:

> Start a library. You can get hold of one. You can get the nucleus of a good library now. It does not require a great number of books. Persons who have been well read through the medium of books; they have read them well, have looked up all the references, all the characters, all the cities mentioned, and the person therefore who reads one book thoroughly will become educated, indeed he is an educated person. (Washington 1972, vol. 3, 94)

Prior to 1900, only four HBCUs (Historically Black Colleges and Universities) had free-standing libraries: Booker T. Washington's alma mater, Hampton Institute; Lincoln University (Pennsylvania); Claflin College; and St. Augustine's College (Kaser 1994). Instead of free-standing buildings, most Black colleges used existing facilities for their libraries. Tuskegee followed this model, as the first library at Tuskegee was in the former principal's home.

In addition to the responsibilities previously mentioned, Logan served as Tuskegee's first librarian.

According to Alexander (2021), she carefully crafted the collection:

> Adella collected whatever she could that was written by, for, or about people of African ancestry. She knew that white folks sometimes appropriated and mocked their black culture but nonetheless enjoyed Joel Chandler Harris's recently published Uncle Remus Tales, since he'd been reared in a county adjoining Hancock and his stories quite resembled her grandmother's. She especially, however, sought out works that bore relevance for their women, such as the enslaved Phillis Wheatley's Revolutionary-era poetry, William Wells Brown's novel *Clotel: The President's Daughter*, Frances Ellen Watkins Harper's diverse oeuvre, and even *Adela, the Octoroon*, a maudlin novel by a white man named H. L. Hosmer. (96–97)

She cataloged the books from her grandfather, Judge Nathan Sayre's library, and added them to the collection. She was known to donate materials she thought would be beneficial to the students, such as suffrage materials she acquired from a trip to New Orleans (Alexander 2021).

Very soon, Logan's collection of books grew to the point where additional space was required. Her husband provided her with a ten-by-twelve-foot space next to his office, and students built shelves on three sides to accommodate the books (Alexander 2021). According to Washington's appeal letter to Andrew Carnegie requesting funds to construct a free-standing library at Tuskegee, by 1900, the seed that Logan planted had grown to twelve thousand "books, periodicals, etc., gifts from our friends" (Washington 1972, vol. 1, 316).

As Logan's family responsibilities grew, her responsibilities shifted. In her lifetime, she would give birth to nine children. Although her formal roles at Tuskegee ceased, she assumed many informal capacities that allowed her to have an impact on the students, the community, and the larger world. One of the primary vehicles for Logan's work was the Tuskegee Women's Club. She was a charter member of the organization that was founded on March 2, 1895, by Margaret Murray Washington, Booker T. Washington's third wife (Harris 2021, 81).

Like other women's clubs, the Tuskegee Women's Club took on causes such as juvenile delinquency, prison reform, and health care. As early as 1897, the club took interest in and developed a free public library in downtown Tuskegee, which was accessible to white and Black patrons alike. Washington (1972, vol. 4, 338) bragged about this feat. In a letter to industrialist Edward Atkinson, he stated: "The book which I send you belongs to the public library in Tuskegee which has just been opened in town. It is, so far as I know, the only public library free to all races in Alabama." In addition to the libraries that she helped to develop at the institute and through the Tuskegee Women's Club, Logan served as the chair of the club's Suffrage Department and was personally responsible for developing a "suffrage library" that was available to members of the club (Washington 1972, vol. 8, 480).

By the turn of the century, Logan's attention shifted from collecting information to disseminating it. By 1912, her relationship with W.E.B. Du Bois had developed to the point where she was invited to write in a special issue of the *Crisis* dedicated to women's suffrage. She joined writers such as Paul Lawrence Dunbar, Mary Church Terrell, Bishop

John Hurst of the AME Church, and Charles Waddell Chestnutt (Yellin 1973).

Her essay was entitled "Colored Women as Voters." In it, she opined as follows: "More and more colored women are studying public questions and civics. *As they gain information* [emphasis added] and have experience in their daily vocations and in their efforts for human betterment they are convinced, as many other women have long ago been convinced, that their efforts would be more telling if women had the vote" (Logan 1912, 242). She also wrote on the topic of suffrage for Black women for the *Colored American* and the National American Woman Suffrage Association's *Women's Journal*. Clearly, in Logan's eyes, information was a vehicle for social uplift.

Death and Legacy

The year 1915 would prove to be consequential for Adella Hunt Logan. She suffered what has been described as a "nervous breakdown" and, with Booker T. Washington's assistance, spent time at the Battle Creek Sanitarium at Battle Creek, Michigan, returning to the campus of Tuskegee shortly before Washington would pass away on November 14, 1915. Despite a lifetime dedicated to women's suffrage issues, she had recently learned that the opportunity to have the question decided on the ballot had been rejected by the Alabama legislature, dimming the possibility that she and other Black women would gain access to voting during her lifetime. On Friday, December 10, 1915, she fell from the roof of Tuskegee's main academic building. Her daughter transported her to the institute's hospital, where she lay in a ward overseen by Nella Larsen before dying at 6:20 p.m. (Hutchinson 2006, 97–98; Alexander 1983).[3]

An obituary in the *Tuskegee Student* memorialized her. Logan was funeralized and buried quietly in the school cemetery on Sunday morning, December 12, 1915 (a public memorial for Booker T. Washington was held later the same day). Pallbearers included Washington's personal aide and confidant, Emmett J. Scott, and Robert Taylor, the MIT-educated architect who designed Tuskegee's Carnegie library and several other HBCU library buildings. In addition to her husband and children, the service was attended by several of her siblings, including

Henry A. Hunt Jr., principal of the Fort Valley High and Industrial School, Fort Valley, Georgia, and friend of both W.E.B. Du Bois and Booker T. Washington. Adele Logan Alexander, Logan's granddaughter through her son Warren, alludes that the fate of the main character in Larsen's acclaimed novel *Passing*, Clare Landry, may have been inspired by her grandmother's life and death. Much like the death of Clare, "no one ever knew for certain if Adella Hunt Logan jumped, fell, or tried to fly away" (Alexander 2021, 313).

While the circumstances surrounding her death remain an enigma, Adella Hunt Logan's legacy of collecting and disseminating information toward social justice for Black women is no longer a mystery. She joins an extensive line of Black women librarians who have merged their social justice activism with the vocations of writing and librarianship.

Notes

1. The Black family spells its surname *Dixon*; the white family spells its surname *Dickson*.

2. Toomer's novel, *Cane*, is loosely based on the town of Sparta. His mother, Nina Pinchback, was also a woman of mixed-race heritage, being the daughter of P.B.S. Pinchback, the first and only Black governor of Louisiana. Pinchback was born in nearby Macon, Bibb County, Georgia.

3. Prior to her career as a librarian and author, Larsen lived and worked as a nurse in Tuskegee from 1915 to 1916. See Hutchinson (2006) for more information.

Bibliography

Alexander, A. L. 1983, November. "How I Discovered My Grandmother . . . and the Truth about Black Women and the Suffrage Movement." *Ms.* 12, no. 5: 29–37.

Alexander, A. L. 1991. *Ambiguous Lives: Free Women of Color in Middle Georgia, 1789–1879*. University of Arkansas Press.

Alexander, A. L. 1995. "Adella Hunt Logan, the Tuskegee Woman's Club, and African Americans in the Suffrage Movement." In *Votes for Women! The Woman Suffrage Movement in Tennessee, the South, and the Nation*, 71–104, edited by M. S. Wheeler. University of Tennessee Press.

Alexander, A. L. 2021. *Princess of the Hither Isles: A Black Suffragist's Story from the Jim Crow South*. Yale University Press.

Annual Meeting of the Trustees. 1903. *Bulletin of Atlanta University* 138, 1.

Ardizzone, H. 2007. *An Illuminated Life: Belle Da Costa Greene's Journey from Prejudice to Privilege*. W.W. Norton & Company.

Culp, D. W. 1902. *Twentieth Century Negro Literature*. J. L. Nichols.

Harris, S. 2021. *Margaret Murray Washington: The Life and Times of a Career Clubwoman*. University of Tennessee Press.

Hochman, B. 2018. "Filling in Blanks: Nella Larsen's Application to Library School." *PMLA* 133, no. 5: 1172–90.

Hutchinson, George. 2006. *In Search of Nella Larsen: A Biography of the Color Line*. Harvard University Press.

Kaser, D. 1994. "Andrew Carnegie and the Black College Libraries." In *For the Good of the Order: Essays in Honor of Edward G. Holley*, 119–33, edited by D. Williams. JAI Press.

Leslie, Kent Anderson. 1995. *Woman of Color, Daughter of Privilege: Amanda America Dickson, 1849–1893*. University of Georgia Press.

Logan, A. H. 1912, September. "Colored Women as Voters." *Crisis*: 242–43.

"Mrs. Logan's Death." 1915, December 25. *The Tuskegee Student*: 3.

"Personal." 1916, February. *The Crisis*: 167.

Pollock, C. M., and S. P. Haley. 2018. "'When I Enter': Black Women and Disruption of the White, Heteronormative Narrative of Librarianship." In *Pushing the Margins: Women of Color and Intersectionality in LIS*, 15–60, edited by R. L. Chou and A. Pho. Library Juice Press.

Sanders, C. R. 2021. "'We Very Much Prefer to Have a Colored Man in Charge': Booker T. Washington and Tuskegee's All-Black Faculty." *Alabama Review* 74, no. 2: 99–128.

Schultz, M. R. 1999. "The Unsolid South: An Oral History of Race, Class, and Geography in Hancock County, Georgia, 1910–1950." Doctoral diss. Retrieved from ProQuest Dissertations and Theses. (UMI No. 304547653).

Smith, T. D., and S. J. Zepeda. 2009. "Adella Hunt Logan: Educator, Woman's Suffrage Leader, and Confidant of Booker T. Washington." In *The Varieties of Women's Experiences: Portraits of Southern Women in the Post-Civil War Century*, 151–70, edited by L. E. Rivers and C. E. Brown Jr. University Press of Florida.

Washington, Booker T. 1972. *The Booker T. Washington Papers Collection: Volumes 1–14*. University of Illinois Press.

Whitmire, E. 2014. *Regina Andrews, Harlem Renaissance Librarian*. University of Illinois Press.

Williams, S. 2021, May 4. "Bess Bolden Walcott." *Encyclopedia of Alabama.* http://encyclopediaofalabama.org/article/h-4274.

Yellin, J. 1973. "Dubois' 'Crisis' and Woman's Suffrage." *The Massachusetts Review* 14, no 2: 365–75.

PART II

CELEBRATING COLLECTIVE AND INDIVIDUAL IDENTITY

CHAPTER FIVE

"I'm Rooting for Everybody Black"

A Labor of Love

Jina DuVernay

The third episode of *Blackish*, entitled "The Nod," aired in 2014. In the episode, Dre becomes very concerned that his son did not nod at another Black child. Dre proceeds to explain to his biracial wife "the nod is important," declaring that it is "basic Black." He continues his explanation by stating that "the nod" is "the internationally accepted yet unspoken sign of acknowledgement of Black folks around the world."

This acknowledgment is a knowing exchange between Black people that is an important form of community building. It is in this quick, intentional recognition that one affirms the other in the space that they take up. The motivation for this acknowledgment of other Black people, particularly in non-Black spaces, is that of seeing and embracing the other individual. It is creating community, and it is what Black librarians do tirelessly and lovingly for Black patrons in addition to their everyday work. Black librarians who spend that extra bit of time listening to and engaging with Black students, faculty, and members of the community usually find that these patrons eventually come back to see them, and only them, for assistance and sometimes just to chat. Certainly, it is typical for patrons to seek out the librarian who assisted them previously if, of course, they had a positive experience. However, Black library users often go to the Black librarian whom they have spotted out of familiarity and the community, if you will, that they share.

This results in additional labor for the Black librarian, albeit, a labor of love.

Of course, not all Black librarians engage in this extra labor. In fact, some library workers may come across as condescending and/or inconvenienced for having to assist patrons. I am not stating that all Black librarians give special attention to Black patrons. As a Black consumer and library user, I have encountered my fair share of downright bad customer service from Black people that at times felt intentional. I am referencing those who make the choice to look out for Black patrons. Many times, librarians do this out of a sense of responsibility to overcompensate for the less than stellar service that Black patrons may receive from other non-Black librarians. Additionally, Black librarians might also simply be positively responding to the racial sameness of the patron.

Any librarian of any racial background can do their job correctly and excellently. Yet the Black librarian's choice to be attentive and responsive and to share all their skills and knowledge with a Black patron goes beyond merely being nice or exhibiting model behavior on the job. Instead, this behavior is reserved, consciously or unconsciously, for Black library users as a celebration of collective identity. As a result, both parties may generally feel more comfortable with one another. Again, this is due to the respect and validation that the librarian gives to Black patrons through their acknowledgment of them. Oftentimes, the Black librarian fosters a sense of familiarity with Black patrons. If the librarian works with a patron repeatedly and forges a relationship with the individual, it would not be surprising if that relationship seemed almost familial for both parties.

As with "the nod," Black people see each other. Black librarians see Black patrons, and they know the history of libraries and how there was a time Black people were not even allowed inside of libraries. They know that the library can be intimating for all patrons but especially Black students, who all too often do not even feel welcomed on campus let alone the library. Black librarians read the news reports that continue to illustrate the latest incident of library workers calling the police because a Black person was too loud or looked like they did not belong. Similarly, Black librarians can relate to being discriminated against such as when patrons bypass them to go to other non-Black

"I'm Rooting for Everybody Black"   ~   69

library personnel only to be directed right back to the Black librarian. As a result, Black librarians frequently associate with Black patrons in familial ways. Consequently, a sense of kinship means that the Black student escorted out of the library is reminiscent of their own son, brother, or cousin (their mother's best friend's son).

Black librarians who are especially supportive and nurturing to Black library users can foster an environment in which they feel seen, heard, and respected. They accomplish this in a number of ways that can include advocating for Black student workers, bringing in their own resources to share with Black patrons, and offering information on helpful services outside of the library. The celebration of collective identity that informs the work of Black librarians helps Black patrons feel welcomed in the library but also results in added labor.

The following questions will help to identify whether one is partaking in the additional labor.

1. Do Black patrons want to see only you and ask others if you are around to assist them instead of someone else?
2. Do Black patrons frequently state that you remind them of family or friends?
3. Are Black patrons comfortable with you? Do they laugh or cry in your presence? Do they share personal details about their life with you?
4. Do you feel responsible for ensuring that Black library users have a positive experience in the library?
5. Do colleagues and/or library administrators question your productivity?
6. Do you find it difficult to provide evidence/statistics of your engagement with and service to library users?

The answers to the above-mentioned questions can determine whether one is taking on the extra labor to care for Black library users by validating them with a listening ear and a helping hand, all the while creating community for them. The extra work that Black librarians undertake is tremendously valuable and reveals both challenges and benefits. Their work is vital in helping to shape new perspectives about libraries. This is especially critical in changing the reasonably negative perspective that Black people oftentimes have regarding libraries. Such perspectives of Black library users include not feeling as though they are welcomed and wanted in the library and that the resources do not adequately reflect their research needs and interests.

Additionally, the efforts of Black librarians can undoubtedly have a direct correlation to school retention. This is due to the community building that Black librarians work to develop with Black faculty and students. Black librarians cultivate a celebration of collective identity with Black library users through acknowledgment, engagement, encouragement, and trust. Trust is earned, not given; thus, there is work involved in garnering trust from Black library users. The time, effort, and care bestowed on Black patrons establishes their trust that the Black librarian is giving them the very best library service with respect. This level of care encourages Black library users not just to return to the library but also to stay in school. After all, the library's mission is to support teaching and learning. By intentionally making Black faculty and staff feel welcomed in the library, soliciting their research resource needs, and actively addressing them and not discriminating against them, Black librarians support the library's mission and in turn contribute to campus-wide retention efforts.

Yet, regardless of what the additional labor of Black librarians produces by way of benefits, challenges exist as well. Such challenges are accusations from library administrators and colleagues of not working productively, the difficulty of documenting the additional labor, and the unfortunate emotional toll that the added work and opposition from others in the library take on Black librarians.

Extra time spent with Black faculty and students might spur discontented remarks from library administrators and colleagues toward Black librarians. Black librarians who have labored to forge friendly working relationships and who typically make time for a conversation with Black library users may be discouraged from providing that additional time and space for patrons. This is because the labor of community building on the part of the Black librarians is unseen. The camaraderie that Black librarians have with Black students and faculty is often misunderstood and unvalued.

Furthermore, when Black librarians attempt to document the additional time and effort expended in working with Black patrons, it can be very difficult to do. Establishing community, building trust, and working to ensure that Black patrons feel welcomed in the library do not always bode well when it comes to recording one's use of time to establish productivity. Still, it is important for library administrators to understand the value in the extra labor of Black librarians. Their efforts help to make the library inclusive, which is imperative for the success of the library, as it should be relevant and welcoming to all Black students and faculty.

However, when that additional labor is underestimated and/or disregarded, Black librarians may feel incredibly discouraged. On the one hand, colleagues and library administrators proclaim that they are being unproductive in their work. On the other hand, they know what it takes to interact with Black patrons to make them feel welcomed in the library. They need to engage in conversation, show interest in their research or inquiry, provide some sort of assistance, and be personable in a way that makes them feel comfortable. This requires intentionality; care; and, most of all, time—time that goes beyond the normal day-to-day duties and tasks involved with one's role in the library. Stress can result from having to get all things done while still giving extra time and assistance to some Black library users who sometimes seek out Black librarians to vent or to get advice. It would not be unusual for Black librarians to feel compelled to give them their undivided attention or careful feedback.

In recent years, Pew Research Center surveys "show that most black adults feel that they are part of a broader black community."[1] Additionally, "Black adults who said they feel strongly connected to a broader black community are more likely . . . to have engaged with organizations dedicated to improving the lives of black Americans by donating money, attending events or volunteering their time" (Barroso 2020). Thus, if Black librarians feel part of the broader Black community and their job is to assist patrons, the probability of their giving more of their time is high, and yet their additional labor is all too often overlooked. The stress of being overworked and undervalued can take an emotional toll on Black librarians. The extra care that Black librarians provide to Black library users could and should be provided to them as well.

Conclusion

It is important to recognize and value the unseen added labor of Black librarians who care for Black library users by creating community for them and helping to make them feel welcomed in all library spaces, fostering new perspectives about libraries, and contributing to school retention. Library administrators would benefit from being able to identify whether Black librarians are undertaking additional labor. Likewise, they should find ways for that labor to count toward their productivity. Black librarians who expend extra labor for Black library users are overworked and at times under stress yet oftentimes still find a way to be welcoming and attentive to Black library users in an intentional and nurturing manner. They should be recognized and compensated for their extraordinary efforts.

Note

1. Amber Barroso, "Most Black Adults Say Race Is Central to Their Identity and Feel Connected to a Broader Black Community," *Pew Center Research*, March 20, 2020, https://www.pewresearch.org/fact-tank/2020/02/05/most-black-adults-say-race-is-central-to-their-identity-and-feel-connected-to-a-broader-black-community/.

Bibliography

Amanda Barroso. (2020, February 5). "Most Black Adults Say Race Is Central to Their Identity and Feel Connected to a Broader Black Community. *Pew Center Research.* https://www.pewresearch.org/fact-tank/2020/02/05/most-black-adults-say-race-is-central-to-their-identity-and-feel-connected-to-a-broader-black-community/.

CHAPTER SIX

Assumed Identity

Realities of Afro-Caribbean Librarians

Twanna Hodge, Kelsa Bartley, and Kenya Flash

In libraries, the presumption that Black racial identity equates to African American heritage belies a struggle that often goes unseen by most. Afro-Caribbean library workers occupy a space that is constantly in question, rooted in the fact that they do not often share the same historical context of African Americans around them, and yet Afro-Caribbeans share the same contemporary socioracial treatment as African Americans.

In this chapter, we aim to explore distinct experiences of Afro-Caribbean library workers, their place in advocacy for themselves and African Americans, and the challenges of navigating "who actually counts as Black." We represent several English-speaking islands, territories, or countries from the Caribbean: the US Virgin Islands, Trinidad and Tobago, and Jamaica. As early-career librarians working in academic/research and health sciences libraries who arrived in the mainland United States at various life stages, we view the world and Black librarianship in similar but also distinctive ways. We plan to take readers through our experiences of presumed African American heritage in librarianship, the impact of culture on our personal and professional lives, our pathways to librarianship, and finally our approaches to the profession in an attempt to shed light on the diversity within Black librarianship.

Survey on Afro-Caribbean Presence in Black Librarianship

Between January 6 and February 16, 2021, an anonymous survey was created and disseminated to explore how many librarians identify as Afro-Caribbean or of Afro-Caribbean heritage living in the mainland United States. There were one hundred responses. Of these, 58 percent ($n = 58$) expressed Afro-Caribbean heritage, and 40 percent ($n = 40$) consider themselves to be Afro-Caribbean. The countries that had the greatest representation in the survey are Jamaica, the Dominican Republic, Puerto Rico, Haiti, and Trinidad and Tobago. The primary languages spoken were English, Spanish, and Haitian Creole. Participants indicated that they recognized creolization as unique languages within the survey. Many respondents are multilingual, with heritage from different islands, and over 40 percent racially identify as Black. Of respondents, 57 percent ($n = 57$) were born on the mainland, with 47 percent ($n = 47$) identifying as second-generation children of immigrants, 58 percent ($n = 58$) being primarily raised in the mainland United States.

Eighty-three percent ($n = 83$) were able to engage with their Afro-Caribbean culture as they grew up (which aligns with our experiences), 46 percent ($n = 46$) have lived in the mainland United States their entire life, with 40 percent ($n = 40$) residing in the United States for more than twenty years. Finally, respondents predominantly worked in academic libraries and public libraries. This data provided a sense of the size of the Afro-Caribbean library community but has also revealed that further study needs to be conducted. Some of our experiences align with the results above, and we are only three experiences of hundreds—possibly thousands—of Afro-Caribbean library workers' experiences and identities. Our chapter is, thus, part exploratory, part ethnographic. We hope you either see yourself and your community in this book or learn about how Afro-Caribbean librarians are similar to and different from African American librarians.

Authors' Experiences and Positionality

In the subsequent sections, each author will introduce the island she is from and then describe her experiences as an Afro-Caribbean librarian. The chapter will then move on to responses from two interviewees. We conclude with a discussion of shared experiences.

Twanna Hodge: A Virgin Islander's Story
St. Thomas is a part of the US Virgin Islands (USVI). The territory spans thirty-two square miles. March 31 marks Transfer Day to commemorate the transfer of power from Danish rule ended (from Denmark-colonized West Indies) to the US occupation (now in its 104th year). According to the CIA Factbook, the St. Thomas population totals 105,870 with racial/ethnic breakdown as Black (76 percent), White (15.6 percent), Asian (1.4 percent), other (4.9 percent), and mixed (2.1 percent). The main languages are English (71.6 percent), Spanish/Spanish Creole (17.2 percent), French/French Creole (8.6 percent), and more. It is an unincorporated organized territory of the United States with local self-government with the Revised Organic Act of the Virgin Islands, which functions as our constitution.[1] The colonial legacy from the Danish West Indies and now the United States is still alive and infused in the cultural, political, and economic structures. The primary economic industries are tourism, watch assembly, and rum distilling.[2]

I, Twanna, identify as a Virgin Islander, Afro-Caribbean, Caribbean American, and Black. I choose these identifiers in this specific order based on my upbringing on the island of St. Thomas, my African cultural influences, and ancestry. My identity is also shaped by the aftermath of the trans-Atlantic slave trade, my maternal and paternal connections to other Caribbean islands, and the impacts of migration from other Caribbean islands. Although I, like other US Virgin Islanders, was granted birthright citizenship and am thus a US citizen, my salient identity is predominantly centered on my upbringing. I use born and raised together since people can be born in one place and raised in one or many places, which impacts how they perceive the world and the identities claimed or ascribed to them.

After living on the island of St. Thomas for close to twenty-three years, earning my bachelor's degree from the University of the Virgin Islands[3] (UVI), a Historically Black College and University (HBCU), in September 2013, I came to the mainland for graduate school to pursue a master's in Library and Information Science from the University of Washington. I connected with Caribbean communities throughout graduate school, during my diversity residency, afterward when I returned to St. Thomas for a full-time position. I have since returned to the United States, holding positions at the State University of New York

Upstate and now at the University of Florida. When I returned home, it felt like a burden/pressure was relieved. I no longer had to code switch, represent the Virgin Islands, be a walking encyclopedia on all things Virgin Islands, nor an exotic being. I did not have to disclose my origins when others detected or guessed at an accent. Oftentimes, St. Thomas was confused with Jamaica among those who had never heard of it.

Eventually, in spite of my ability to fit in culturally and linguistically, my personal interests, career interests, trajectory, and growth set me apart in unexpected ways. I came to realize that my island home was not home for me anymore, though St. Thomas will remain my childhood home. While in St. Thomas, there was no conscious thought of engaging in Afro-Caribbeanness; it was ever present in the food, the music, and the Creole language. It was woven into my friendships and my connections. Now on the mainland, I keep in close contact with my friends and family from the islands, listen to traditional Afro-Caribbean music (soca, reggae, calypso, and more), patronize Caribbean restaurants, and support Caribbean LIS workers through collaborations. I am committed to continuing to learn about the Virgin Islands and Caribbean history and by simply being myself.

Though I carry my Afro-Caribbean identity wherever I go, it took a backseat when navigating Black librarianship. This dynamic began in 2014 when I joined the Black Caucus of American Library Association.[4] I have served on several committees for several years, and now I'm cochairing the National Conference of African American Librarians[5] XI Program Committee. I have been exposed to much of Black librarianship and have felt embraced. Still, there is always a gap in the representation of Afro-Caribbean heritage and identity. My decision to become a librarian in middle school was influenced by mostly Caribbean and Black library workers as role models. I did not know that the US library profession is over 86 percent white or that I would engage with so few Afro-Caribbean library workers. My initial engagement in the iSchool Inclusion Institute[6] and the Smithsonian Minority Awards Program[7] introduced core concepts and provided research and work experiences, while also ingraining my racially minoritized status in the United States. With the help of diversity recruitment programs such as the ALA Spectrum Scholarship[8] and the now defunct Association of Research Libraries Career Enhancement Program,[9] I became a part of communities that supported my growth and development in the profession. I specifically connected with other Black library workers to learn how to negotiate a historically, traditionally, and predominantly white profession without sacrificing my authentic self. I ultimately recognized that my social identity is not inferior to my professional identity.

Settler colonialism, systematic and institutional racism, colorism, tokenism, racial battle fatigue, deauthentication, emotional and cultural labor, imposter syndrome, the characteristics of white supremacy, and especially erasure and silences have plagued my experiences on the US mainland. Exclusionary practices are built within these systems and structures that we are only now (somewhat) acknowledging. To be included in this acknowledgment, you have to identify within the recognized categories that dehumanize and reinforce pariah-like status, based on race/ethnicity, access to resources, and more.

As I reflect on Black and Afro-Caribbean librarianship, I operate within both spheres while still learning how to balance the two identities. There are times when I operate within one identity. This reality is magnified by the fact that the Caribbean is divided by water and politics but connected by culture, colonialism, imperialism, colorism, geographic location to Africa, the specter of hurricanes, and global neglect and abuse. We are invisible in ways similar to Black Americans but also different. We are judged based on our accents/patois/creole/languages, mannerisms (too aggressive or forthright), and environmental, familial, and individual experiences. Afro-Caribbean identity is complex, nuanced, beautiful, lyrical, all while impacted by historical factors. There are as many ways of being Afro-Caribbean as there are Afro-Caribbeans. This is one story out of many, and other stories need to be shared.

Kelsa Bartley: A Trinidadian American's Story
The twin island Republic of Trinidad and Tobago is the southernmost nation in the Caribbean Island chain. Trinidad, the larger of the two islands, located just seven miles north of Venezuela, comprises an area of about 1,850 square miles. Tobago spans roughly 115 square miles.[10] The discovery of oil in Trinidad in 1910 made the nation one of the most prosperous in the Caribbean,[11] with petroleum and natural gas production sustaining the economy. Tourism closely follows, generated

by the pre-Lenten, postcolonial celebration of Carnival and the idyllic beaches of Tobago. The islands have a diverse mix of ethnicities due to their unique colonial legacy from plantation slavery and indentured servitude. The islands' approximately 1.3 million people are mostly of East Indian (35.4 percent) and African (34.2 percent) descent, with 22.8 percent of mixed ancestry, including those of both African and East Indian heritage.[12] The other 8 percent includes people of Chinese and Syrian origin, Caribs—descendants of one of the native indigenous tribes—and people descended or expatriated from a variety of European countries. Only 0.6 percent of Trinbagonians identify as white. Trinidad and Tobago gained independence from Britain on August 31, 1962, becoming a republic in 1976 and fully separated from British rule. Trinidad and Tobago has its own constitution, a president as head of state, and a democratic system of government led by a prime minister. Prominent Americans of Trinbagonian heritage include civil rights activist Stokely Carmichael, actors and entertainers such as Geoffrey Holder, Heather Headley, Nia Long, Nikki Minaj, Winston Duke, Alfonso Ribeiro, and many others.

I consider myself Trinidadian American and Black. Born and raised on the island of Trinidad, I migrated to the United States in my midtwenties. I've spent most of my adult life as a legal immigrant; almost fifteen years later, I am an American. A bachelor's degree in photography was my initial entry point into the United States. I wanted to further my education in the field as a master photographer and teacher. Pursuing higher education was expected and vigorously encouraged as part of my upbringing. My grandfather was a journalist and instilled the value of education into our family. I chose America because my mother migrated here in the late 1980s. After she became a US citizen, she sponsored my eventual citizenship. Her courage and sacrifice forged a pathway for future success for my younger brother and me and gave me the opportunity for a deviation from island life.

My fully formed Trinbagonian identity influenced my migration to the United States and made it easier to hold on to my "Trini-ness" for the first few years, without feeling obligated to embrace an American or African American identity. Miami, the city I live in, is known as a US gateway to the Caribbean and Latin America. This also made it easier to connect with other Trinbagonian Americans and Afro-

Caribbean people but also exist contently as a person from somewhere else, as so many others exist and live in South Florida. Much of my continued connection in the early part of my American experience had been driven by my immigrant status. I had to prove that I was still connected to the islands in order to remain in status. Once I got permanent residency, however, I then had to prove myself worthy of American citizenship. My ties to the island have weakened as my allegiances shifted. Being in the United States for such a long time, with the strong societal pressure to assimilate into American culture—expectedly into African American culture—I sometimes feel my Trinidadian identity melting away with every code switch. Acculturation is happening regardless how much I resist it. Added to the vulnerability of being Black in America, I often have conflicting thoughts about who I am and my place in this country.

I was keenly aware of my Blackness early in life. As a postcolonial, multicultural society, Trinidad and Tobago has its own racial and socioeconomic tensions that make racism, colorism, and classism unavoidable. But no one would be surprised by whichever career path I chose. Being a librarian in Trinidad and Tobago is as normal a career path as choosing to be a doctor, lawyer, politician, or engineer; it is not unique. You just get your education, get a job, and go on living life. However, a Black librarian in the United States, particularly within academia, and in medical libraries specifically, is essentially considered of unicorn status.

Because of the diverseness of South Florida, my first engagement with Black librarians and library workers happened early in my library career. When I started my library career as a paraprofessional at the University of Miami, there was an African American librarian and several Black library workers on staff who made me feel welcome. There was even an Indo-Trinidadian librarian on staff. Both librarians are still my colleagues today. I had interacted with Caribbean library workers while living in Trinidad and working as a photography cataloger in a television station media library as I awaited US residency. My supervisor then was a Jamaican librarian. These experiences did not prepare me for librarianship in the United States, a majority white profession, even though Blacks comprise a racial minority group in America. My first hint was discovering highly competitive "minority" scholarships. I applied for all of them, not fully realizing the gravity of why they were there in the first place. It was jarring for me to hear over sixty Spectrum Scholars express their experiences of microaggressions, implicit bias, isolation, and overt racism in the profession while attending my first major library conference. It then became clear that I needed to align myself with colleagues of color if I wanted to thrive in libraries.

Subsequently, I became a member of the African American Medical Librarians Alliance (AAMLA) Caucus[13,14] of the Medical Library Association (MLA);[15] I currently serve as chair for 2020–2021. AAMLA has been my professional home since joining MLA after receiving its scholarship for underrepresented students while in library school. I was mentored by the then incoming MLA president, Beverly Murphy, the first African American person to hold the office. Later, I had the opportunity to meet the first woman and African American Librarian of Congress, Carla Hayden, as an ALA Spectrum Scholar. These two experiences early in my librarian career really impressed upon me the importance of having a seat at the table as a Black librarian and emphasized the responsibility of paving the way for future librarians of color in decision-making roles in our profession. AAMLA has nurtured the sense of belonging that seems missing in other spheres of my burgeoning librarian career. However, I experienced an intense identity crisis and imposter syndrome after becoming the chair of the group of African American librarians as an Afro-Caribbean librarian. I was a new librarian, a new American, and by extension, a new African American. I assumed this role less than a year before the onslaught of COVID-19 and its devastating effects on the Black community that were directly linked to health disparities caused by racism. My term as chair began just a couple weeks after the murder of George Floyd due to systematic racism and police brutality. Suddenly, I was spearheading racial justice initiatives, as I was also beginning to discern what being an African American really meant in the contexts of libraries and in society. I immediately recognized that my experiences made my viewpoint and reactions to injustices and structural inequity different from those of my Black colleagues while being acutely aware that those same issues also affect me directly because in America I am Black first, anything and everything else after.

Afro-Caribbean librarians have to balance the idea of an "exceptional immigrant" with their presumed identities as African Americans. Exceptionalism has always been rewarded in the immigration system, but the pressure to maintain this ideal of the perfect immigrant continues long after the immigration process is over. Sometimes, I feel like I am overcompensating with my achievements. I am seeking the same drive that I had when I first migrated. I struggle with the notion that I am considered less capable because I come from a so-called Third World country. In spite of AAMLA's nurturing atmosphere, the urge to prove myself worthy of being an African American librarian still persists, especially when exploring social justice issues that affect Black communities. Experiences such as these can cause additional stressors for Afro-Caribbean immigrant library workers; this strain remains unspoken among peers and potentially unrecognized in ourselves. Our stories as Afro-Caribbean librarians will uncover these challenges and highlight the distinctiveness of our lived experiences.

Kenya Flash: A Jamaican American's Story
Jamaica spans 4,243 square miles.[16] In spite of its size,[17] the island has had a huge global footprint. According to the CIA Factbook, Jamaica has approximately 2.8 million residents, with 92.1 percent of residents identifying as Black, 6.1 percent as mixed, 0.8 percent East Indian, 0.4 percent other, and 0.7 percent unspecified as of 2011. Jamaica boasts an 88.7 percent literacy rate. In spite of celebrating independence on August 6, 1962, Jamaica still identifies as a parliamentary democracy with the governor general of Jamaica representing the Queen of England. The colonial legacy from England is still very much alive in social and class interactions. Jamaica has seven national heroes: Nanny of the Maroons, Sam Sharpe, Marcus Mosiah Garvey, George William Gordon, Paul Bogle, Norman Washington Manley, and Sir Alexander Bustamante.[18]

I identify as Jamaican American because I have lived in the United States so long that I cannot separate whether I am more Jamaican or American. I lived in several places throughout my youth where there were some Jamaicans and, in some cases, no Black people. I was surrounded by a large family, which helped me maintain my identity, but it was hard. Additionally, Blackness was not highlighted during my short time living in Jamaica. Almost as soon as I entered the United States, the need to assimilate was burned into my mind. It was on my first day in the American school system. My classmates in my predominantly Black middle school called me "Kunta Kinte" because of my Jamaican accent. Standing out was not acceptable, and I believe it still is not. Yet, even though I came to the United States as a child, I do not see myself moving back. This is because the Jamaica I knew when I was a child does not exist as I knew it.

The silence regarding Afro-Caribbean identities within Black librarianship is to me reminiscent of the way I worked to curb the edges of my speech, to blend, so the students could not hear inflections that set me apart. I do not mean to say that this is required in Black librarianship. Indeed, this does not even seem to be expected as much by Black librarians as it does by well-meaning white "allies" who want to understand the Black experience or how Black people feel about certain things. In my institution, I am expected to speak more for African Americans than I am for immigrants, and what gets missed is that my world is a mashup of the two.

In the context of librarianship this ultimately means I have to be thoroughly engaged with issues and expectations of Black librarians. I attempt to do this by speaking with Black librarians, by supporting Black students (in my institution, I am the most public-facing Black librarian specifically among only three Black librarians), and I explore Black librarianship through literature. I think Afro-Caribbean librarianship is a bit more nuanced, as an Afro-Caribbean librarian where to focus your energy is split between the Black community, the immigrant/non-Black Caribbean communities, and the community at large.

One of the conversations I have with many women of Caribbean American descent is the impact that culture has on their personal and professional lives. In my experience, it is rare to find a Caribbean person who has not considered the effect that their position has on the family and the way it is seen within their family. Many of our countries rely on remittances and/or migration to boost the economy and to help the livelihoods of those who remain behind. The phenomenon is so acute that a researcher in Jamaica coined the term "barrel children."[19] The idea that the younger generation or those abroad would take care of older family members is one that affects many of us. Indeed, the expectation around success and job choice is not simply one that is individual, but a family choice impacting whether one is considered "successful" or "worthless."

I started working in libraries as a paraprofessional in a public services role. I worked in three different positions at two institutions while I got my library degree and then took on an adjunct position at a small university. Even with that experience and two master's degrees, I received interviews for only diversity residency positions. I worked as a diversity resident at the University of Knoxville and then as their social sciences librarian for political science and sociology. Since then, I started working at Yale University as the librarian for political science, global affairs, and government information.

In my current and previous roles, I have connected with those who embrace the immigrant community more strongly than other groups. This is perhaps because, at one point, I was told by a faculty member early in my higher education career, which goes further back than my library career, that I could not speak for the Black experience because I was not born here. Or it may come from the fact that as an international undergraduate student I was more accepted within the international community. I cannot explain where it comes from. However, I connect with those who question what home is and who have had to leave their past and ancestors behind to forge a new life. This does not mean I do not connect with African Americans; I do. It is just a bit more tenuous primarily due to the worry that I am inauthentically associated with the African American experience. I wish others knew that Afro-Caribbean identity is core to who we are and it cannot be separated. The fact that it is muted through the profession hurts.

Presumed Black from Our Perspectives

We, the authors, have all been presumed African American within our organizations, our social lives, and in American society. One salient thing that happens when you have been raised here or have lived here for a while is that your identity as a person from the Caribbean is in question. How well you speak patois, which Caribbean enclave you belong to, how often you travel back home to the Caribbean—these factors all become questioned as part of your Caribbean-ness. And even that does not save you from the statement that you "are foreign" in the eyes of "real" Caribbean people. Between this sentiment and the need to blend, we find ourselves in three worlds, but none of our choosing. The first is trying to represent ourselves in corporate America (where we are expected to be African American), the second is within the African American world itself, and finally, the need to prove that we are Caribbean enough and have not abandoned our roots. For us, this is complicated by our inability to control how we can stay immersed in Afro-Caribbean culture.

There is an emotional and psychic toll one engages when existing in these spaces. In the constant code switching, we fight to retain our own identities and our own authenticity in the midst of persistent erasure. We acknowledge that race was not a limiting factor in the spaces where we originated to the same extent as the United States. Subsequently, advocacy or promotion of ideals where this knowledge is expected becomes awkward. Once our identities are known, we are expected to speak for cultures that constantly shift due to migration and labor flows. Like many African Americans within our circles, we deal with the perception of "African American-ness" from the outside and yet are categorized as different from African Americans. Between this perception and the cultural need to be successful, we are shaped into model minorities. There is a unique isolation that results from attempting to balance all of these roles while also at times being the only one from your culture in the room. One adapts, and perhaps assimilates, while silently balancing these thoughts.

We are here. We matter. We are not a monolith. We are not representatives, spokespersons, or role models of or for our island, country, or culture. Afro-Caribbean identity is incredibly complex like other identities, and it morphs over time. It is acknowledging and connecting to our African ancestors, understanding the influences and impact of being in the Caribbean and the forces that lead us to be there, claiming our heritage, choosing and defining what it is. It is being proud of our past and present and working toward a liberatory future for us and others. Our message is to not exclude or "other" us when you hear our accent, patois, or creole languages. Please do not say that our difference equals oppression and that we are not American or do not belong. Let us push back against Caribbean stereotypes and generalizations that widen instead of close ethnic divides.

Conclusion

We hope this chapter has shed some light on a few of the heretofore silent experiences of Afro-Caribbean librarians within Black librarianship. By recognizing and highlighting the experiences of Afro-Caribbean librarians, the authors hope to advocate for a holistic and inclusive approach to Black librarianship that engages dialogue with members of the Pan-African diaspora. Our general survey and discussions with the interviewees lead us to the conclusion that this work is worth further study and exploration. This includes questions of identity, desire (lack thereof) to return to the Caribbean, and definitions of home among other things.

The limitations of this book chapter include the fact that the librarians do not represent as much diversity within Afro-Caribbean librarianship as the authors hoped to capture. As noted, the authors are all female-identifying librarians from Anglophone Caribbean countries who work in academic/research or medical libraries. We invite our readers to explore the experiences of two male Afro-Caribbean librarians interviewed for this project (http://bit.ly/interview2macl). We were not equipped to discuss other intersections of Afro-Caribbean librarian identity—for example, LGBTQ Afro-Caribbean librarians—among other variances. We close this chapter with the strong encouragement for more open conversations and research on identity within Black librarianship.

Notes

1. US Department of the Interior, "Definitions of Insular Area Political Organizations," accessed January 19, 2021, https://www.doi.gov/oia/islands/politicatypes.
2. US Central Intelligence Agency, "Virgin Islands—the World Factbook," accessed January 19, 2021, https://www.cia.gov/the-world-factbook/countries/virgin-islands/.
3. University of the Virgin Islands, "Home Page," accessed January 19, 2021, https://www.uvi.edu/default.aspx.

4. Black Caucus American Library Association (BCALA), "Home," accessed January 19, 2021, https://www.bcala.org/.

5. National Conference of African American Librarians, "11th National Conference of African American Librarians," accessed January 19, 2021, http://www.ncaal.org/.

6. iSchool Inclusion Institute, "Home Page," accessed January 19, 2021, http://www.i3-inclusion.org/.

7. Smithsonian Office of Fellowships and Internships, "Diversity Awards Program—Internship (Formerly the Minority Awards Program)," accessed January 19, 2021, https://www.smithsonianofi.com/minority-internship-program/.

8. American Library Association Office of Diversity," Spectrum Scholarship Program—About Spectrum," accessed January 19, 2021, http://www.ala.org/advocacy/spectrum.

9. Association of Research Libraries, "Career Enhancement Program Application Deadline Extended," accessed January 19, 2021, https://www.arl.org/news/career-enhancement-program-application-deadline-extended/.

10. David Watts et al., "Trinidad and Tobago: People, Culture, Language, Map, Population, & Flag," *Encyclopedia Britannica*, accessed February 11, 2021, https://www.britannica.com/place/Trinidad-and-Tobago.

11. US Central Intelligence Agency, "Trinidad and Tobago—the World Factbook," accessed February 11, 2021, https://www.cia.gov/the-world-factbook/countries/trinidad-and-tobago/.

12. David Watts et al., "Trinidad and Tobago: Ethnic Composition," *Encyclopedia Britannica*, accessed February 11, 2021, https://www.britannica.com/place/Trinidad-and-Tobago/People#/media/1/605453/210035.

13. African American Medical Librarian's Alliance Caucus, "Home Page," accessed February 11, 2021, https://sites.google.com/view/aamla-mla/home.

14. Medical Library Association, "African American Medical Librarians Alliance Caucus," accessed February 11, 2021, https://www.mlanet.org/page/caucus-aamla.

15. Medical Library Association, "Home Page," accessed February 11, 2021, https://www.mlanet.org/.

16. "Jamaica—Location, Size, and Extent," *Nations Encyclopedia*, accessed January 17, 2021, https://www.nationsencyclopedia.com/Americas/Jamaica-LOCATION-SIZE-AND-EXTENT.html.

17. Small compared to the United States, but we are the third largest island in the Caribbean.

18. "Heroes," *Jamaica Information Service*, accessed January 17, 2021, https://jis.gov.jm/information/heroes/.

19. Melissa Noel, "Jamaica's 'Barrel Children' Often Come Up Empty with a Parent Abroad," *NBC News*, accessed January 30, 2021, https://www.nbcnews.com/news/nbcblk/jamaica-s-barrel-children-often-come-empty-parent-abroad-n830636.

Bibliography

African American Medical Librarian's Alliance Caucus. "Home." Accessed February 11, 2021. https://sites.google.com/view/aamla-mla/home.

American Library Association Office of Diversity. "Spectrum Scholarship Program—About Spectrum." Last modified March 29, 2017. Accessed January 19, 2021. http://www.ala.org/advocacy/spectrum.

Association of Research Libraries. "Career Enhancement Program Application Deadline Extended." Last modified October 16, 2013. Accessed January 19, 2021. https://www.arl.org/news/career-enhancement-program-application-deadline-extended/.

Black Caucus American Library Association (BCALA). "Home." Last modified October 30, 2019. Accessed January 19, 2021. https://www.bcala.org/.

Britannica Academic, s.v. "Trinidad and Tobago," accessed February 12, 2021, https://www.britannica.com/ place/Trinidad-and-Tobago/People#/media/1/605453/210035.

iSchool Inclusion Institute. "Home Page." Accessed January 19, 2021. http://www.i3-inclusion.org/.

Jamaica Information Service. "Heroes." Last modified August 12, 2013. Accessed January 17, 2021. https://jis.gov.jm/information/heroes/.

Medical Library Association. "African American Medical Librarians Alliance Caucus." Accessed February 11, 2021. https://www.mlanet.org/page/caucus-aamla.

Medical Library Association. "Home Page." Accessed February 11, 2021. https://www.mlanet.org/.

National Conference of African American Librarians. "11th National Conference of African American Librarians." Accessed January 19, 2021. http://www.ncaal.org/.

Nations Encyclopedia. "Jamaica—Location, Size, and Extent." Accessed January 17, 2021. https://www.nationsencyclopedia.com/Americas/Jamaica-LOCATION-SIZE-AND-EXTENT.html.

Noel, Melissa. "Jamaica's 'Barrel Children' Often Come Up Empty with a Parent Abroad." *NBC News*. Last modified December 27, 2017. Accessed January 30, 2021. https://www.nbcnews.com/news/nbcblk/jamaica-s-barrel-children-often-come-empty-parent-abroad-n830636.

Smithsonian Office of Fellowships and Internships. "Diversity Awards Program—Internship (Formerly the Minority Awards Program)." Accessed January 19, 2021. https://www.smithsonianofi.com/minority-internship-program/.

University of the Virgin Islands. "Home Page." Accessed January 19, 2021. https://www.uvi.edu/default.aspx.

US Central Intelligence Agency. "Trinidad and Tobago—the World Factbook." Accessed February 11, 2021. https://www.cia.gov/the-world-factbook/countries/trinidad-and-tobago/.

US Central Intelligence Agency. "Virgin Islands—the World Factbook." Accessed January 19, 2021. https://www.cia.gov/the-world-factbook/countries/virgin-islands/.

US Department of the Interior. "Definitions of Insular Area Political Organizations." Last modified June 12, 2015. Accessed January 19, 2021. https://www.doi.gov/oia/islands/politicatypes.

Watts, David, Arthur Robinson, Raymond Napoleon, and Bridget M. Brereton. "Trinidad and Tobago—People." *Encyclopedia Britannica*. Accessed February 11, 2021. https://www.britannica.com/place/Trinidad-and-Tobago.

Watts, David, Arthur Robinson, Raymond Napoleon, and Bridget M. Brereton. "Trinidad and Tobago—People, Culture, Language, Map, Population, & Flag." *Encyclopedia Britannica*. Accessed February 11, 2021. https://www.britannica.com/place/Trinidad-and-Tobago.

Recommended Reading

Chancellor, Renate L. "Racial Battle Fatigue: The Unspoken Burden of Black Women Faculty in LIS." *Journal of Education for Library and Information Science* 60, no. 3 (2019): 182–89.

Diggs, Gregory A., Dorothy F. Garrison-Wade, Diane Estrada, and Rene Galindo. "Smiling Faces and Colored Spaces: The Experiences of Faculty of Color Pursuing Tenure in the Academy." *The Urban Review* 41, no. 4 (2009): 312–33.

Durr, Marlese, and Adia M. Harvey Wingfield. "Keep Your 'N' in Check: African American Women and the Interactive Effects of Etiquette and Emotional Labor." *Critical Sociology* 37, no. 5 (2011): 557–71.

Flors, Juan, and Miriam Jiménez Román. "Triple-Consciousness? Approaches to Afro-Latino Culture in the United States." *Latin American and Caribbean Ethnic Studies* 4, no. 3 (2009): 319–28.

Foner, Nancy, ed. *Islands in the City: West Indian Migration to New York*. University of California Press, 2001.

Hall, Stuart. "Cultural Identity and Diaspora." Master's thesis, 1990. https://warwick.ac.uk/fac/arts/english/currentstudents/postgraduate/masters/modules/asiandiaspora/hallculturalidentityanddiaspora.pdf.

Hao, Richie Neil, Bryant Keith Alexander, Bernadette Marie Calafell, Kate Willink, Amy Kilgard, and John T. Warren. "Building Community in the Academy through Mentoring: Reflections and Directions." *Liminalities: A Journal of Performance Studies* 8, no. 5 (2012): 30–55.

Jaschik, Scott. "Who Counts as a Black Student?" *Inside Higher Ed.* October 9, 2017. https://www.insidehighered.com/admissions/article/2017/10/09/cornell-students-revive-debate-whom-colleges-should-count-black.

Louis, Dave A., Keisha V. Thompson, Patriann Smith, Hakim Mohandas Amani Williams, and Juann Watson. "Afro-Caribbean Immigrant Faculty Experiences in the American Academy: Voices of an Invisible Black Population." *The Urban Review* 49, no. 4 (2017): 668–91.

Onyenekwu, Ifeyinwa, and Chrystal A. George Mwangi. "'Who Counts as a Black Student' Is Not a New Debate." *Inside Higher Ed.* November 27, 2017. https://www.insidehighered.com/admissions/views/2017/11/27/debate-about-who-counts-black-student-not-new-essay.

Patton, Tracey Owens. "Reflections of a Black Woman Professor: Racism and Sexism in Academia." *Howard Journal of Communications* 15, no. 3 (2004): 185–200.

Rivera, Petra R. "Triple Consciousness." *Transition* 105, no. 1 (2011): 156–63.

Smith, Patriann, S. Joel Warrican, Alex Kumi-Yeboah, and Janet Richards. "Understanding Afro-Caribbean Educators' Experiences with English across Caribbean and US Contexts and Classrooms: Recursivity, (Re)Positionality, Bidirectionality." *Teaching and Teacher Education* 69 (2018): 210–22.

Vickerman, Milton. "Tweaking a Monolith: The West Indian Immigrant Encounter with 'Blackness.'" In *Islands in the City: West Indian Migration to New York*, edited by Nancy Foner, 237–56. University of California Press, 2001.

Wingfield, Adia Harvey. "Are Some Emotions Marked 'Whites Only'? Racialized Feeling Rules in Professional Workplaces." *Social Problems* 57, no. 2 (2010): 251–68.

CHAPTER SEVEN

The Western Librarian

Community and Collective Individualism

James Allen Davis Jr.

Black librarianship is often situated within the Deep South and Eastern corridor of the United States. Considering the historic familial ties and migration patterns among the Black population, it is understandable to think of Black librarianship in the context of the Southern and Eastern states. African Americans' strong and fascinating presence in the American West is often left out of the American story, and the case is the same for library information science. The one hundredth anniversary of the brutal Tulsa, Oklahoma, massacre in 2021[1] reminded us that the American West once offered hope, prosperity, and progress for African Americans before a white mob's deadly, terrorous rampage. African Americans too were Western pioneers. This chapter spotlights Black contributions to library development in Denver, Colorado, a city that comprises only 9 percent Blacks.

The pioneering of library services to Black communities is an interesting journey. According to the Alabama Slave Code of 1833, "any person who attempts to teach any free person of color or slave to spell, read or write shall be fined not less than $250 and not more than $500."[2] Many other states adopted antiliteracy laws similar to this because they believed teaching slaves to read could result in slave revolts. Fundamentally, Black people were deemed inferior. It is not a stretch to surmise that, given this historical context, public libraries were never created with the Black, indigenous, and people of color (BIPOC) community in mind. Stories of the Greenville Eight in South Carolina and the Tougaloo Nine in Jackson, Mississippi,[3] demonstrated two things: first, that "libraries mirrored the social conditions" of that century, as stated by Stuart A. P. Murray in *The Library: An Illustrated History*; and second, that Blacks were tired of being subjugated by systems that did not mind using their tax dollars and exploiting them as labor, while at the same time denying them equal access to the municipalities their tax dollars supported.[4]

We witness this racist tension between public funding and denial of service to Blacks. Carnegie-funded libraries often came with a requirement to subsidize their libraries with an annual amount of 10 percent. For example, in Richmond, Virginia, Carnegie agreed to give $100,000,00 to the building of a library as long as the city agreed to furnish the site and tax itself an annual $10,000 believing that the community would take an active role in support of the library. The library was a center for reading, learning, culture, and civic engagement, a place to share and exchange ideas; however, several Carnegie-funded libraries were segregated rather than grant Blacks access to the same libraries. A comparatively small amount of money was given to build separate libraries for Black community members.

Such was the case in Denver, Colorado, where I now serve as a Black male librarian. The community had to take an active role in advocating for library services for their community, and as the community began to grow and change demographically, the library could not remain neutral and aloof if it wished to be part of the community it was serving. When asked about this reality, Terry Nelson, a notable and celebrated librarian in Colorado, shared:

> Nothing came easily; everybody had to work on addressing the needs of the Black community: working to get the academic, educational, and recreational materials in the library. The staff had to really listen to what the community was saying.[5]

The Warren Library opened on May 21, 1913, and was the first branch of the Denver Public Library; it opened after the city secured funding from the Andrew Carnegie Corporation. Later, due to population growth and the changing needs of the community, there was a need for a new branch. With the help of community members and library officials, the Warren Library branch was relocated and renamed the Ford Warren Library, named after Dr. Justina Ford, Denver's first Black physician, and the former Warren name, named after Bishop Henry White Warren, an American Methodist Episcopal bishop credited for cofounding the Iliff School of Theology in Denver, Colorado.[6]

It is very important that those who work in communities that are predominantly BIPOC work toward advocating for services that will meet the needs of the community they serve.

Currently, there has been more emphasis placed on hearing the voice of the customer and tailoring library services to meet the needs of the community. In 2016, the Denver Public Library started looking at more deliberate ways in connecting with the communities they serve in the city of Denver. They decided to develop a team to work on their initiative of community engagement by choosing a few of their staff to go through the Harwood Training program and attend a few "turned outward trainings," which were a key part of the Hardwood model. Throughout the following years, they started having community conversations at all of their branch locations. Doing this allowed them to hear the voices in their community and to understand the shared aspirations of the community, which would help them have a greater impact on the services they provide to several of their communities. The Pauline Robinson branch of the Denver Public Library is located in a predominantly African American community and is named after Pauline Robinson, Denver Public Library's first African American librarian. Leslie Williams, senior librarian of the Pauline Robinson Branch, shared the following:

> My work with the community conversations will be one of many highlights of my career here. To give more context, there are two library branches serving the same neighborhood in Denver, in a neighborhood called Park Hill. Our locations were selected to dive deeper into community aspirations because we share the same neighbors and customers. We are literally a mile apart, serving over 5,000 residents. Bridging the community together between the Park Hill and Pauline Robinson branch libraries was not as hard as we thought it would be.[7]

Importance of Representation in Public Libraries

For me, it meant a great deal to be able to serve the communities that I worked in and at times resided in. I am what you call a "Denverite," someone who is born in the city of Denver, the capital of the State of Colorado. According to the US Census, Colorado's population is about 6 million people and of that 6 million people 6.4 percent of them are Black. The total population in the city of Denver is about 727,000, and Blacks make up about 9.8 percent of that population. I am within that number, a relatively small number of Blacks within the State of Colorado.[8]

Given the relatively small number of Blacks in Colorado, it was not uncommon to find yourself being the only Black person in certain spaces, especially those areas outside of the community you worked in. It is interesting to me how much these spaces would mirror the demographic makeup of the state of Colorado, just a few Blacks in the white spaces that served the Black community; the majority of these spaces were not positions of leadership.

The first Black male librarian in a position of leadership I met was Danny Walker, who lived on the same block as I did; the day I met him we were both working in our yards.

Generally, our discussions would be casual exchanges either about the weather or about house maintenance, but as time went on we forged quite a friendship and learned more about each other. During one of our conversations, we talked about our jobs, and he informed me that he managed the African American Research Library in the historical Five Points neighborhood of Denver, a neighborhood affectionately referred to as the "Harlem of the West."

It was through these conversations that I learned more about what librarians do. It went beyond checking out books or reader's advisory. Libraries and those who worked as librarians had a connection to the community and contributed greatly toward building a strong and vibrant community. I asked Danny Walker about his time at the Denver Public Library and here's what he shared with me:

> I started at DPL February of 1995. There was only one Black male I know who got a library degree during the early years of my time there and he left after a few months.

However, for over ten years I was the only African American male who managed a branch library for the Denver Public Library, ironically the African American Research Library. For thirteen years I was the only African American male senior librarian supervisor and one of only two African American male librarians for fifteen years.

I loved being a librarian at the Denver Public Library, but for African American male librarians, the library lacked the ability to recruit, retain, or promote in any impactful manner.

As a librarian, I believed it was important for the Black community to see an African American male librarian and to understand that the profession was more than a little old white lady telling a bunch of rowdy kids to be quiet. I took pride in the expression on people's faces when I told them I was a librarian. I felt it was my mission to take off the veil of secrecy the library had for when it came to its most valuable resources, resources that could change people's lives from patent research to business ratios.[9]

According to the diversity counts table from ALA, Black male librarians still represent a very small percentage of the population of credentialed librarians across the nation, so one can only imagine what the percentage of male librarians would be in Denver.[10] If overall Black male librarians make up less than 1 percent of the total population of librarians, it adds perspective to Danny's experience as an African American librarian and even more so as an African American male who managed a branch in the Denver Public Library, one of twenty-four branches.

On a personal level, I began to see Black librarianship as a viable field; before then my career track was teaching and community development, which quite honestly, I was able to see a balance of both in the field of information science. I am a firm believer that what libraries add to a community can only become more beneficial when libraries represent a diverse staff, especially in positions of leadership.

I often thought about the faces and positions you see at career days in high schools or the lack of recruitment that happens among Black males to the field of library science, and to be honest, unless I was exposed to a Black male who held a leadership position in the library and who was able to communicate what the Black male librarian represents to the community, I wouldn't have given this field a second thought.

Because of the conversation I had with Danny Walker, I pursued a career in libraries, a career that has opened up so many opportunities for me to work in the community I grew up in, the community I love, and the community I identified with.

Programs and Information Literacy in BIPOC Communities

In 1921, the ALA Roundtable met in Swampscott, Massachusetts, and the topic of discussion was "A Service to Negroes Roundtable." This discussion was led by Ernestine Rose, a white librarian of the Harlem Branch Library, 135th Street Branch. According to ALA's page the purpose of this meeting was to encourage outreach to the Black community as stated, "The roundtable began to examine the state of equitable access to library materials for African-Americans."[11] There were two meetings held, one in 1921 in Swampscott, Massachusetts, and one in 1922 in Detroit's Main Library. At the conference in Detroit, there was a discussion around a 1922 questionnaire that was sent to 122 libraries in which 98 responses were collected.

According to the 1922 *Bulletin of the American Library Association*, this questionnaire explored the size of the Black population in some cities, accommodations made to serve Black populations, availability of library collections to the Black population, the training and representation of Black library assistants, and whether there was Black representation on the governing board. According to ALA, the roundtable faced challenges among libraries in the North and South, based on differences about how library services should be conducted to the Black community. The discussions became so intense that the roundtable was eventually discontinued.

Almost one hundred years later, the results of the 1922 questionnaire are still relevant today. We are still addressing issues around library services to BIPOC communities, issues that are often based on what the library believes the community needs, without community engagement. How far removed are we from the damage caused by antiliteracy laws of the 1830s? What impact did they have on white perceptions of the Black population and how white institutions engage with BIPOC members of their community?

I am not discrediting the work that has been done throughout the early developing years of library services to the Black community. Rather, I am affirming the focus that was placed on opening up the opportunity for training Black library assistants; promoting Black librarians and Black representation on library boards if anything was and is the impetus to relevant programs that enhance information literacy in BIPOC communities. Throughout the eighteen plus years of my career in library services, I have seen firsthand how progressive institutions become when they center voices of BIPOC staff and are more intentional in hearing the voices of BIPOC members of their community. Doing this will make the library one of the most progressive institutions in developing more vibrant communities where information sharing and community engagement flourish.

Personal Introduction to the Field of LIS

Unlike a few of my colleagues, my time wasn't spent in libraries poring through collections and absorbing knowledge. I wish that were the case. I had a lot of catching up to do. I was an information seeker. I loved learning new things and had a very active imagination. I enjoyed learning new things and was very inquisitive, but that meant exploring places in the streets, not in the library.

My introduction to the library, quite honestly, started out of necessity. I needed another job because I left my job as a program coordinator for before- and after-school programs. My focus in college was teaching K–6 at the time, and after a few practicums, I was quickly dispelled of my desire to teach and went on to pursue youth mentoring and running after-school programs. However, after I met Danny Walker, as mentioned earlier, I decided to give the library a try.

I started in the circulation and security departments at the Ford Warren branch and became enamored by the services and opportunities to connect with the community that I identified with. Although I was warned by several white and Black security officers, "That library is in a rough neighborhood; you are going to have a rough time," it was the total opposite. The community was lively and full of life. The teens were simply ordinary teens, and people were engaged with the staff at the library. All the managers were white; the librarians were white, even the on-call librarians. Yet the neighborhood was mainly made up of BIPOC families. Some of the branch managers were problematic, to put it nicely; others were fully engaged and wanted to make a difference. Becky Brazil is one such example; she took the time to mentor me and guide me toward pursuing a degree in library science. When the opportunity presented itself for a LIS Fellowship grant through the Urban Librarians Council, I took it and went on to become a librarian, serving three locations of the Denver Public Library because of staff shortages.

My journey into leadership came when I attended a JCLC conference and saw firsthand African American managers and directors. I was so impressed that I became a member of the Black Caucus of the American Library Association and went back to Denver with a newfound vision and understanding of what it meant to be a Black librarian.

Collectivism and Personal Accountability

Early into my career, I knew we as information professionals have the tools for increasing information literacy in our communities. I knew there was a special responsibility to build strong BIPOC communities given the effect of political and socioeconomic disparities caused by structural and institutional racism. For this reason, my goal became to pursue leadership and management with the Denver Public Library. I connected with those who held leadership positions and took advantage of leadership opportunities that presented themselves. Despite opposition from white gatekeepers, I went on to push past the many roadblocks intentionally placed in my way. Since mentoring was part of my background, I welcomed opportunities to mentor others. I sought mentors for myself and eventually was accepted into the Denver Public Library's Leadership Academy, which allowed me to connect with others who had a passion for leadership.

I am now a branch manager at one of our twenty-four branches of the Denver Public Library. I have joined the BCALA Executive Board, and along with a few of my colleagues have started the Colorado Black Librarians Association in support and advocacy of Black librarians in Colorado.

Advocating for EDI Initiatives

Given the long and sordid history of racism in American society, it is not difficult to realize that public libraries are simply an extension of a deeply painful national sin of racism and slavery. The field lauds how progressive it is and has established the ALA Bill of Rights and Code of Ethics to guide its work in library and information science. History reveals the tedious journey that has been undertaken to hold the ALA accountable to the values that are presumed to be foundational: "We provide the highest level of service to all library users through appropriate and usefully organized resources; equitable service policies; equitable access; and accurate, unbiased, and courteous responses to all requests."[12]

One of the projects I had the privilege of working on in DPL's Leadership Academy was to write a proposal for an equity, diversity, and inclusion (EDI) consultant to help guide the Denver Public Library's work in their Diversity and Equity initiative. We assisted in helping the library establish the work along with a dedicated EDI committee. Thanks to the committee's work, a dedicated EDI manager was hired, and we have now started an EDI task force. Given its national reputation, there is no debate that the Denver Public Library is one of the most progressive libraries in terms of providing services to the unhoused, collaborating on community reentry programs for the recently incarcerated, new Americans, and those in need of job assistance. There is even an Older Adults Library with a dedicated Community Resource department with trained social workers and community advocates. There is now a greater push to "Lead with Race," or to realize that all these populations are affected by these growing disparities. Race is still the dominating factor across intersections of underserved communities. These programs are an extension of the pioneering spirit that characterizes Colorado and the West. It is great to observe a connection between our city's progressive ideals and the fundamental creed of human rights, which is, indeed, richly interwoven with African American values.

I am also a member of the GARE library interest team. GARE stands for Government Alliance of Race and Equity, a national alliance of government agencies that work to "achieve racial equity and advancing opportunities for all." Libraries can start by joining with other organizations that are doing this work in addition to learning about the importance of this work and communicating the importance of this work to their supporters.[13] The Denver Public Library exemplifies that libraries should spark conversations around racial disparities rather than hiding behind the guise of neutrality. History has shown at those times when libraries have attempted to be neutral, they have caused greater harm to the communities they serve. In 2015 before we started our EDI work, a few of my colleagues and I started a social book group called RADA, which stands for read, awareness, dialogue, and action. This was in response to a hurting community that was affected by ongoing police brutality and the murder of BIPOCs. The library could not in good conscience remain neutral while the community they claim to serve and be a part of was suffering. We started meeting and discussing issues like mass incarceration, mental illness in the Black community, immigration, gentrification, the school-to-prison pipeline, and so much more. We hired a strategic illustrator to capture these conversations and began developing workshops on race and privilege.

The community was very receptive to these conversations. Later, the Denver Public Library adopted the Harwood model and began to have further conversations within the communities we serve. These conversations have helped in charting the course for future work of DPL by helping to better communicate its values internally and externally and establish commitments to make the most vulnerable members of our communities a priority.

Conclusion

As a Black librarian, I understand that there is a shared history between myself and members of the communities I serve. This history is a part of the American fabric in every community I work in, whether or not the setting is predominantly BIPOC. My presence is still a reminder of this shared history. Though I and other Colorado librarians are physically distant from the majority of Black librarians who reside in the southern and eastern United States, we are nonetheless united through a shared mission and identity. I am an individual, but the work that I do is still connected to our collective Black librarian identity. My salient identity is that of an African American male in a proportionately white state, predominantly white field, and majority white library system. Although I identify as a cis-gendered male, it does not negate the many areas of intersectionality that BIPOC librarians have to navigate. The work that is being done in BIPOC communities must acknowledge the need of having leaders of color to represent various perspectives and heritages throughout organizations.

Notes

1. Madigan, Tim. *The Burning: Massacre, Destruction, and the Tulsa Race Riot of 1921*. Macmillan, 2001.
2. "Selections from Alabama's Laws Governing Slaves," *Social History for Every Classroom*, February 13, 2021, https://shec.ashp.cuny.edu/items/show/1640.
3. Preer, Jean L. "'This Year—Richmond!': The 1936 Meeting of the American Library Association." *Libraries & Culture* (2004): 137–160.
4. Stuart Murray, *The Library: An Illustrated History* (Chicago: Skyhorse, 2012), 207.
5. Terry Nelson, email message to the author, February 13, 2021.
6. "Historical Narrative of the Ford Warren Library," Denver Public Library, Western History Collection, July 1988.
7. Leslie Williams, email message to the author, February 13, 2021.
8. "Quickfacts: Denver County, Colorado," US Census Bureau, accessed February 14, 2021, https://www.census.gov/quickfacts/denvercountycolorado.
9. Danny Walker, email message to the author, February 13, 2021.
10. "Diversity Counts 2009–2010 Update," American Library Association, September 18, 2012, http://www.ala.org/aboutala/offices/diversity/diversitycounts/2009-2010update.
11. "1921," American Library Association, January 23, 2013, http://www.ala.org/aboutala/1921.
12. "Code of Ethics," American Library Association, January 22, 2008, http://www.ala.org/advocacy/sites/ala.org.advocacy/files/content/proethics/codeofethics/Code%20of%20Ethics%20of%20the%20American%20Library%20Association.pdf.
13. "Why Lead with Race?" *Local and Regional Government Alliance on Race & Equity*, February 13, 2021, https://www.racialequityalliance.org/about/our-approach/race/.

Bibliography

American Library Association. "1921." January 23, 2013. Accessed February 12, 2021. http://www.ala.org/aboutala/1921. Document ID: bc81ec00-2f2b-29e4-25ab-525f2b115230.

American Library Association. "Code of Ethics." January 22, 2008. http://www.ala.org/advocacy/sites/ala.org.advocacy/files/content/proethics/codeofethics/Code%20of%20Ethics%20of%20the%20American%20Library%20Association.pdf.

American Library Association. "Diversity Counts 2009-2010 Update." Accessed September 18, 2012. http://www.ala.org/aboutala/offices/diversity/diversitycounts/2009-2010update.

Denver Public Library. "Historical Narrative of the Ford Warren Library." Western History Collection, July 1988.

Local and Regional Government Alliance on Race & Equity. "Why Lead with Race?" Accessed February 13, 2021. https://www.racialequityalliance.org/about/our-approach/race/.

Momodu, S. "The Tougaloo Nine (1961)." October 6, 2019. Accessed February 14, 2021. https://www.Blackpast.org/african-american-history/the-tougaloo-nine-1961/.

Murray, Stuart. *The Library: An Illustrated History.* Chicago: Skyhorse, 2012.

Preer, Jean L. "'This Year—Richmond!': The 1936 Meeting of the American Library Association." Libraries & culture (2004): 137–160.

Social History for Every Classroom. "Selections from Alabama's Laws Governing Slaves." Accessed February 13, 2021. https://shec.ashp.cuny.edu/items/show/1640.

US Census Bureau. "Quickfacts: Denver County, Colorado." Accessed February 14, 2021. https://www.census.gov/quickfacts/denvercountycolorado.

CHAPTER EIGHT

Margins of the Margins of the Margins
On Being Black with Disabilities and/or Neurodivergence in Libraries and Archives
Kai Alexis Smith

"I am sick and tired of being sick and tired!"

—Fannie Lou Hamer[1]

"Just like we cannot afford to forget the names of those victims, we also must not erase their disabilities."

—Sarah Kim[2]

Sandra Bland. Eric Garner. Freddie Gray. What is overlooked with the tragic killings of so many Black lives is that they also experienced mental illness or developmental disabilities. A third to half of individuals killed by police officers experience disabilities.[3] According to the US Census, almost a quarter of the Black population has some form of disability.[4] Data supports that the Black population has an increased rate of mental health concerns, including anxiety and depression.[5] These conditions may go untreated as a result of a lack of access to appropriate and culturally responsive mental health care, historical trauma from unethical experimentation by the medical field, and everyday prejudice and racism. This also prompts Black people with invisible disabilities to hide their conditions to mitigate judgment and bias at the expense of equitable support.

Just as disability is left out of discussions about police brutality, it is also left out of the conversations on Black library professionals, library workers, or librarians. These conditions are compounded in the very white profession of librarianship, causing Black and disabled librarians to not receive the same access as their counterparts. These individuals experience further marginality or inequities and simply feel dually invisible.

The idea for this book chapter grew out of my own experiences with disabilities at the intersection of my Black womanhood. In 2020, just after we went into lockdown during two pandemics, I discovered that I had been living my life with a visual disability. With this new knowledge, I am learning to live my life in a whole new way while learning about disability communities and spaces where I might find myself welcomed and supported as a Black woman with disabilities.

Terminology

Before exploring the concepts in this chapter, I will define key terminology. While researching this chapter, I discovered the vastness of terminology in the disability and Black communities. I learned that, while the dominant culture in the disability community prefers the term *disability*, many Black librarians that I informally interviewed for this chapter preferred to be called differently abled or neuroatypical. I wondered why that was and who determined what everyone should refer to themselves as. I am always interested in whether Black people were a part of the conversations when these decisions were being made. While in no way is this chapter comprehensive about this topic, some of this is uncovered in the section "A Look Back and Forward: Black Activists and Librarians with Disabilities and Neurodiversity" further along.

I am still new to exploring this part of my identity. I understand how the disability justice activists and community does not prefer the terminology of *differently abled*. For my own interest and the purpose of this chapter, I have immersed myself in the works of Black disability studies and Black disabled artists' works. I found that Black women in particular (which I identify as) do not regularly use the term *disabled* in their work[6] and they describe and celebrate Black bodies in different ways. I struggle with the word/label of *disabled* as I explore the intersection of my own Blackness and disabilities in my art. According to the Harriet Tubman Collective, "The phrase 'differently abled' suggests that we are the locus of our disability when we are, in fact, disabled by social and institutional barriers. Not only is this term offensive, but it also reifies the marginalization that Black Disabled/Deaf people face on a regular basis by and within our own communities and oppressive state institutions."[7] When I do use the term *disability*, I will use the Americans with Disabilities Act definition of disability, which is "A person with a disability is a person who has a physical or mental impairment that substantially limits one or more major life activity. This includes people who have a record of such an impairment, even if they do not currently have a disability. It also includes individuals who do not have a disability but are regarded as having a disability."[8] I use this term in the context of disability justice activists community norms and when referring to the medical model used to define the term.

For the term *neurodiversity*, I will use the combined definitions by Australian sociologist Judy Singer,[9] who coined the term, along with the National Symposium on Neurodiversity's definition:[10] "A concept where neurological differences are to be recognized and respected as any other human variation. These differences can include those labeled with Dyspraxia, Dyslexia, Attention Deficit Hyperactivity Disorder, Dyscalculia, Autistic Spectrum, Tourette Syndrome, and others." While I have used the term *disabled* up until now, I will use the phrase "people with disabilities" or "people who are neurodiverse" instead of "disabled people" or "neurodiverse people" to front load the "personhood of people living with physical impairments, chronic illnesses, psychosocial disabilities, and cognitive/intellectual disabilities."[11]

A Look Back and Forward: Black Activists and Librarians with Disabilities and Neurodiversity

"Instead of inviting disabled people to inaccessible meetings and marches, pour into the activism and advocacy we've already started. Stop asking why we didn't come to your twenty-mile march; let's move forward using a diversity of tactics, holding each in equal respect."

—Cyree Jarelle Johnson[12]

"We do not live single issue lives."

—Audre Lorde[13]

In the past few years, there have been more open discussions and contributions to library literature around mental health in the library profession. Key thinkers and scholars on disabilities in libraries include J. J. Pionke, Karina Hagelin, and Alana Kumbier, all of whom are a part of the dominant culture. After the COVID-19 pandemic onset and protests in March 2020, it became crucial for Black Indigenous People of Color (BIPOC) librarians to have a space to discuss mental health and issues related to disabilities and seek support within the community. The Facebook group We Here[14] and conferences like BIPOC in LIS Mental Health Summit,[15] to name a few, created spaces for these necessary discussions and provided supportive environments. This chapter seeks to build on these efforts and centers works by Black disabled librarians, activists, and advocates that are not readily discussed in library literature or MLIS curricula. In addition to research, I informally interviewed Black librarians, library workers, and library professionals who identified as having a disability and/or are neurodiverse. These discussions helped me to better understand the unique and common struggles Black librarians with disabilities face every day in the profession and how these experiences may or may not correspond with the literature. Some of the questions that came up while doing research for this chapter included Where are the Black librarian activists with disabilities? Are they choosing between their disability or their Blackness to advocate for or can they do both?

Structural racism, heteropatriarchy, and ableism all shape the lenses of disability in the United States, making it particularly hard for Black people with disabilities to navigate the social structures that have very real effects on their everyday experiences and access to resources. Fobazi Ettarh (2014) explains in *Making a New Table: Intersectional Librarianship*:[16]

> It can be more dangerous for POC [people of color] to speak up or "lean in" at the workplace. Compounded with other identities such as disability (disability justice) or gender, to visibly be their whole selves can seem impossible. Fear of job loss or not hiring; fear of not being allowed to use

appropriate restrooms; or even fear of physical violence are just a few of the very real issues that are swept under the rug when loud and explicit advocacy are offered as blanket advice. The "Lean In" advice is, in fact, about how to have it all, while offering precisely zero guidance on how to dismantle the structural barriers.

White supremacy is the backbone of the United States, and both the disability movement and librarianship have roots in this violent history. Disability activists reframed their approach to advocacy from the charity and medical model to the civil rights model,[17] repositioning disabled people from the poor or diseased minority citizens to that of a socially constructed state of oppression. This paradigm shift relied on the *Brown v. Board of Education* ruling to lay the groundwork for the rights of people with disabilities. The Black rights movement and the disability rights movement developed alongside each other; however, similar to the women's rights movement, the disability rights movement initially centered on whiteness, with white activists and advocates at the forefront.

Shancia Jarrett writes in *Lost and Found: The Stories of Blacks with Disabilities Found in the Community*, "The predominant theories of disability which disregard the experiences of Blacks undermine the impact and existence of disability within minority communities. Disability is a non-discriminatory reality; anyone can acquire a disability. Thus, theories which deny the non-discriminatory reality of race fail to adequately represent disability."[18] It is not possible to choose between being Black or a person with a disability as a single issue to address in the complex social systems we live in today. Despite the foundation of the disability movement on a single-issue base and centering white experiences,[19] Black disability rights activists and advocates did and do exist. They have to straddle a tightrope between the two movements and identities of being Black and being disabled.

Black disability rights activists like Johnnie Lacy and Donald Galloway had the unique perspective of seeing both sides at their best and worst. In a 1998 University of California Berkeley oral history archive interview, Lacy spoke of how the Black community promoted oppression without realizing that they were promoting the same behavior and attitudes toward the disabled that white people held toward the

Black community. "This belief in effect cancels out the Black identity they share with the disabled Black person, both socially and culturally, because the disabled experience is not viewed in the same context as if one were Black, and not disabled."[20] She continued that this viewpoint makes it so that Black disabled people were either Black or disabled and not seen as being able to exist wholly as both. Black activists and advocates tried to unify the two movements. For example, the blind Black activist Galloway tried to integrate the Center for Independent Living in the 1970s by bringing Black people into positions at the center. He advocated to start a Black caucus to make sure their voices were heard. Sadly, he was dismissed from the board of directors. However, he was later successful in getting the Black Panther Party to ally with disability rights activists around political advocacy. Ultimately, he shared Lacy's thoughts about the divide between the two movements. Scholar John Lukin captures it best in *Disability and Blackness*:

> That "difference" is central to the conflict between the two movements—whenever one group said, "We are the same," the other group said, with some insight "No. You are exploiting my group's experience just so you can have a metaphor for your own." And individuals who occupied both groups [Black and disabled] were caught in the crossfire. The tension created by one group feeling that its experience was being reduced to a metaphor still occurs in situations where people with disabilities seek representation alongside racial and ethnic minorities.[21]

In the 1990s, disability scholar-activist Mike Oliver created the phrase "social model of disability" noted by scholars Alana Kumbier and Julia Starkey in their article "Access Is Not Problem Solving: Disability Justice and Libraries." They position his framework as "shift[ing] from individual persons' medical diagnoses and impairments toward the material, physical, and social environments that impose limitations or create barriers for people with impairments. By reframing disability as an experience that is shaped by social, cultural, historic, political, and economic factors, disability scholars and activists are able to explore how these factors impact people's lived experience of impairment."[22] Disability as a social construct in relation to the effects of power is explored by scholar Garland-Thomson.[23] In the 2000s, the above-noted scholars and more contributed to the canon that lays a framework for

Black and Brown activists and scholars to address oppression and colonialism in disability.

With a new generation has come more intersectional activism for Black people with disabilities and neurodiversity. There are spaces now that cultivate Black advocates, activists, and artists to advance anti-ableist agendas in Black movement spaces like the incubator the Harriet Tubman Collective.[24] Black disability rights activists like Keri Gray are using social media to platform and organize around accessibility and rights for Black people with disabilities, most noticeably with the hashtag #Blackdisabledlivesmatter around the Black Lives Matter protests in 2020.

Organizations like National Black Disability Coalition and National Alliance of Multicultural Disabled Advocates were formed to advocate for Black people with disabilities and who are neurodivergent while scholars created and contributed to a new part of the literary canon around disability justice studies. This historical legacy of division between Black rights and the disability rights movements has permeated the policies of libraries and library literature canon through the lack of inclusion of Black people with disabilities as far as storytelling, recruitment, retention, hiring practices, and so much more. Black librarian activists like Ettarh, Jennifer Brown, Stacy Collins, and white collaborators are advancing anticolonial and anti-oppression work by remaining critical of the library profession and trying to evoke change within institutions. Black librarians with disabilities are subsumed within this work. Unfortunately, the area does not receive as much attention, at least in comparison to non-LIS circles, nor are budding young library activists being mentored or supported to do this work. Perhaps the attitude is that advocates should resist detracting from larger issues. There still seems to be that mind-set of "pick one or the other, but not both" in libraries, which must change if we are to realize progress.

Black Librarians for Disability Rights Activism

Lacy and Galloway are pioneers among the Black disability rights activists community. They paved the way for today's and future Black disability rights advocates including Fannie Lou Hamer, Sylvia Walker, Barbara Jones, Jazzie Collins, Audre Lorde, Dr. Nathaniel Marbury, and LeRoy Moore, to name a few. A few Black librarians like Sadie Peterson Delaney and Effie Lee Morris have advanced disability rights in libraries.

Delaney is known as the Godmother of Bibliotherapy,[25] which promotes therapeutic healing through reading books. While serving as the head librarian at the Veterans Administration Hospital in Tuskegee, Alabama, Delaney worked with medical professionals to learn the interests of patients and paired them with books.[26] In addition, she developed outreach to bedridden patients, story hours, the Disabled Veteran's Literary Society, and more. Her work became well known by library school students and librarians in the United States, Europe, and Africa.

Children's librarian and activist Morris is most known for her service as the first Black person who served as president for the Public Library Association. However, she also spent a large part of her career working on advancing services for Black, low-income children and the visually impaired. During the 1950s, she was the first children's specialist for visually impaired patrons at the New York Public Library.[27] Morris accomplished a lot of firsts in her career, including being the first Black woman to work in an administrative position at the San Francisco Public Library as the first children's services coordinator, serving as the first woman chairperson of the Library of Congress as well as president of the National Braille Association for two terms.[28]

What We Can Learn: Exploring Principles, Pedagogy, and Praxis

LIS professionals from all backgrounds can greatly benefit from a better understanding of the connection between libraries and Black disability issues, especially as they relate to broader social, cultural, and historical contexts. This section will introduce frameworks, principles, and praxis that can be used to understand and support Black, disabled, and neurodiverse colleagues and community members. This includes looking at Black disability studies pedagogy, disability justice, trauma-informed practices, Universal Design for Learning Guidelines (UDL), and more.

Black Disability Studies

It is important for the LIS field to better understand Black disability studies as a scholarly field. Black disability studies scholarship developed when activists transitioned careers into the academy. This pedagogy addresses how structural racism and ableism affect the Black community; it recenters disability pedagogy to be more inclusive of Black disabled lives and intersectionalities. This is an ever-growing part of scholarship and education, and it is being incorporated into African American/Black diaspora studies courses across the United States, thus, promoting a more complex understanding of Black disabled people.[29]

Disability Justice

More applicable to all types of institutions and library professionals and workers is the disability justice praxis. Developed and led by queer and gender-nonconforming disabled activists of color, this praxis was started by Mia Mingus[30] and Stacey Milbern, soon to be joined by Leroy Moore, Eli Clare, Patricia Berne, and Sebastian Margaret in 2005 to help normalize disability as a core component of identity. Disability justice comprises ten core principles: intersectionality, leadership of those most impacted, commitment to cross-movement organizing, recognizing wholeness, sustainability, commitment to cross-disability solidarity, interdependence, collective access, collective liberation, and anticapitalist politic. This framework can be used by library administrators to apply a lens to library policies and services across libraries.[31]

Trauma-Informed Pedagogy

According to the Substance Abuse & Mental Health Services Administration (SAMHSA) trauma is "an event, series of events, or set of circumstances that is experienced by an individual as physically or emotionally harmful or threatening and that has lasting adverse effects on the individual's functioning and physical, social, emotional, or spiritual well-being."[32] The Ohio State University communications professor and open education leader Jasmine Roberts[33] reminds us that Black people "are experiencing collective trauma *on top of* collective trauma (systemic racism, anti-Black violence paired with the COVID-19 pandemic)" and effects of pandemic (economic, health) are unevenly distributed.

Trauma-informed pedagogy, as practiced and discussed by higher education educator Karen Costa and grounded in science by Dr. Mays Imad, has been adopted by librarians and applied to library services and teaching in the recent past (most notably during the 2020 coronavirus pandemic). The Centers for Disease Control's Office of Public Health Preparedness and Response, in collaboration with SAMHSA's National Center for Trauma-Informed Care, describes six approaches: safety; trustworthiness and transparency; peer support; collaboration and mutuality; empowerment voice and choice; and cultural, historical, and gender issues. While this approach requires organizational-level implementation, this can be adopted in library service, reference interaction, and instruction—if not comprehensively incorporated by upper administrators within libraries of all types.[34]

Universal Design for Learning Guidelines

Keeping in mind both invisible and visible disabilities and different ways of thinking and learning, this framework is aimed at postsecondary institutions and curriculum, but the guidelines mapped out can be applied to policies and services at any type of library to support a variety of neurodivergent thinkers and to meet accessibility needs. Based on scientific insight into how humans learn, these guidelines serve as a tool with which to critique and minimize barriers inherent in curriculum and provide support and increase opportunities for people who are neurodivergent. The three guidelines include Engagement, which is the "why" of learning that can materialize as expectation setting during the instruction session or reference consultation before getting started. There is Representation, which is the "what" of learning, or clarifying syntax, defining terms, and spelling out acronyms for library patrons and trying to be mindful of Westernized tones and slang in any of the service interactions and instruction sessions. Then there is Action and Expression, which is the "how" of learning and can look like considering multiple forms of communication for different types of learners and providing access to tools and assistive technologies, such as alt texting your images in your slides and presentations for those who use screen readers.[35]

An understanding of these praxis, principles, and pedagogy can help library workers, librarians, professionals, and administrators shift power in libraries. It represents advancement toward reimagining collection development policies, acquiring donations and gifts that align with these frameworks, and redesign services to support inquiries from the community. These praxis and pedagogies can support change in library policies and administrative practices with a more inclusive and equitable lens including recentering those most impacted in leadership roles.

More than Just Access: A More Inclusive Future

"Disability Justice is a vision and practice of a yet-to-be, a map that we create with our ancestors and our great grandchildren onward, in the width and depth of our multiplicities and histories, a movement towards a world in which every body and mind is known as beautiful."

—Patricia Berne[36]

COVID-19 brought to the forefront the routine racism that Black people experience in all spaces in America and the correlative effects on our health. Examples of this in libraries include the open letter[37] by the Concerned Black Workers of The Free Library of Philadelphia, which highlighted that Black library workers routinely experience racism, microaggressions, and ableism, and Kaetrena Davis Kendrick's research[38] on the low morale of library workers and library professionals in the conservative landscape of libraries. The shift happening in the activist community influencing legislation, laws, and policy changes has not reached the libraries across the United States yet. A sea change is needed to shift the medical approach in libraries that draws from the ADA's definition of disability as invalid, defective, or deviant bodies, to the social model of disability with an intersectional approach. Kumbier and Starkey point to disability studies literature and activists when summarizing approaches to use like the "both/and" approach (a way of thinking indebted to Chicana theorizations of third-space consciousness): librarians and library workers need to recognize that disability is experienced by individuals in specific ways, requiring particular (material) accommodations, and that disability is a "fluid, contextual social relation" that exceeds technological solutions, changes to a built environment, or better symbols of inclusion.[39]

As we think about what we want the future of libraries to look like beyond access, first, there must be a lot of unlearning and learning among library leaders and professionals. To address systemic change, I agree with Kumbier and Starkey that there needs to be a "mindshift from just problem-solving accessibility and reframing the approach to accessibility as a part of the larger project to dismantling ableism and white supremacy to transform libraries, organizations and the profession." The praxis and pedagogies developed by activists and scholars can frame advocacy in libraries around Black and disabled library workers and the community. There is a great but unrealized potential for partnered training with community disability centers or campus disability offices that emphasize disability justice principles in training for library professionals. "Services to People with Disabilities: An Interpretation of the Library Bill of Rights"[40] already applies core principles of disability justice focused on services and facilities. Strategies can be developed around more inclusive policies that use the UDL for learning guidelines and scaffolding reference and instructional services with trauma-informed approaches. Redevelopment of services, strategic plans, visions, and policies is vital to engaging Black disabled library workers in decision-making and service design planning. We must also be mindful to recruit, educate, mentor, and cultivate Black disabled library workers and librarians into leadership positions. As South African disability rights activists Michael Masutha and William Rowland shouted, "Nothing about us without us."[41]

Notes

1. Fannie Lou Hamer, "I'm Sick and Tired of Being Sick and Tired—Dec. 20, 1964," December 20, 2019, https://awpc.cattcenter.iastate.edu/2019/08/09/im-sick-and-tired-of-being-sick-and-tired-dec-20-1964/.

2. Sarah Kim, "Black Disabled Lives Matter: We Can't Erase Disability in #BLM," *Teen Vogue*, July 3, 2020, https://www.teenvogue.com/story/Black-disabled-lives-matter.

3. David M. Perry and Lawrence Carter-Long, "The Ruderman White Paper on Media Coverage of Law Enforcement Use of Force and Disability," *Ruderman Family Foundation*, March 2016, http://rudermanfoundation.org/wp-content/uploads/2017/08/MediaStudy-PoliceDisability_final-final.pdf.

4. Danielle M. Taylor, "Americans with Disabilities: 2014," *US Census Bureau*, November 2018, 5, https://www.census.gov/content/dam/Census/library/publications/2018/demo/p70-152.pdf.

5. Thomas A. Vance, "Addressing Mental Health in the Black Community," *Columbia University Department of Psychiatry*, February 8, 2019, https://www.columbiapsychiatry.org/news/addressing-mental-health-Black-community.

6. Anna Hinton, "Refusing to Be Made Whole: Disability in Contemporary Black Women's Writing," PhD diss., Southern Methodist University, 2018, https://scholar.smu.edu/hum_sci_english_etds/5.

7. "Disability Solidarity: Completing the 'Vision for Black Lives,'" Harriet Tubman Collective, accessed February 15, 2021, https://harriettubmancollective.tumblr.com/post/150415348273/disability-solidarity-completing-the-vision-for.

8. "What Is the Definition of Disability under the ADA?" ADA National Network, accessed May 14, 2021, https://adata.org/faq/what-definition-disability-under-ada.

9. Judy Singer, "'Why Can't You Be Normal for Once in Your Life?' From a 'Problem with No Name' to the Emergence of a New Category of Difference," in *Disability Discourse*, ed. Corker Mairian and French Sally (London: McGraw-Hill Education, 1999), 64.

10. "What Is Neurodiversity?" National Symposium on Neurodiversity at Syracuse University, April 8, 2011, https://neurodiversitysymposium.wordpress.com/what-is-neurodiversity/.

11. Alana Kumbier and Julia Starkey, "Access Is Not Problem Solving: Disability Justice and Libraries," *Library Trends* 64, no. 3 (2016): 473. https://doi.org/10.1353/lib.2016.0004.

12. Cyree Jarelle Johnson, "Black Cripples Are Your Comrades, Not Your Counterpoint," *HuffPost*, February 10, 2017, https://www.huffpost.com/entry/Black-cripples-your-comrades-not-counterpoint_b_589dbb37e4b094a129ea32b8.

13. Audre Lorde, "Learning from the 60s," in *Sister Outsider: Essays and Speeches* (Berkeley, CA: Crossing Press, 2007), 138.

14. "We Here," Facebook, accessed February 15, 2021, https://www.facebook.com/groups/librarieswehere/.

15. Kaetrena Davis Kendrick, "BIPOC in LIS Mental Health Summit," *Renewals* (blog), April 1, 2020, https://renewerslis.wordpress.com/2020/04/01/bipoc-mental-health-summit-panel-resources/.

16. Fobazi Ettarh, "Making a New Table: Intersectional Librarianship," *In the Library with the Lead Pipe* (July 2, 2014), https://www.inthelibrarywiththeleadpipe.org/2014/making-a-new-table-intersectional-librarianship-3/.

17. Josh Lukin, "Disability and Blackness," in *The Disability Studies Reader*, ed. Lennard J. Davis, 309–15 (New York: Taylor & Francis, 2013).

18. Jane Dunhamn et al., "Developing and Reflecting on a Black Disability Studies Pedagogy: Work from the National Black Disability Coalition," *Disability Studies Quarterly* 35, no. 2 (May 19, 2015), https://doi.org/10.18061/dsq.v35i2.4637.

19. Patty Berne, "Disability Justice—A Working Draft by Patty Berne," *Sins Invalid*, June 9, 2015, https://www.sinsinvalid.org/blog/disability-justice-a-working-draft-by-patty-berne.

20. Johnnie Lacy, "Director, Community Resources for Independent Living: An African-American Woman's Perspective on the Independent Living Movement in the Bay Area, 1960s-1980s," *Online Archive of California*, 1998, accessed February 15, 2021, https://oac.cdlib.org/view?docId=kt0p30012x&brand=oac4&doc.view=entire_text.

21. Lukin, "Disability and Blackness," 311.

22. Kumbier and Starkey, "Access Is Not Problem Solving," 473.

23. Rosemarie Garland-Thomson, "Feminist Disability Studies," *Signs: Journal of Women in Culture and Society* 30, no. 2 (January 1, 2005): 1557–87, https://doi.org/10.1086/423352.

24. "Disability Solidarity."

25. Words Heal, Inc., accessed February 15, 2021, https://wordshealinc.weebly.com/.

26. Betty K. Gubert, "Sadie Peterson Delaney: Pioneer Bibliotherapist," *American Libraries* 24, no. 2 (1993): 124–30.

27. "Effie Lee Morris," *The History Makers*, accessed February 15, 2021, https://www.thehistorymakers.org/biography/effie-lee-morris-41.

28. Binnie Tate Wilkin, ed., "Effie Lee Morris: Retired Children's Services Coordinator, San Francisco Public Library," in *African American Librarians in the Far West: Pioneers and Trailblazers* (Lanham, MD: Scarecrow Press, 2006), 154.

29. Dunhamn et al., "Developing and Reflecting on a Black Disability Studies Pedagogy."

30. In addition, decision-makers should consider reviewing questions from the essay "Reflection toward Practice: Some Questions on Disability Justice,"

which library administrators can ask themselves as they visit policies and services with a lens of disability justice in "collaboration or partner[ship with] people with disabilities and members of other nonprivileged/nondominant groups." Mia Mingus, "Reflection toward Practice: Some Questions on Disability Justice," *Criptiques*, ed. Caitlin Wood (2014), 107–15, https://criptiques.files.wordpress.com/2014/05/crip-final-2.pdf.

31. One can learn more about these principles here: "10 Principles of Disability Justice," *Sins Invalid*, September 17, 2015, https://www.sinsinvalid.org/blog/10-principles-of-disability-justice.

32. "SAMHSA's Concept of Trauma and Guidance for a Trauma-Informed Approach," Substance Abuse & Mental Health Services Administration, July 2014, https://ncsacw.samhsa.gov/userfiles/files/SAMHSA_Trauma.pdf.

33. Jasmine Roberts, "White Academia: Do Better," *Medium*, June 8, 2020, https://medium.com/the-faculty/white-academia-do-better-fa96cede1fc5.

34. Learn more about these principles here: "6 Guiding Principles to a Trauma-Informed Approach," Centers for Disease Control and Prevention, accessed February 15, 2021, https://www.cdc.gov/cpr/infographics/6_principles_trauma_info.htm.

35. Learn more about UDL here: "The UDL Guidelines," Universal Design for Learning Guidelines, accessed February 15, 2021, https://udlguidelines.cast.org/.

36. Berne, "Disability Justice—A Working Draft."

37. "An Open Letter from Concerned Black Workers at the Free Library of Philadelphia," Concerned Black Workers of The Free Library of Philadelphia, *Google Drive*, accessed February 15, 2021, https://drive.google.com/file/d/17LEyjd7-_UVOR6kZwDqIlgOrA8uyKdiI/view?usp=embed_facebook.

38. Kaetrena Davis Kendrick and Ione T. Damasco, "Low Morale in Ethnic and Racial Minority Academic Librarians: An Experiential Study," *Library Trends* 68, no. 2 (2019): 174–212, https://doi.org/10.1353/lib.2019.0036.

39. Kumbier and Starkey, "Access Is Not Problem Solving," 19.

40. "Services to People with Disabilities: An Interpretation of the Library Bill of Rights," American Library Association, February 2, 2009, http://www.ala.org/advocacy/intfreedom/librarybill/interpretations/servicespeopledisabilities.

41. James I. Charlton, *Nothing about Us without Us: Disability Oppression and Empowerment* (Berkeley: University of California Press, 1998), 3.

Resources

Ableism Is the Bane of My Motherfuckin' Existence. https://vimeo.com/216562627. https://bcrw.barnard.edu/videos/ableism-is-the-bane-of-my-motherfuckin-existence/.

Black Disabled Women Who Made a Powerful Impact in Life & Self Love. https://thebodyisnotanapology.com/magazine/14-Black-disabledwomen-re minding-us-of-our-power/.

Crip Lit: Toward an Intersectional Crip Syllabus. https://www.autostraddle.com/crip-lit-an-intersectional-queer-crip-syllabus-333400/.

Disability 101: Learn about Your Communities. https://www.blackdisabledandproud.org/disability-101.html.

Faking Sick or FAKING WELL [CC]. https://www.youtube.com/watch?v=1iruRLGhmv0&list=PLk3zILm6mXo49HFNoGGKxMVXz7vXxODqK&index=100.

Intersectionality of Identities with Disability. https://www.nccsdclearinghouse.org/intersectionality-of-identities.html.

My Body Doesn't Oppress Me, Society Does. https://www.youtube.com/watch?v=7r0MiGWQY2g.

National Black Disability Coalition. http://www.Blackdisability.org/.

Showing Up for Racial Justice. https://www.showingupforracialjustice.org/disability-justice.html.

Trauma Informed Pedagogy/Pedagogy of Care. https://sabresmonkey.wixsite.com/pedagogiesofcare#:~:text=Pedagogies%20of%20Care%3A%20Open%20Resources%20for%20Student%2DCentered%20%26%20Adaptive,Higher%20Education%20book%20series%20from.

Bibliography

ADA National Network. "What Is the Definition of Disability under the ADA?" Accessed May 14, 2021. https://adata.org/faq/what-definition-disability-under-ada.

American Library Association. "Services to People with Disabilities: An Interpretation of the Library Bill of Rights." February 2, 2009. http://www.ala.org/advocacy/intfreedom/librarybill/interpretations/servicespeopledisabilities.

Berne, Patty. "Disability Justice—A Working Draft by Patty Berne." *Sins Invalid.* June 9, 2015. https://www.sinsinvalid.org/blog/disability-justice-a-working-draft-by-patty-berne.

Centers for Disease Control and Prevention. "6 Guiding Principles to a Trauma-Informed Approach." Accessed February 15, 2021. https://www.cdc.gov/cpr/info graphics/6_principles_trauma_info.htm.

Charlton, James I. *Nothing about Us without Us: Disability Oppression and Empowerment.* Berkeley: University of California Press, 1998.

Dunhamn, Jane, et al. "Developing and Reflecting on a Black Disability Studies Pedagogy: Work from the National Black Disability Coalition." *Disability*

Studies Quarterly 35, no. 2 (May 19, 2015). https://doi.org/10.18061/dsq.v35i2.4637.

Ettarh, Fobazi. "Making a New Table: Intersectional Librarianship." *In the Library with the Lead Pipe* (July 2, 2014). https://www.inthelibrarywiththeleadpipe.org/2014/making-a-new-table-intersectional-librarianship-3/.

Facebook. "We Here." Accessed February 15, 2021. https://www.facebook.com/groups/librarieswehere/.

Garland-Thomson, Rosemarie. "Feminist Disability Studies." *Signs: Journal of Women in Culture and Society* 30, no. 2 (January 1, 2005): 1557–87. https://doi.org/10.1086/423352.

Gubert, Betty K. "Sadie Peterson Delaney: Pioneer Bibliotherapist." *American Libraries* 24, no. 2 (1993): 124–30.

Hamer, Fannie Lou. "I'm Sick and Tired of Being Sick and Tired—Dec. 20, 1964." *Iowa State University*. December 20, 2019. https://awpc.cattcenter.iastate.edu/2019/08/09/im-sick-and-tired-of-being-sick-and-tired-dec-20-1964/.

Harriet Tubman Collective. "Disability Solidarity: Completing the 'Vision for Black Lives.'" Accessed February 15, 2021. https://harriettubmancollective.tumblr.com/post/150415348273/disability-solidarity-completing-the-vision-for.

Hinton, Anna. "Refusing to Be Made Whole: Disability in Contemporary Black Women's Writing." PhD diss. (Southern Methodist University, 2018). https://scholar.smu.edu/hum_sci_english_etds/5.

The History Makers. "Effie Lee Morris." Accessed February 15, 2021. https://www.thehistorymakers.org/biography/effie-lee-morris-41.

Johnson, Cyree Jarelle. "Black Cripples Are Your Comrades, Not Your Counterpoint." *HuffPost*. February 10, 2017. https://www.huffpost.com/entry/Black-cripples-your-comrades-not-counterpoint_b_589dbb37e4b094a129ea32b8.

Kendrick, Kaetrena Davis. "BIPOC in LIS Mental Health Summit." *Renewals* (blog). April 1, 2020. https://renewerslis.wordpress.com/2020/04/01/bipoc-mental-health-summit-panel-resources/.

Kendrick, Kaetrena Davis, and Ione T. Damasco. "Low Morale in Ethnic and Racial Minority Academic Librarians: An Experiential Study." *Library Trends* 68, no. 2 (2019): 174–212. https://doi.org/10.1353/lib.2019.0036.

Kim, Sarah. "Black Disabled Lives Matter: We Can't Erase Disability in #BLM." *Teen Vogue*. July 3, 2020. https://www.teenvogue.com/story/Black-disabled-lives-matter.

Kumbier, Alana, and Julia Starkey. "Access Is Not Problem Solving: Disability Justice and Libraries." *Library Trends* 64, no. 3 (2016): 468–91. https://doi.org/10.1353/lib.2016.0004.

Lacy, Johnnie. "Director, Community Resources for Independent Living: An African-American Woman's Perspective on the Independent Living Movement in the Bay Area, 1960s-1980s." *Online Archive of California.* 1998. Accessed February 15, 2021. https://oac.cdlib.org/view?docId=kt0p30012x &brand=oac4&doc.view=entire_text.

Lorde, Audre. "Learning from the 60s." In *Sister Outsider: Essays and Speeches.* Berkeley, CA: Crossing Press, 2007.

Lukin, Josh. "Disability and Blackness." In *The Disability Studies Reader*, edited by Lennard J. Davis, 309–15. New York: Taylor & Francis, 2013.

Mingus, Mia. "Reflection toward Practice: Some Questions on Disability Justice." *Criptiques*, edited by Caitlin Wood (2014), https://criptiques.files.wordpress.com/2014/05/crip-final-2.pdf.

Neurodiversity Symposium. "What Is Neurodiversity?" National Symposium on Neurodiversity at Syracuse University, April 8, 2011. https://neurodiversitysymposium.wordpress.com/what-is-neurodiversity/.

Perry, David, and Lawrence Carter-Long. "The Ruderman White Paper on Media Coverage of Law Enforcement Use of Force and Disability." *Ruderman Family Foundation.* March 2016. http://rudermanfoundation.org/wp-content/uploads/2017/08/MediaStudy-PoliceDisability_final-final.pdf.

Roberts, Jasmine. "White Academia: Do Better." *Medium*, June 8, 2020. https://medium.com/the-faculty/white-academia-do-better-fa96cede1fc5.

Singer, Judy. "'Why Can't You Be Normal for Once in Your Life?' From a 'Problem with No Name' to the Emergence of a New Category of Difference." In *Disability Discourse*, edited by Corker Marian and French Sally. London: McGraw-Hill Education, 1999.

Sins Invalid. "10 Principles of Disability Justice." September 17, 2015. https://www.sinsinvalid.org/blog/10-principles-of-disability-justice.

Substance Abuse & Mental Health Services Administration. "SAMHSA's Concept of Trauma and Guidance for a Trauma-Informed Approach," July 2014. https://ncsacw.samhsa.gov/userfiles/files/SAMHSA_Trauma.pdf.

Tate Wilkin, Binnie, ed. "Effie Lee Morris: Retired Children's Services Coordinator, San Francisco Public Library." In *African American Librarians in the Far West: Pioneers and Trailblazers.* Lanham, MD: Scarecrow Press, 2006, 154.

Taylor, Danielle M. "Americans with Disabilities: 2014." *US Census Bureau.* November 2018. https://www.census.gov/content/dam/Census/library/publications/2018/demo/p70-152.pdf.

Universal Design for Learning Guidelines. "The UDL Guidelines." Accessed February 15, 2021. https://udlguidelines.cast.org/.

Vance, Thomas A. "Addressing Mental Health in the Black Community." *Columbia University Department of Psychiatry.* February 8, 2019. https://www.columbiapsychiatry.org/news/addressing-mental-health-Black-community.

Words Heal, Inc. Accessed February 15, 2021. https://wordshealinc.weebly.com/.

CHAPTER NINE

Uhuru Celebration of Individual and Collective Healing and Empowerment

Five Lessons from an Activist Librarian-Author-Griot

Roland Barksdale-Hall

Our Harps Hang on The Willows
by Roland Barksdale-Hall

They brought us over here,
And we ran,
And they said,
"Take us to the championship."

They brought us over here,
And we danced,
And they said,
"They got rhythm."

They brought us over here,
And we sang,
And the angels . . .
In heaven cried.

—Roland Barksdale Hall

I visited the Farrell Public Library in my childhood hometown, witnessed my photo mounted on the library's Wall of Community Heroes, and reflected on the journey. As a child, I often posed questions to my mom, a proud 1937 Farrell High School graduate, who would reply, "I do not have the answers to all your questions. But I will take you to the public library, where you can find answers." She drove me there and affirmed the power of reading.

As part of a fifth-grade book assignment, I elected to meet an "uneducated" character, Bigger Thomas, in Richard Wright's *Native Son*; experienced a reawakening; and further inhaled the power of reading. I found Bigger Thomas an intriguing yet unfamiliar character because my Pops, a union man, Southern migrant with a sixth-grade education grounded in a rich understanding of Black history, purchased for me a multivolume set of Black history books through *Crisis* magazine, provided a positive image of a Black male. Pops was viewed as a hero and quintessential Uhuru fighter by community members. Uhuru is a Swahili word that means *freedom*. The Library's Black Studies Special Collection too beckoned with a "'*uhuru—welcome*' in a thousand ways." Wendell Wray, cofounder of the Association of College and Research Library's African American Studies Librarians Section, wrote in *The Handbook of Black Librarianship*, "[T]he rhythms and vibrations of the community should be able to seep into the building."[1]

"How can you become a community hero?" I pondered. I paused for reflection and recognized a significant interconnectedness between freedom moments between my journey as a BCALA librarian-author-griot and the broader library field, in particular, the evolving BCALA village. Kelvin Watson, BCALA president, presented me with the 2015 BCALA Leadership Award at the Ninth National Conference of African American Librarians (NCAAL) in St. Louis, Missouri. I presented a paper, "Diverse Books Need Us," in which I recalled high community engagement in the Kwanzaa Community Book Festival. I cherished memories of children looking at the face of an African American hero on the front book cover while hugging the zawadi (gift book).[2] My being named president emeritus of JAH Kente International, Inc., culminated twenty-one years of service as president to this DC-based cultural arts organization that included a youth theater. This lifetime achievement honor caught me by surprise.[3]

In the midst, a flurry of freedom moments came back to me. During the 1990s I served as Penn State head librarian, presented results of a national survey of library and cultural groups collaborative relationships at the Second NCAAL, met with the challenge of an antiquated library, and oversaw program plans and development of a newly renovated facility and spatial utilization. The transformation of the former steelworker's union hall from a place where once I saw Santa and received holiday treats to a modern library and technology center was an honor. Even with these accomplishments, I received letters of harassment, lacked a sense of empowerment, and shared my experiences with a trusted BCALA mentor Gladys Smiley Bell.[4]

Ball explains, "many minorities feel that many events in their lives are in the control of powerful others or external."[5] I made some decisions before my departure: (1) Empowerment and collective healing, albeit fleeting at times, seemed worth pursuing; (2) be a leader and unleash the power of freedom in all my travels; (3) ally with antiracists; and (4) leave the world a better place. In what follows, I share five lessons on pursuing a leadership path.

Lesson 1: Know and Heal Yourself

What are your core values? You can discover them through journal reflection. Dr. E. J. Josey, BCALA's founder, advised, "Be who you are. This will lead to the next opportunity." Through journaling I gained valuable insight: I am an activist scholar librarian-author-griot not because someone told me so but because I *chose* to travel the path. Where do you *choose* to travel?

I fashioned librarianship as a way station. I initially planned to be a biomedical librarian. A January 20, 1984, journal entry recounted: "I *choose* library work as my craft, history will be my art . . . enrolling in a PhD program . . . My vision to teach, to write," and "research . . . a people without a vision are lost." An August 6, 1984, entry, over halfway through the LIS program, records developed interest in the politics of information, social exclusion, and equity in access: "Racism, classism and elitism are pervasive throughout my culture. . . . The gatekeepers of information, impervious to the needs of others, attempt to monopolize" information. "By limiting their youth, a primary resource, the country hurts itself. When that realization comes, true social progress can then follow."

Figure 9.1. Mary Lewis (1924–2011) at the Allegheny Branch Carnegie Library of Pittsburgh. Photography by Roland Barksdale-Hall.

I urge newer librarians to sit with an elder, listen about their struggle, and gain perspective on leadership. I developed lasting bonds of fidelity with BCALA members, as recorded in a Labor Day 1999 entry: "[C]alled, my good friend, Ida Mary Lewis. We talked for a long time. Ms. Lewis said, 'My only brother Anderson passed. But I think of you

Figure 9.2. Rillis Hall receives zawadi (gift book) at Kwanzaa celebration. Photography by Roland Barksdale-Hall.

as a younger brother.'" Ida Mary Lewis, recognized as the first African American junior library apprentice at the Carnegie Allegheny Library in 1945, was a pioneer, pre–civil rights era Pittsburgh librarian. She became a litigant in a suit against the University of Pittsburgh and received recognition for her contributions to women's rights, human rights in the area of arts, African American culture, and librarianship. In Lewis, I "recognized a kindred spirit with an insatiable love of books and learning," "shared conversations with me on many topics, ranging from race to librarianship." Ida Mary Lewis and I teamed up to reawaken genealogy and local history outreach to fifth graders in Pittsburgh public schools. I sat down and interviewed Ida Mary Lewis as part of the Black Librarian Pioneers Oral History Project,[6] which culminated in the *Ida Mary Lewis Memorial Lecture: Celebrating a Life of Advocacy and Service Is Held at the Hill District Carnegie Library of Pittsburgh*. The struggle of Bongiwe Nkabinde, from a political prisoner to Johannesburg Public Library manager, published as part of our Black Librarians Pioneers Oral History Project, provided a global perspective.[7]

My message here is to let us give honor to whom honor is due. Journaling can help with appreciation of others. Among my BCALA author and library mentors are Tony Rose of Amber Books, E. J. Josey, Wendell Wray, Gloria Reaves, Loretta Parham, Gladys Smiley Bell, Barbara Ann Williams, James Welbourne, and Salvador Waller. Who have been your mentors? Take a moment to thank them.

My goals changed over time, simply dropped out based on relevancy or awaited the right time and place. Yet most have grown deep roots. My project *People in Search of Opportunity: The African-American Experience in Mercer County* challenged myths. The long-awaited exhibit I researched, designed, and felt stalled took six years to realize implementation, opened at the courthouse rotunda, and demonstrated the power of librarians in freedom.[8] Other projects were challenging. I realized that my writing threatened the establishment, I published as an independent scholar twelve encyclopedia signed entries on topics ranging from slave status and Juneteenth to entrepreneurs and inventors, and I wrote the guide *Leadership under Fire* (2016).

In *What Black Librarians Are Saying*, Welbourne emphasized the significance of the struggle of African Americans bringing their lenses to the "interpretation of issues and problems" and "the Black experience."[9] The persistence of racial stereotypes was evidenced in a remark by Jared Kushner during the 2020 election that African American people first must "want to be successful." It prompted me to reflect on how my research project *People in Search of Opportunity* was met with perplexing comments—"against everything you stand for" "feel sorry for you," "your fuzzy, political correctness"—and an attack on our home. Despite this, I encourage African Americans to be bold, chart their journey, and make a *choice* to honor their personal freedom.

Lesson 2: Choose to Help and Heal Others

How can you help promote health and wellness? Do you know what health conditions run in your family? If so, it likely runs in other folks' families too. These ruminations prompted me to serve as coordinator of Black Health History at the Stokes Medical Library and ponder. I was driven by the question, "How can I encourage early detection of breast cancer?" My mother died of breast cancer. She failed to go to the doctor upon feeling discomfort in her breast. I wondered about championing preventive steps to change the outcome for other sisters, mothers, and daughters.

Reflections from a combination of spirituality, sheer determination, and perseverance led to my desire to impact health awareness. This produced a deep stirring in my spirit, as recorded in a September 21, 1988, personal journal entry: "[P]rovidence again has shown on me . . . evening I woke up having talked with God . . . I woke with a determination to become a famous writer." Within a week I wrote "Breast Cancer: Lightning Does Strike Twice," which I prepared to submit to *Essence* magazine. I interviewed a researcher at the Howard University Cancer Center and took a family system approach (see figure 9.4) in trying to encourage disease prevention. Rejected by *Essence*, I realized the piece appealed to an older audience and resubmitted it without any changes to *Sisters*. I received an acceptance phone call and, through my author talks, shared this story as a lesson on resilience and empowerment. *Sisters* circulated the issue with my essay at the international women's conference in Cairo, Egypt.

Lesson 3: Pull Together and Take Responsibility for Ourselves and Our Communities

How do you *choose your* talents to create a better world? I served as an HIV/AIDS educator; collaborated with a public health physician, Dr. Pamela Payne Foster; and published a community awareness guide, *Is There a Balm in Black America?: Perspectives on HIV/AIDS in the African American Community*.[10] A drive to increase awareness about the role of prevention led to research on identities and roots and joint roles as contributor and coeditor of *Practice Prevention: How to Be Healthy and Whole* (2013).

I was inspired by Jason Alston's address on the evolving role of BCALA; he noted "collective concerns," including "erasing the educational gap between Black and white students, addressing crime and poverty in Black-majority communities, addressing higher rates of obesity, diabetes, heart disease, cancer, and HIV/AIDS, and other issues."[11] I, an activist librarian-author-griot, collaborated with a public health physician, nurse, clergy, social worker, and psychiatrist to produce a culturally sensitive holistic resource *Practice Prevention* and a session at the Eighth National Conference of African American Librarians held in Cincinnati, Ohio. I later worked as a professor, introduced curricular enhancements with a health emphasis, and presented on "Teaching Information Literacy to Marginalized Communities" at the Georgia Conference on Information Literacy. I sought to train trainers on increasing awareness of racial health disparities.[12]

In the same vein, I promoted literacy, supported intergenerational storytelling at the Quinby Street Resource Center, a library serving people who live in public housing through a BCALA Reading Is Grand! grant, which not only grew numerically but greatly impacted lives.[13] "Who? *You're* an author?" a young person once asked me, pleasantly surprised that I had written books. I count myself blessed to be an author and griot. "I am a man on a mission," I responded. Later, young people began to give me a shout-out in the neighborhood. "Are you still on a mission?"

I applied this same drive to my involvement in BCALA. "Why don't you get more involved in BCALA?" Dr. Stanton F. Biddle asked me. I got more involved; extended the radius of trust; published a piece about a cultural study trip to Africa; and, after being recruited by then BCALA president Gladys Smiley Bell, served a five-year stint as editor of the *BCALA News*, introducing features Issues and Action, Off-the-Press Section with reviews of print and nonprint materials, and Interviews with notables, including W. Paul Coates, librarian and founder of Black Classic Press; Tracie D. Hall, then ALA Office for Diversity director; Haki Madhubuti, Third World Press publisher; and Sharon Flake, young adult author. I continued as a regular contributor under the editorship of Dr. Jason Alston.

BCALA has been a pillar of strength for me. During a community crisis, I found BCALA information workers to be a moral support. I was able to commiserate via the BCALA listserv, generated great ideas and talking points, and shared my final update: "Thank you so much for your helpful suggestions and responses. . . . Grassroots community/library activism still works. The resignation of the police chief was in the best interest of our community, in particular our youth. Young people had expressed agitation about how slow the process was moving.

Our young people thought we as elders had lost our minds in accepting 'things as usual.' I hope the peaceful resolution to an unpleasant situation helps to build for our youth some confidence in the elders to do the right thing at the right time."

Lesson 4: Find Community Partners and Set Communities at Liberty

How can we advance progress and liberate our communities? During my BCALA News editorship, I focused on global allyship by renewing interest in the Progressive African Library and Information Activists' Group (PALIAct).[14] Together with forward-thinking Black librarians, I identified community needs (e.g., self-sufficiency, landlord/tenant relations, policing, drug awareness, domestic abuse, and beautification) and addressed crime and poverty in Black-majority communities.[15] I developed plans through examination of the kindred international healthy cities concept with integrated education, housing, and employment. I sought to find better answers with national elected Black officials such as president Russel Neal Jr., who implemented an innovative model of service delivery to people living in poverty, supported by a combination of empirical data, statistics, focus groups, interviews, and PALIAct model's meeting basic human needs (e.g., tools and seeds).[16] In addition, I developed a reawakening Life Empowerment program, identified community partners (e.g., social workers, health workers, bankers, police, legal aid, and others). Participants engaged in forums with police and public service attorneys.

What are rewards? I witnessed once incorrigible young people graduate and become productive citizens. I have seen dreams the once dormant realized. I have also turned vacant spaces into sustainable Community Unity Gardens, with fresh produce and weekly storytelling. I worked for equal access to health care, contributed to improved health in my urban community, and presented on the community transformation at the Tenth National Conference for African American Librarians in Atlanta, Georgia.[17] Through collaboration, we can meet pressing challenges and set communities at liberty.

Figure 9.3. Quinby Street Resource Center. Photography by Roland Barksdale-Hall.

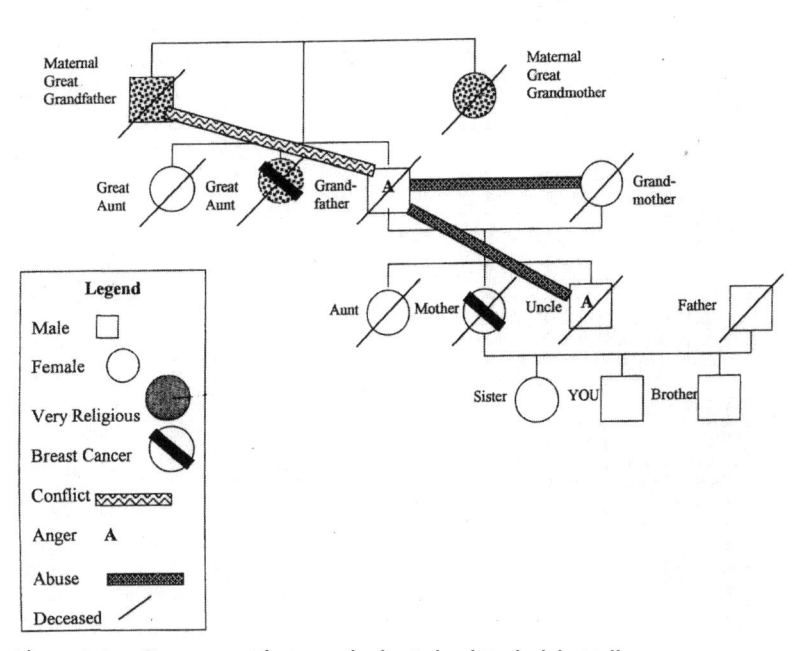

Figure 9.4. Genogram. Photography by Roland Barksdale-Hall.

Lesson 5: Celebrate Individual and Collective Identities, Tell Our Stories

Assign yourself to works that liberate others. Harriet Tubman went back and led others to freedom. However, when Harriet Tubman became free, she did not rest in freedom. In the spirit of Harriet Tubman, I in tandem with BCALA and its allies have gone back and fetched what was lost and sparked a youth reawakening. We therefore urge our brothers and sisters to tell their individual and collective leadership stories.

Through a BCALA Reading Is Grand! Reading Is Great! initiative, I became a teaching artist at Farrell school, spearheading creative computer design and magazines. High schoolers researched topics, designed magazine features, and wrote essays about topics ranging from teen pop heroes to self-identities. Through this program, they participated in mock interviews, came with résumés, dressed in business attire, filled out job applications, and received awards for best design and overall magazine publication.[18] This experience edified me as well; I became a transformational leader, empowered others, and found high satisfaction. I served as magazine editor for QBR *Black Book Review*; participated in the Harlem Book Fair opening session, "My Favorite Book Story: Bring Your Story"; and joined in an *uhuru celebration* by New York BCALA affiliate and past BCALA president Andrew P. Jackson (Sekou Molefi Baako), another celebrated community leader and major donor to the Quinby Street Resource Center. I also shared connections to the people and places developed during my youth and summer visits, all the while remembering how Langston Hughes remains my favorite poet.

Some might associate griots with an image of storytelling, singing, and playing a kora, a musical string instrument. In Africa, griots are held in high esteem; they are leaders and integral to the social fabric. I embraced my griot identity and the correlative call to soulful artistry by deploying music for liberation by initiating reawakening courtyard storytelling with puppetry for youth living in public housing, publishing storybooks such as *Under African Skies* and *Lion Pride*, participating in the Birmingham NCAAL author pavilion and other communal networks of griots and the Cleveland Association of Black Storytellers, and attending my first National Association of Black Storytellers (NABS) Conference in Winston-Salem. I purchased my cowtail, balaphone, and other griot resources.[19]

Around the time of the airing of Alex Haley's *Roots*, the TV miniseries, my mother pressed into my hand a newspaper clipping with an image of my enslaved ancestor and urged me to "keep and preserve," which provided a reawakening for insights into the past and inspiration for my now classic *The African-American Family's Guide to Tracing Our Roots: Healing, Understanding and Restoring Our Families*.[20] I researched my enslaved ancestors, developed a genogram from my family system as a learning tool (see figure 9.4), organized and served as first president of the Pittsburgh Chapter Afro-American Historical and Genealogical Society (AAHGS), incorporated genealogy and local history into community engagement, and celebrated freedom moments.[21]

What is your mission? Ask yourself a question about unmet needs in our communities. Research the issue, find better answers, and be open to allyship. I practice this, bringing leadership, energy, enthusiasm, and love for people along with a passion for literacy, listening to issues from the heart. Naturally, Uhuru community celebrations followed: Life Empowerment social transformation through 2019 Pennsylvania Housing Finance Agency (PHFA) Caught-in-the-Act award-winning community Thanksgiving dinner, community store, and car giveaway.[22] Like E. J. Josey, Ida Mary Lewis, and Sekou Molefi Baako, I *chose* to travel along a leadership path and found my mission in a life of advocacy and service.[23] I served as Frontiers International national youth director and inspired youth through a program called freedom's exploration. When I was on a freedom's exploration project, Farrell public librarian ally Margaret Orchard passed on a publisher's author query for a book about Farrell. I recognized the role of hidden bias in storytelling, sought participation, actively listened to the participants' stories, and told three divergent viewpoints of a deadly labor strike. Young people tell me public school teachers now are using my books *Farrell*[24] and *African Americans in Mercer County*[25] in the social justice classroom.[26] *Farrell*, celebrated for capturing a multiethnic peopling of America, challenged myths about people of color, immigrants, and Black males. The book, like this chapter, was intended to affirm our shared freedom journeys and my existence as an activist scholar librarian-author-griot.[27]

Notes

1. Wendell Wray, "Library Services to Black Americans," in *Handbook of Black Librarianship*, ed. E. J. Josey and Marva L. DeLoach (Littleton, CO: Libraries Unlimited, 1977), 91.
2. Roland Barksdale-Hall, *Leadership under Fire: Advancing Progress, Communicating, Teaching and Setting Communities at Liberty* (Phoenix, AZ: Amber Books, 2016), 60–70.
3. T. Sherman, "A Passion for History," *Valley Voices* (2019): 18–25.
4. Roland Barksdale-Hall, "Building Dialogic Bridges to Diversity: Are We There Yet?" in *Where Are All the Librarians of Color?: The Experiences of People of Color in Academia*, ed. Rebecca Hankins and Miguel Juárez, 265–98 (Sacramento, CA: Library Juice Press, 2015).
5. Patricia Ball, "African American Male Library Administrators in Public and Academic Libraries," *College and Research Libraries* 56, no. 6 (1995): 543.
6. Roland Barksdale-Hall, "Developing Critical Thinkers for Today and Tomorrow," *Information, Equality, Africa: Newsletter of the Progressive African Library and Information Activists' Group* 2 (2006): 9–13; Barksdale-Hall, "Building Dialogic Bridges to Diversity," 269–74, 276.
7. Jocelyn Poole, "From Political Prisoner to Johannesburg Public Library Manager: An Interview with Bongiwe Nkabinde," *Journal of Pan African Studies* 3, no. 1 (2009): 2–8.
8. H. Gwin, "College Librarian Begins Project to Record Area's Black History," *The Vindicator* (March 20, 1994): B1–B2; A. Thompson, "Courthouse Celebrates Black History," *Allied News* (March 8, 2000): A-11.
9. James Welbourne, "The Information Potential in the Liberation of Black People," in *What Black Librarians Are Saying*, ed. E. J. Josey (Metuchen, NJ: Scarecrow Press, 1972), 53–56.
10. Pamela Payne Foster and Roland Barksdale-Hall, eds., *Is There a Balm in Black America?: Perspectives on HIV/AIDS in the African American Community* (Montgomery, AL: AframSouth, 2007).
11. Jason Alston, "The Importance of Librarian Ethnic Caucuses and the Slander of 'Self-Segregation,'" in *Librarians with Spines: Information Agitators in an Age of Stagnation*, ed. Max Macias and Yago S. Cura (Los Angeles: Hinchas Press, 2017), 56.
12. Pamela Payne Foster and Roland Barksdale-Hall, eds., *Practice Prevention: How to Be Healthy and Whole* (Cherry Hill, NJ: Africana Homestead Legacy Publisher, 2013), 82.
13. Karen Lemmons, "Reading Is Grand! Reading Is Great!" *BCALA Newsletter* 40, no. 1 (2012–2013): 5.

14. Shiraz Durrani, "The PALIAct Story," *Information, Equality, Africa: Newsletter of the Progressive African Library and Information Activists' Group* 1 (2006): 7–9.

15. Alston, "The Importance of Librarian Ethnic Caucuses," 56.

16. Healthy Cities, World Health Organization, 2014, accessed January 10, 2021, https://www.euro.who.int/__data/assets/pdf_file/0007/262492/Healthy-Cities-promoting-health-and-equity.pdf.

17. L. Duhl and T. Hancock, "Promoting Health in the Urban Context," *WHO Healthy City Papers*, no. 1 (Copenhagen: FADL Publishers, 1986).

18. Lemmons, "Reading Is Grand!"

19. Karen Lemmons, "Karen Lemmons Reviews Children's Book *Lion Pride*," *BCALA Newsletter* 40, no. 1 (2012–2012): 7.

20. Barksdale-Hall, Roland C. 2005. *The African American Family's Guide to Tracing Our Roots: Healing, Understanding and Restoring Our Families* (Phoenix: Amber Books. 2015).

21. Roland Barksdale-Hall, "Community Engagement Stimulates Collaboration and Innovation for Local History and Genealogy Programming to Public Housing Residents," in *Genealogy and the Librarian: Perspectives on Research, Instruction, Outreach and Management*, ed. Carol Smallwood and Vera Gubnitskaia, 60–68 (Jefferson, NC: McFarland and Company, 2018).

22. Lemmons, "Reading Is Grand!"; David L. Dye, "She Had a Dream: A Meal for Anybody," *Sharon Herald* (November 22, 2018), https://www.sharonherald.com/news/local_news/she-had-a-dream-a-meal-for-anybody/article_3282215e-eddf-11e8-98fb-2b3ef5cb015a.html; Patricia Adams, "Congratulations to Roland Barksdale-Hall and Malleable Heights, You Were 'Caught in the Act,'" *PHFA Quick Connections* (January 2019): 1.

23. Roland Barksdale-Hall, "Navigating the New Frontier: African American Librarians and Service," *Urban Library Journal* 11, no. 2 (2002): 47–60.

24. Roland Barksdale-Hall, *Farrell* (Arcadia Publishers, 2012).

25. Roland Barksdale-Hall, *The African American Family's Guide to Tracing Our Roots: Healing, Understanding and Restoring Our Families* (Phoenix: Amber Books. 2015).

26. A. B. Mitchell, "Review of *Farrell* by Roland Barksdale-Hall, *Journal of the Afro-American Historical and Geological Society* 28 (2010): 135.

27. Patricia Adams, "Photo Book Captures Farrell's Ethnic Heritage," *Life and Times* 4, no. 7 (2012): 3.

Bibliography

Adams, Patricia. "Congratulations to Roland Barksdale-Hall and Malleable Heights, You Were 'Caught in the Act.'" *PHFA Quick Connections* (January 2019): 1.

Adams, Patricia. "Photo Book Captures Farrell's Ethnic Heritage." *Life and Times* 4, no. 7 (2012): 3.

Alston, Jason. "The Importance of Librarian Ethnic Caucuses and the Slander of 'Self-Segregation.'" In *Librarians with Spines: Information Agitators in an Age of Stagnation*, edited by Max Macias and Yago S. Cura. Los Angeles: Hinchas Press, 2017.

Ball, Patricia. "African American Male Library Administrators in Public and Academic Libraries." *College and Research Libraries* 56, no. 6 (1995): 543.

Barksdale-Hall, Roland. *The African American Family's Guide to Tracing Our Roots: Healing, Understanding and Restoring Our Families*. Phoenix: Amber Books, 2015.

———. "Building Dialogic Bridges to Diversity: Are We There Yet?" In *Where Are All the Librarians of Color?: The Experiences of People of Color in Academia*, edited by Rebecca Hankins and Miguel Juárez, 265–98. Sacramento, CA: Library Juice Press, 2015.

———. "Community Engagement Stimulates Collaboration and Innovation for Local History and Genealogy Programming to Public Housing Residents." In *Genealogy and the Librarian: Perspectives on Research, Instruction, Outreach and Management*, edited by Carol Smallwood and Vera Gubnitskaia, 60–68. Jefferson, NC: McFarland and Company, 2018.

———. "Developing Critical Thinkers for Today and Tomorrow." *Information, Equality, Africa: Newsletter of the Progressive African Library and Information Activists' Group* 2 (2006): 9–13.

———. *Farrell*. Arcadia Publishers, 2012.

———. *Leadership under Fire: Advancing Progress, Communicating, Teaching and Setting Communities at Liberty*. Phoenix, AZ: Amber Books, 2016.

———. "Navigating the New Frontier: African American Librarians and Service." *Urban Library Journal* 11, no. 2 (2002): 47–60.

Duhl, Leonard, and Trevor Hancock. "Promoting Health in the Urban Context." *WHO Healthy City Papers*, no. 1. FADL Publishers, 1986.

Durrani, Shiraz. "The PALIAct Story." *Information, Equality, Africa: Newsletter of the Progressive African Library and Information Activists' Group* 1 (2006): 7–9.

Dye, David. "She Had a Dream: A Meal for Anybody." *Sharon Herald* (November 22, 2018). https://www.sharonherald.com/news/local_news/she

-had-a-dream-a-meal-for-anybody/article_3282215e-eddf-11e8-98fb-2b3ef5cb015a.html.

Gwin, H. "College Librarian Begins Project to Record Area's Black History." *The Vindicator* (March 20, 1994), B1–B2.

Lemmons, Karen. "Karen Lemmons Reviews Children's Book *Lion Pride*," *BCALA Newsletter* 40, no. 1 (2012–2012): 7.

———. "Reading Is Grand! Reading Is Great!" *BCALA Newsletter* 40, no. 1 (2012–2013): 5.

Mitchell, A. B. "Review of *Farrell* by Roland Barksdale-Hall." *Journal of the Afro-American Historical and Geological Society* 28 (2010): 135.

Payne Foster, Pamela, and Roland Barksdale-Hall, eds. *Is There a Balm in Black America? Perspectives on HIV/AIDS in the African American Community*. AframSouth, 2007.

———. *Practice Prevention: How to Be Healthy and Whole*. Cherry Hill, NJ: Africana Homestead Legacy Publisher, 2013.

Poole, Jocelyn. "From Political Prisoner to Johannesburg Public Library Manager: An Interview with Bongiwe Nkabinde." *Journal of Pan African Studies* 3, no. 1 (2009): 2–8.

Sherman, T. "A Passion for History." *Valley Voices* (2019): 18–25.

Thompson, A. "Courthouse Celebrates Black History." *Allied News* (March 8, 2000), A-11.

Welbourne, James. "The Information Potential in the Liberation of Black People." In *What Black Librarians Are Saying*, edited by E. J. Josey. Metuchen, NJ: Scarecrow Press, 1972.

World Health Organization. "Healthy Cities." 2014. Accessed January 10, 2021. https://www.euro.who.int/__data/assets/pdf_file/0007/262492/Healthy-Cities-promoting-health-and-equity.pdf.

Wray, Wendell. "Library Services to Black Americans." In *Handbook of Black Librarianship*, edited by E. J. Josey and Marva L. DeLoach. Littleton, CO: Libraries Unlimited, 1977.

PART III

~

BLACK LIBRARIANS ACROSS SETTINGS

CHAPTER TEN

Building Community through Digital Innovation

@BlackLibrarians and WOC+Lib

Shannon Bland and LaQuanda Onyemeh

Since the inception of the World Wide Web, Black internet users have been customizing and expanding digital communities. Black women especially have coconstructed digital norms and contributed to representing Black aesthetics, expertise, and empowerment.[1] Black librarians, who are key to knowledge and information exchange, are expanding the boundaries of digital possibilities for all BIPOC groups. Black librarians defy expectations and narratives that suggest marginalized groups are digitally inept.

In this chapter, we describe our journeys as Black women digital content creators who are refashioning library and information science professionalization, discourse, and networking. We, Shannon Bland and LaQuanda Onyemeh, will share why and how we established two Black librarian cybercultures: @BlackLibrarians and WOC+Lib, respectively. The common thread that binds WOC+Lib and @BlackLibrarians is a previously unfilled niche in librarianship—a space where librarians of color can begin to build our own shared communities. In what follows, we take turns describing our rationale, process, and impact.

Beginnings

@BlackLibrarians—Shannon

If there was ever a year that taught us the importance of technology, it was 2020. The COVID-19 pandemic stripped us of life as we know it with America's favorite places—school, church, the movies, the mall, restaurants—all closed. After a few weeks of the unknown, we realized that what we thought would be a brief time-out from the hustle and bustle of life was now our new reality. With this newfound revelation, we had to pivot. Technology played a tremendous role in that shift. Through technology we were able to "reopen" schools, bring church congregations back together, and continue to support local restaurants via delivery apps. More importantly, we were able to bring family and friends together again *virtually* via digital platforms like Zoom. If you hadn't learned the importance of the digital community before, you definitely ended 2020 knowing.

Long before the pandemic, it was the importance of the digital community that pushed me to create the @BlackLibrarians platform. The community started on Instagram in January 2018. I've always been a visual person, and I found myself constantly scrolling Instagram. My timeline consists mostly of Black art, Black hair, Black love, well just Blackness overall. I loved following accounts that shared stories of Black excellence. I also enjoyed following accounts that showcased Black people venturing in new areas. (Shout-out to pages like @afroswimmers and @browngirlsurf!) As a final-semester graduate student working toward her MLIS at the time, I longed for a page like that to follow that showcased Black librarians, and I couldn't find one. On a whim I mentioned the idea of creating such a community in a group chat composed of other library workers of color. I shared that I was thinking of creating not just a page but a community. They heavily encouraged me to do so; in fact, I think I would have gotten into trouble with them had I not followed through!

WOC+Lib—LaQuanda

A lightbulb went off. I started to grasp the power it could bring to librarians of color if we began to publish online and share our own stories without the rampant censorship and elitism that exists within the sphere of academic publishing. The goal was to establish a digital platform that allowed Black librarians and librarians of color to publish and disseminate digital scholarship. The idea was to empower gallery, library, archive, and museum (GLAM) professionals in various areas of librarianship. It was of utmost importance for the platform to highlight a variety of different perspectives: emerging library and information studies (LIS) student-researchers, activist non-MLIS degree-holding staff, seasoned LIS educators, archival and museum employees, and so forth. These voices are often omitted from mainstream LIS conversations. My goal was to have Black, Indigenous, People of Color (BIPOC) librarians like myself in full control of our content without the censorship of Whiteness gaslighting our feelings of marginalization and minimizing our perspectives within librarianship. WOC+Lib was founded by Lorin K. Jackson and LaQuanda T. Onyemeh and launched in April 2019. WOC+Lib began as a web-based digital writing resource created to nurture and encourage open dialogue about BIPOC experiences. Our space exists to express innovative ideas, share personal experiences, and disseminate original research that promotes marginalized voices and the intersectional identities of Women of Color (WOC) and People of Color (POC) in the field. During the first month of launching, WOC+Lib had 2,672 unique visitors and over 6,339 page views, and it continued to grow. WOC+Lib has visitors represented in more than twenty-four different countries including the United States.

Building Blocks

@BlackLibrarians—Shannon

Why did I choose Instagram? Of all the major social media platforms in existence, Instagram is my personal favorite. Preference aside, I knew I wanted image-based content. My goal was to feature Black librarians from everywhere by displaying their pictures and sharing the work that engaged them. Representation via imagery is extremely impactful. In addition to creating an online support community for Black librarians in the LIS field, I also wanted to showcase our distinctiveness to the masses. Revealing how eclectic and cool Black librarians are—hopefully inspiring others to take interest in the field was my purpose. I found the perfect graphic on Google that said "Black Librarians Rock." I made it our profile photo and started searching the hashtags #black librarians and #blacklibrariansrock to find other profiles to follow, and those profiles returned the love. Thus @BlackLibrarians was born.

WOC+Lib—LaQuanda

I chose to create a digital writing platform because I was heavily influenced by my scholarly communication rotation during my first year as a resident librarian. I began researching scholarly communication and digital humanities from my mentor, Sarah Potvin, cofounder of DH+Lib. I learned about various types of scholarly communications and their influences. The article "Blogs as Infrastructure for Scholarly Communication," by Matt Burton, heavily influenced my perceptions of scholarly blogs, open access, and open publishing. Through this research, I learned how creating a digital platform to launch scholarly communication could establish credibility in the field by lending itself to digital humanities and digital autoethnography of BIPOC librarians. That is to say, I realized that BIPOC library workers need opportunities to share experiences, foster critical commentary, propagate transformative works, and advance professional literature. I envisioned a means for us to help our LIS community by creating opportunities for professional development. The impetus of WOC+Lib's creation was to use technology and the power of the written word to encourage digital publishing scholarship among BIPOC librarians through an official website.

To garner support for WOC+Lib, I knew that we had to establish credibility to attract an audience as well as potential contributing writers. Both Lorin and I invested our own money that went to hiring a top-tier graphic designer to make the WOC+Lib logo, cover the domain-hosting fee, and pay for the digital platform so that the site could be seen as a serious contender in the field. I created the original site in 2019 and redesigned it for the fall 2020 relaunch to give it a modern look and showcase our impact and new submission guidelines.

Filling a Need

@BlackLibrarians—Shannon

Both @BlackLibrarians and WOC+Lib have birthed much-needed cybercultures that help to fuel conversations about racism and exclusion within libraries. According to the Department for Professional Employees,[2] over 83 percent of librarians were white, non-Hispanic in 2019. Library technicians and assistants were slightly more diverse. Among library technicians and assistants, 68.9 percent identified as white, non-Hispanic in 2019. Just 5.3 percent of librarians identified as Black or African American. Clearly, there is a lack of racial and ethnic diversity in the field of librarianship. According to the American Library Association, 86.7 percent of its members identified as white in a 2017 Member Demographics Study. With so few Black people making up the library and information science profession, many are, unfortunately "the only" in their work environments. This racially siloed way of working and living perpetuates feelings of isolation—namely, a lack of community support and concerns of being unheard. Shortly after its inception, the @BlackLibrarians audience started to grow, and our few followers at the time would share the page with other librarians they knew. People began engaging with each other, and some started asking about in-person meet-ups. This request became an opportunity to build a bridge between digital and traditional community settings. That spring, just three months after starting the page, we held our first in-person meeting at a local Washington, DC, cafe.

WOC+Lib—LaQuanda

Lorin and I decided to launch WOC+Lib during the 2019 Association of College and Research Libraries (ACRL) Conference to take advantage of its substantial visibility and high attendance to gain momentum for our site and mission. WOC+Lib went live with a feature written by me called "The Importance of Professional *Friendships*: WOC + Librarianship." I created a Twitter page to assist with promotion. Initially, we only had a few followers. However, as of this writing, we currently have over 1,700. During the ACRL conference, WOC+Lib hosted a social hour with the help of my academic library colleagues at the time. I created and circulated business cards to engender a sense of professionalism and credibility for WOC+Lib. I want to acknowledge and thank Emile Algenio for her coordinating skills; she helped find the restaurant and arrange the social hour. Stephanie Graves, Sarah Lemire, and Sarah Potvin pitched in to sponsor the food for the event. The WOC+Lib social event was a hit. Many attendees expressed their excitement about the space and shared experiences of having their writing censored in the past. Many of them were enthusiastic to write with our platform. I began recruiting editors who also believed in the mission and vision of WOC+Lib to assist with WOC+Lib. These women continue to serve as our founding editors, and they are Jaena Rae Cabrera, Malikkah Hall, and Juanita Thacker.

Audience Reach and Growth

@BlackLibrarians—Shannon

The digital community continues to grow. In just three years @BlackLibrarians has grown from an Instagram page in its infancy to a platform with over thirty thousand followers, an official logo, a domain, in-person and virtual meet-ups, merchandise, and mentorship. The @BlackLibrarians community has not only become popular among its target audience, but trusted throughout the LIS field as well. During the height of mainstream concern about all things #blacklivesmatter (aka June 2020), the American Library Association issued its "Libraries Respond: Black Lives Matter" statement. In it, they named @BlackLibrarians and WOC+Lib as Black voices in LIS that ALA was committed to "center(ing) and support(ing)" through "amplify(ing) the voices of Black library workers and support(ing) their community spaces with donations and membership."[3] All eyes were now on us as the keepers of diversity and inclusion; I just wanted to create a platform to celebrate us. My target audience is Black people who work in libraries, archives, museums, and other information center settings. Now, we have found ourselves with masses of white followers flocking to us to learn how to be a better ally, but we are not here for performative allyship. We are here for our people. I wanted to create a space where we could be our full selves, sharing ideas that are commonly censored or iced out of traditional spaces uncensored.

The year 2020 was definitely big for @BlackLibrarians. We were able to transition from in-person meet-ups, in a time of social distancing, into virtual game nights connecting with our LIS "cousins" from all across the globe. We held a virtual commencement ceremony to celebrate those in our community who were graduating and could not celebrate that triumph in person with their family, friends, and colleagues. With this exponential growth, the question then becomes How can this digital community be sustained?

WOC+Lib—LaQuanda

The WOC+Lib platform continues to grow in two years since its inception. We are currently up to eighteen thousand unique visitors with over thirty-seven thousand page views. We have had over twenty-five authors and counting contribute to the site. During the Black Lives Matter protests in the summer and fall of 2020, WOC+Lib responded by posting an antiracist statement and taking an unapologetic stance against oppression and injustice on Twitter. The WOC+Lib (@Wocandlib) Twitter page launched a social media campaign showcasing everyday library workers and LIS students both past and present. We shared meaningful LIS history and promoted awareness about BIPOC library people. The WOC+Lib social media campaign served to encourage our diverse audience during the global pandemic through powerful testimonials calling attention to the reasons that we all chose librarianship!

During the pandemic, WOC+Lib decided to continue to operate to create a safe place for the WOC+Lib community internally and externally. I made sure to check in on team members periodically because many were siloed in different parts of the United States. I created a vent channel on our WOC+Lib slack channel for our team members. This allowed them to be vulnerable and have a safe place to discuss their feelings, especially after George Floyd's death. The goal was to encourage members to decompress and feel comfortable to take up space and establish friendships with other team members. When our team members need to rest, we encourage them to relax and take the required time to rest. Externally, we continue to market the WOC+Lib brand and recruit writers who will unapologetically show up as their authentic selves.

Our target audience at WOC+Lib is people, especially women, of color. We aspire to feature content that will assist in the creation of a collective platform for diverse voices, experiences, and ideas otherwise ignored or marginalized in the literature about the field. That is WOC+Lib's primary mission and goal! We also strive to offer an equal representation for library workers, students, and volunteers from intersectional BIPOC backgrounds. And yes, our platform is open to cis-gendered men too.

Establishing a Community in the Profession

Testimonials

"Thank you for organizing this community and bringing people together. I'm so grateful!"

—@BlackLibrarians follower

"I am so proud and humbled to have had my first professional piece of writing featured on the WOC+Lib blog. How refreshing to have such support and guidance from these womxn. I cannot say enough about the value it has given me as a Chicana academic. Órale, mi gente."

—WOC+Lib Contributor

WOC+Lib and Censorship

WOC+Lib's mission is to provide a digital presence for uncensored dialogue and commentary in the field. Our goal is to counteract the narrative that libraries (and discussions about them) are neutral. Any discussion about libraries is a discussion about *all* perspectives—not just those espoused by Whiteness. Everyone has a right to weigh in and be heard. For example, the *Journal of the Medical Library Association* recently issued an apology for significantly changing five Black librarians' article submissions on an article about anti-Blackness; the submission had originally been accepted for publication. During the revision process, major changes were made "without track changes or previous mention of required revisions." These included changes in the capitalization of words like "Black" and "white supremacy." The concerns by the authors were ignored, and they ultimately decided to pull their piece from the publication.[4]

Unfortunately, I have heard similar stories from my peers like this during our WOC+Lib social hour and informal conversations with writers. Many BIPOC librarians face censorship because the publishing establishment view their honest, unflinching work through the lens of white supremacy. WOC+Lib's platform is a space to speak out on hot-button issues in the field, discuss taboos within the profession, and acknowledge lesser-known roles in librarianship that usually are disregarded. Some of the topics we have highlighted to date have been Whiteness in Technical Services, intersectional power dynamics in the library, racist microaggressions, the imposter syndrome, and LGBTQIA+ community members' experiences, to name a few.

Sustainability

@BlackLibrarians—Shannon

@BlackLibrarians remains the volunteer operated hub it started as, with the founder still as its nucleus. I am very grateful for the members of the community as they indirectly develop content with their colorful commentary, recommended reads, sharing of experiences, and direct messages. Sustainability to me looks like expanding into a team of like-minded librarians interested in contributing to the cause, expanding into different platforms of digital community (e.g., podcast and video content), and continuing to build the brand's identity and finances through merchandising and potentially sponsorships as well. Most importantly, I want to continue to increase the number of Black librarians highlighted, connect people to each other, and inspire others to enter the field. If in the future, just one person direct messaged the account and said I just enrolled in an LIS program because of the @BlackLibrarian community, I will consider it a job well done.

WOC+Lib—LaQuanda

WOC+Lib is a volunteer-based grassroots organization that is operated by group LIS workers who donate their time to serve as administrators, editors, content creators, contributing writers, and social media managers. WOC+Lib thrives due to the immense love and support from our writers, readers, and LIS communities. As a founder and the executive director, one of my concerns is how to maintain and advance this platform in years to come for the future of BIPOC librarianship. We are looking at multiple ways to sustain WOC+Lib financially and grow our organization for the next generation of library workers to continue to feel seen. We are excited about how we have been able to contribute to the profession and give space to BIPOC writers. We receive many messages of gratitude for creating a space and exercising a high level of care with our BIPOC writers. Many writers have excelled in their career and have gone on to publish more work thanking us for opening doors for them! Please make sure to visit and support the WOC+Lib mission and values so that we can continue at wocandlib.org.

Special Note from LaQuanda T. Onyemeh, Executive Director, WOC+Lib

I'd like to take a moment and acknowledge the work of our WOC+Lib team members and give a special thanks to Lorin K. Jackson, Jaena Rae Cabrera, Juanita Thacker, Malikkah Hall, Narcissa Haskins, Eva Rios-Alvarado, Jessica Tingling, Jina DuVernay, and Stephanie Rose and our honorary member Ray Pun for contributing their time, expertise, and creativity to the WOC+Lib platform and our mission, values, and goals.

I would also like to thank all of our contributing writers who have entrusted us with their voices, original research, and more! Thank you to our donors (big and little contributions) and our readers and loyal supporters who signal boost, bring awareness to our platform to make sure we are here to stay!

Special Note from Shannon Bland, Founder, @BlackLibrarians

I want to give a special shout-out to the group chat for encouraging me to create @BlackLibrarians: Jennika, Alonzo, Jonnetta, Koree, and Dauveen. Because of you the village we have among ourselves has been able to reach across the globe!

Notes

1. André Brock et al., "Cultural Appropriations of Technical Capital: Black Women, Weblogs, and the Digital Divide," *Information, Communication & Society* 13, no. 7 (2010): 1040–59.
2. Department for Professional Employees, "Library Professionals: Facts and Figures," June 2021. Accessed February 6, 2021 https://static1.squarespace.com/static/5d10ef48024ce300010f0f0c/t/60c24d4d903e4a17f8629234/1623346509173/Library+Workers+Facts+%26+Figures+2021+%282%29.pdf.
3. American Library Association, "2017 ALA Demographic Study," January 11, 2017, accessed February 6, 2021, http://www.ala.org/tools/sites/ala.org.tools/files/content/Draft%20of%20Member%20Demographics%20Survey%2001-11-2017.pdf.
4. Jasmine Clark, "On JMLA, Conflict, and the Failed Diversity Efforts in LIS," December 22, 2020, https://jasminelelis.medium.com.

Bibliography

American Library Association. "2017 ALA Demographic Study." January 11, 2017. Accessed February 6, 2021. http://www.ala.org/tools/sites/ala.org.tools/files/content/Draft%20of%20Member%20Demographics%20Survey%2001-11-2017.pdf.

American Library Association. "Libraries Respond: Black Lives Matter." June 3, 2020. Accessed February 6, 2021. http://www.ala.org/advocacy/diversity/librariesrespond/black-lives-matter.

Brock, Andre. "Critical Technocultural Discourse Analysis." *New Media & Society* 20, no. 3 (2018): 1012–30.

Brock, André, Lynette Kvasny, and Kayla Hales. "Cultural Appropriations of Technical Capital: Black Women, Weblogs, and the Digital Divide." *Information, Communication & Society* 13, no. 7 (2010): 1040–59.

Clark, Jasmine. "On JMLA, Conflict, and the Failed Diversity Efforts in LIS." December 22, 2020. https://jasminelelis.medium.com.

Department for Professional Employees. "Library Professionals: Facts and Figures." June 2021. Accessed February 6, 2021. https://static1.squarespace.com/static/5d10ef48024ce300010f0f0c/t/60c24d4d903e4a17f8629234/1623346509173/Library+Workers+Facts+%26+Figures+2021+%282%29.pdf.

CHAPTER ELEVEN

Empowerment through Access

Fostering Youth STEM Engagement with Culturally Reflective Library Services

Teresa A. Quick, Cheryl R. Small, and Amalia E. Butler

> "Libraries are a cornerstone of democracy where information is free and equally available to everyone. People tend to take that for granted, and they don't realize what is at stake when that is put at risk."
>
> —Dr. Carla Hayden, Fourteenth Librarian of Congress and the first woman as well as the first African American to hold the post

STEM is a part of the larger Black legacy and a source of true power. The creations and ideas of Black people have proven to be of value, but often this value is presented as separate or fully removed from the creator. Many of the conveniences of modern life in the United States, from the seemingly everyday to the technologically advanced, were created by or improved upon by Black people.[1] Benjamin T. Montgomery, an enslaved man, created an angled boat propeller in 1864, which allowed for safe navigation in shallow waters. Sarah Breedlove, perhaps best known as Madame CJ Walker, used the scientific method to create a line of Black hair care products. Garett Morgan invented, among other things, the three-color traffic signal and the gas mask. Lonnie Johnson, a NASA scientist, engineered the Super Soaker water gun toy. Mark Dean led the team that significantly improved computer processor speeds with the development of the first gigahertz processor after working with the team that built the first IBM PC a few years earlier. Lisa Gelobter, who served as the chief digital service officer for the US Department of Education under the Obama administration, developed the animation used to create the GIF and other video technology. The simple act of highlighting contributions such as these can foster strong personal connections to the material and empower youth and their families to become more deeply involved in STEM.

In light of our most recent history, the time is now to recognize the exigency of information among underserved communities, especially communities of color. The COVID-19 pandemic brought forward concerns regarding equitable access to technology, health care, science-based information, food, and socioeconomic security.[2] The need for diversified perspectives to assist communities with awareness, caregiving, and policy became increasingly evident during the many crises of 2020. There is a dire need for diverse perspectives in many areas of STEM,[3] for example, books that honor and acknowledge the accomplishments of Black, Indigenous, and People of Color (BIPOC) and resources to inspire future generations to join the ranks of scientists, doctors, engineers, and mathematicians.

The escalating COVID-19 crisis in the midst of the unending media stream of blatant abuses against Black people further highlighted systemic disparities, which only serve to compound these issues and create a literal disconnect from the youth whom we serve. The shift to virtual learning and programming due to COVID-19 presents its own set of challenges. When everyone is separated, it is even more important to be intentional. The stark realization of disproportionate access to technology, which existed pre-COVID, has been laid bare.[4] Digital learning requires (at a minimum) access to a suitable device and the ability to connect to the internet. Some students have a physical device, but they may lack an adequate data plan. Other students may have access to both a device and internet service but need training in how to use the technology. These disparities have been termed the "homework gap."[5] Equitable access not only provides opportunities for enhanced learning but ensures that all have their needs met.

The Black Caucus of the American Library Association (BCALA) "serves as an advocate for the development, promotion, and improvement of library services and resources to the nation's African American community; and provides leadership for the recruitment and professional development of African American librarians."[6] The American Library Association (ALA) pledged its commitment to equity, diversity, and inclusion (EDI) in 2019 with the following statement, "Libraries serve as the cornerstone of our society. Regardless of the type of library, constituency, or region, we stand together to support the efforts of libraries to provide equitable access for all through inclusive collections, resources, services, and programs."[7] This ethos relates to the provision of workforce skill development especially when it comes to racial representation and inclusion in STEM fields. As the last civic organization that serves everyone, the public library has the potential to foster equity within the community through access to quality information in various formats.

This chapter seeks to examine how the availability of STEM programming and diverse materials within school and public libraries can foster culturally reflective critical inquiry among African American youth. The goal is to encourage a love for literacy, learning, and libraries in the minds of all youth. This effort also aims to influence assumptions, challenge ways of thinking, and imagine alternatives for providing high-quality STEM programming and access to resources in libraries.

STEM and Libraries

STEM represents science, technology, engineering, and mathematics. This meld of subject matters brings forward the realization of key skills needed for tomorrow's job force. At present, there is a national deficit of talent across race, ethnicity, gender, and geography within the STEM field. The National Science Foundation's Executive Summary highlights and emphasizes that this shortfall can be addressed within elementary, secondary, and postsecondary schooling.[8] The public library can also serve in this capacity. Andrew Carnegie, philanthropist and industrialist, realized that, with access to knowledge, anyone can be empowered to succeed. His intentional large-scale philanthropy resulted in 1,795 libraries in the United States and 2,509 libraries worldwide.[9] It can thus be said that the industrial or engineering field significantly contributed to the modern library landscape. STEM-focused library programming provides an opportunity to be responsive to the needs of the surrounding community and to form partnerships that leverage public good.[10]

Today, the public library offers many STEM program initiatives that provide tools and access that may not be otherwise accessible to students, especially those in underserved communities. According to Baek, the public library is a place for STEM and should be considered the third place, a place where youth are empowered to discover a new interest that complements the learning that occurs at school and at home.[11] Library programming offers an opportunity to initiate and collaborate through informal and self-guided discovery. These opportunities directly address issues related to inclusiveness, retention, and attrition in STEM as well as the collective ability of librarians to address social challenges through innovation. Libraries can create and help to level a path to STEM opportunities that remains uneven. If librarians initiate this conversation and provide the space for STEM programs with families early and often, then there may be some affinity to and perhaps some interest in STEM later on, which ultimately encourages youth to enter the field and work within their communities.

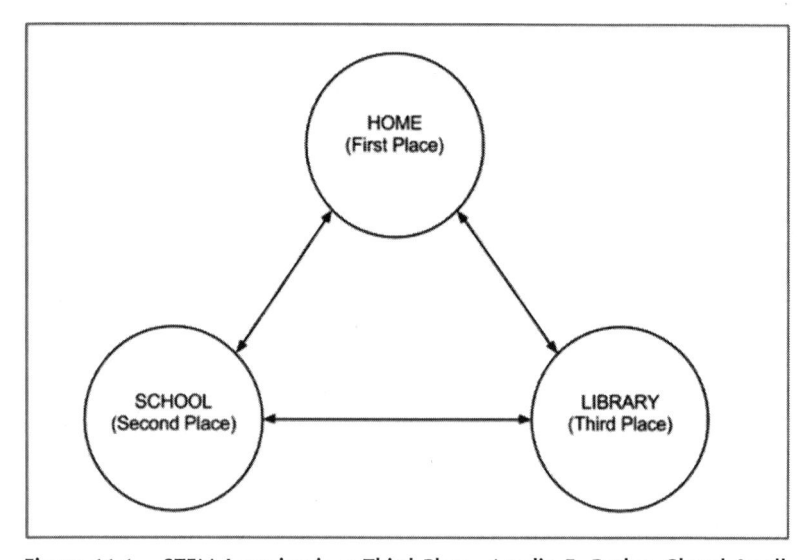

Figure 11.1. STEM Learning in a Third Place. Amalia E. Butler, Cheryl Small, and Teresa A. Quick.[12]

African American librarians can serve as conduits for change by using STEM to build inclusive communities from early education to emerging adulthood, which impacts lifelong social and economic stability and mobility.

Library Materials
Librarians are responsible for content within collections. "Children's literature continues to misrepresent underrepresented communities . . . [resulting in] inaccuracy and uneven quality of some of those books."[13] While the number of books published has increased, there remains a need for books that include BIPOC children written by BIPOC authors. This is of grave concern considering that there are so few people of color as editors.[14] Perhaps even more alarming, there are likely many more writers yet unknown due to gatekeeping. If there were adequate representation of diverse populations in decision-making positions in major publishing houses, then it can be inferred that the representation of diverse creatives and their subsequent works would increase proportionately. These issues continue to contribute to a diversity gap in children's book publishing. In 2018, there were approximately 3,134 children's books published with 712 featuring BIPOC characters;[15] of that number, 301 featured African American/Black character depictions. Furthermore, the number of books created by members from the group that were represented in the books also shows a mismatch across all racial groups. These issues are further compounded when searching for high-quality books that highlight the array of STEM achievements of BIPOC. While there has been a recognition of this need and an emergence of a wider array of biographies and STEM-focused print materials for all ages, there is still a need for further enrichment. Books written by and about familiar names may be well represented in library collections while lesser-known authors and stories are overlooked or remain unknown.

Alternative formats that build upon or move beyond print materials offer opportunity to directly engage the public in STEM and to help address some of the gaps in representation. Kits; tablets; computers; Wi-Fi hotspots; and electronic resources, such as databases, e-books, and subscription websites, can be used for this purpose. Given the influence of technology on the publishing industry and the advent of e-books, there have been concerns for the future of books. However, according to the Association of American Publishers Report, the purchase of print books has remained steady.[16] Pandemic buying patterns changed, showing a spike due to the shift to schooling at home; COVID-19 presented a renewed focus on juvenile fiction, school readiness, and activity books and a 98 percent increase in books for young readers.[17] The disruptions to in-person learning and library service and the shift to digital learning brought about by the coronavirus have not weakened the desire for physical books.

Programming and Readers Advisory

When creating an authentic community through programming and developing collections, we honor human diversity through respect, understanding, and recognition of diverse cultures and communities.[18] In the public library setting, program attendance varies from week to week. There is no guarantee that patrons will return, complete a series of programs, or even finish a recommended title. However, programs and readers advisory sessions can remain intentional and inclusive. To build yearlong sustainable programming within the school setting, cultural competency lessons should be ongoing to ensure that assigned activities create a solid foundation and foster growth over time. Similarly, STEM can be included regularly within all types of programs. STEM programming aims to develop problem-solving skills, critical thinking, and technological advancements with science and creativity as a common goal and community-building capacity.

Libraries can introduce youth and families to STEM through intentional inclusion of topics and vocabulary into story times, other programming, and outreach from a young age.[19] By thoughtfully considering culturally diverse perspectives and experiences within everyday library practices, including STEM-related topics and programs, libraries empower youth of all backgrounds to begin to grow in cultural competence and sensitivity. Youth, especially youth of color, can also feel seen and celebrate their own culture.[20] Using culturally reflective materials in library programs, including STEM programs, invites youth to see a person who looks like them in a previously unknown or unimagined role and encourages them to expand their perception of themselves in a positive way.[21] This is especially important when there is little or no prior exposure to STEM, culturally reflective materials, and/or people of a wide range of backgrounds. Youth of all backgrounds have an opportunity to see their peers in a new light, be exposed to groups with whom they may have little or no contact, and enhance their own worldview.

Organizational and Community Buy-In

Resistance to change and difficulties in overcoming both overt and unconscious bias present very real obstacles. Caregivers, parents, and educators may also have their own objections and reluctance to share unfamiliar topics due to personal discomfort and lack of understanding. This can contribute to cultural insensitivity and historical misunderstanding. On the other hand, sharing and learning about topics in a developmentally appropriate way humanizes and builds empathy by breaking down bias and sharing truth. There is a concept of narrative transparency that speaks to being attuned to the hesitancy to pivot toward science or concerns about the BIPOC narrative centered in library programming. Narrative transparency focuses on the mission and identity over the emotion and does not apologize but leans into a creative solution that moves us forward.

STEM in public libraries and schools should be patron driven and provide youth and their families with real-world experience. Librarians do not necessarily have to master a new skill set or acquire specialized equipment; rather they can collaborate with community experts, such as hospitals, universities, and community colleges. These organizations can also be a source of mentorship and human connection to the topics. Local civic and religious groups may also have members who are connected through their work or social circles. While librarians are not always attuned with the technology or scientific concepts, they understand the needs of future generations and are knowledgeable of the gap in access and representation within the STEM field.

Equipment and Funding

The success model that has been presented is problematic. The ideology of "pulling oneself up by the bootstraps" and a lack of association with a well-funded, socially recognized organization pose significant challenges, especially to underfunded libraries. Fund-raising, especially in a public institution, can be difficult due to restrictions and bureaucracy. Reframing project impacts can effect change through actionable steps and may positively impact grant outcomes, partnership success, and programming attendance. This can also help to gain buy-in and financial support from library foundations. Library leaders must connect and collaborate with the community on a regular basis to build awareness and engagement. In addition, librarians should offer in return name recognition, use of library spaces, gratitude, and inclusion on promotion materials. These incentives may encourage businesses and other organizations to partner on programs or contribute financially. At the same time, libraries must carefully weigh partnership, being mindful that some businesses may not be civic-minded and lack a deeper level of community appreciation and participation.

Libraries do not need to invest heavily or purchase anything to get started. Changes in perspective can seem daunting to initiate. However, a shift in outlook—especially when it comes to overcoming a scarcity mind-set—is possible. Many library systems have closets of what they perceive to be "outdated" equipment. An initial step may be to evaluate what is already in place, though it may not currently be used or understood in the context of STEM. Kits, laptops, tablets, and Wi-Fi hotspots for use on-site in the library space, as well as technology that is available to check out for use at home, can be repurposed. Free online resources that can be used to promote STEM exist on most library websites, and there are a multitude of "unplugged" activities that build skills.

Being adaptable to the changing needs of the public and students in their use of the library is essential to offering services that are responsive and sensitive to their cultural differences, personal norms, and social-emotional needs. Providing a welcoming space and not necessarily a classroom space with a curriculum is key. Programming should be driven by community interests, especially when working with youth. The library space is often visited by choice, and youth should be empowered to foster their own creativity. A welcoming, well-equipped space encourages collaborative exploration and may allow for the library staff to learn as well.

Challenges Faced by Black Librarians

Equity, diversity, and inclusion (EDI) efforts impact every aspect of library services to children, including but not limited to the materials, programming, and readers advisory.[22] In an ideal world, the library would serve as the "great equalizer"—a place that affords every patron the same learning and leisure opportunities to see themselves in any profession. Similarly, there would be equal opportunities for staff to learn and grow within and from their roles. Unfortunately, the reality has been and can be quite different. Segregation laws excluded African Americans from libraries or allowed for only limited subpar services.[23] Librarianship has historically been racially homogeneous and overwhelmingly dominated by white women, while library staff positions are more racially diverse.[24]

Educational costs and time commitment (classes and unpaid internships or student teaching), as well as low compensation relative to educational requirements, are substantial barriers that contribute to the imbalance of representation. At present, no reciprocal training or apprenticeships exist to earn credits toward a library degree.[25] Regional differences of educational requirements and salary disparities at both public and school libraries can pose substantial hindrances. For Black librarians working to promote social justice, systemic limitations such as micromanagement, perceived incredibility, and lack of yearlong sustainable cultural programming are challenges to meaningful change, which beget mental gymnastics and constant code-switching.[26] Black librarians, especially those who are in the racial minority at their institution or relative to their service population, must carefully weigh public perception and the realities against the benefits and the potential outcomes of sharing historical and cultural presentations with children. Perceptions of skin color and physical appearance can trigger implicit and explicit biases as well as presuppositions of personal motives.[27]

The Black librarian has always addressed the social inequality at the front desk, during story time, and beyond policy or policing.[28] Black librarians can empower themselves and one another by continuing to honor and build upon the work of those who came before them. In 1900, Edward Christopher Williams became the first African American to be trained as a professional librarian at New York State Library School. Dorothy B. Porter, Columbia University's first Black library school graduate, worked to reclassify the Dewey Decimal System's misrepresentation of works by Black authors. Charlemae Hall Rollins, an advocate for diverse children's literature, developed criteria for the selection of materials that depict the lives of Black people. Dr. Virginia Lacy Jones, dean of the Atlanta University Library School from 1945 to 1982, trained at least 2,624 African American librarians, more than any other school.[29]

A strong network can foster mutual support. E. J. Josey recognized this truth and thus created the Black Caucus of the American Library Association.[30] The aim is not to be insular, but to highlight, create, and provide ongoing opportunities for learning, mentorship, leadership, and advocacy where they may not otherwise exist. The Joint Council of Librarians of Color (JCLC) has proven over time the value of these networks by providing a space "[t]o promote librarianship within communities of color, support literacy and the preservation of history and cultural heritage, [and] collaborate on common issues."[31] Similarly, with the aim of connectivity and in the absence of having a cohesive national STEM association, states and regions have created their own groups. There is opportunity for these groups to come together to provide quality programming, offer support and scholarships, and provide professional development to librarians.

Call to Action

Many of the problems that exist today, especially with the advent of COVID-19, are threats to world health and endangerments to equitable access resulting in structural disparities.[32] Misinformation and misconceptions about mask use and vaccines are widespread. The health gap is inextricably linked to the information gap such that Black communities are not armed with information, may distrust information, or may mistrust information providers. Historic mistreatment of Black people in medical services and scientific research (e.g., Tuskegee experiment and higher maternal mortality rates) has further complicated trust building. Uneven distribution and inequitable access to vaccination appointments paired with ineffective local communication strategies has further exacerbated health outcomes.[33] The solutions needed are rooted in STEM, and libraries are responding. The public library provides conduits to higher-order learning skills through STEM program opportunities that engender critical thinking, analogical transfer, and evaluation of evidence. The hope is that these informal learning strategies will support the competencies needed to empower youth to explore science fields that lack diversity and lead to long-term involvement in solutions to world issues that all communities face. As public servants on the front line, library staff provide human connection, reliable information, and informational and leisure programs. In some states, library workers help the public navigate COVID-19 vaccine registration, and other staff assist with administrative work at vaccination distribution sites.[34] Libraries empower patrons by partnering with and thereby providing access to community organizations that offer mental health care, food banks, housing resources, employment training, and many other social services in a library setting.

The need for a coordinated national STEM curriculum that is intentionally inclusive of libraries is paramount for the success of our youth. At present there are many avenues for participation but no uniform way to connect to the opportunities or for the presenting organizations to connect with one another.[35] The continued support of initiatives to empower underserved and underrepresented youth is key to prepare them to more fully participate in the global STEM community. These future STEM professionals can then help solve the complex challenges of our world.[36] The future doctors, inventors, and scientists, such as microbiologist Dr. Kizzmekia Corbett, a Black lead scientist for the COVID-19 vaccine, are within our communities. The library programs that are developed and nurtured can impact future generations and shape young people's beliefs about what they can accomplish in life. While we, as librarians, may not necessarily be the experts, we can learn in concert with the youth by contributing to curriculum-building, providing exposure, and giving space alongside resources and mentorship opportunities.

Libraries and educational institutions continue to grapple with ways to increase the recruitment and retention of a more diverse workforce. As racial justice remains in the forefront of social discourse, corporations and organizations have publicly proclaimed their intent to practice EDI.[37] However, intention is not always evident in the outcome. The library exists within society and is not immune to the realities of the world. There is a need to move beyond statements, book lists, or short courses and to impart meaningful change and lasting policies. Our racial identities do not exist in a silo; they influence every part of our lives. EDI is more than a catch phrase, just as "diversity" is more than a face on a page. One story cannot convey the entire experience, but it can contribute a meaningful perspective. More stories contribute to a richer truth. Librarians of all backgrounds, BIPOC included, must also continue to address and guard against harmful personal biases and seek to continuously educate ourselves. By introducing and including culturally reflective materials, perspectives, and access to experts from our communities from a young age, there is a prime opportunity to empower youth and to undo and possibly even to avoid early misconceptions that can later become ingrained beliefs that stunt potential.

Notes

1. Thad Morgan, "Eight Black Inventors Who Made Daily Life Easier," The History Channel, updated February 15, 2021, https://www.history.com/news/8-black-inventors-african-american?li_source=LI&li_medium=m2m-rcw-biography; Katisha Smith, "Thirteen Pioneering Black American Librarians You Oughta Know," *Book Riot*, May 8, 2020, https://bookriot.com/pioneering-black-american-librarians/.

2. "Students of Color Caught in the Homework Gap," Alliance for Excellent Education, July 21, 2020, https://futureready.org/homework-gap/; Clare Bambra, "The COVID-19 Pandemic and Health Inequalities," *Journal of Epidemiology and Community Health* 74, no. 11 (2020): 964–68.

3. "White House Initiative on Education Excellence for African Americans," US Department of Education, accessed February 12, 2021, https://sites.ed.gov/whieeaa/.

4. "Students of Color Caught in the Homework Gap."
5. "Students of Color Caught in the Homework Gap."
6. "About BCALA," Black Caucus of the American Library Association, accessed February 7, 2021, https://www.bcala.org/about-bcala.
7. "ALA and US Library Associations Affirm Commitment to Equity, Diversity and Inclusion," American Library Association, June 17, 2019, http://www.ala.org/news/press-releases/2019/06/ala-and-us-library-associations-affirm-commitment.
8. Beethika Khan, "The State of US Science and Engineering 2020: Executive Summary," National Center for Science and Engineering Statistics, accessed February 12, 2021, https://ncses.nsf.gov/pubs/nsb20201/executive-summary.
9. "Andrew Carnegie: A Legacy of Support for Public Libraries," Carnegie Corporation of New York, accessed February 12, 2021, https://www.carnegie.org/news/articles/andrew-carnegie-legacy-support-public-libraries/.
10. Annette Shtivelband et al., "Exploring 'STEM-Readiness' in Public Libraries," *Journal of Library Administration* 59, no. 8 (2019): 854–72.
11. John Y. Baek, "Public Libraries as Places for STEM Learning: An Exploratory Interview Study with Eight Librarians," National Center for Interactive Learning, October 2013, http://www.nc4il.org/images/papers/Baek_Public%20Libraries%20as%20Places%20for%20STEM%20Learning.pdf; Ray Oldenburg, ed., *Celebrating the Third Place: Inspiring Stories about "Great Good Places" at the Heart of Our Communities* (New York: Harlowe and Company, 2001).
12. Oldenburg, *Celebrating the Third Place*.
13. Sarah Park Dahlen, "Picture This: Diversity in Children's Books 2018 Infographic," *Sarah Park Dahlen PhD* (blog), June 19, 2019, https://readingspark.wordpress.com/2019/06/19/picture-this-diversity-in-childrens-books-2018-infographic.
14. "Where Is the Diversity in Publishing? The 2019 Diversity Baseline Results," Lee and Low Books, *The Open Book* (blog), January 28, 2020, https://blog.leeandlow.com/2020/01/28/2019diversitybaselinesurvey/.
15. Park Dahlen, "Picture This."
16. "Book Publisher Revenue Estimated at $25.8 Billion in 2018," Association of American Publishers, June 21, 2019, https://publishers.org/news/book-publisher-revenue-estimated-at-25-8-billion-in-2018/#:~:text=Washington%2C%20DC%3B%20June%2021%2C,revenue%2C%20representing%202.71%20billion%20units.
17. "Home Life and Educational Books on the Rise as Americans Shelter at Home, The NPD Group Says," NPD Group, March 23, 2020, https://

www.npd.com/wps/portal/npd/us/news/press-releases/2020/home-life-and-edu cational-books-on-the-rise-as-americans-shelter-at-home/.

18. William Welburn et al., "Memory, Authenticity and Cultural Identity: The Role of Library Programs, Services and Collections in Creating Community," presentation 75th World Library and Information Conference, Milan, Italy, August 2009, https://www.researchgate.net/publication/237431413_ Memory_Authenticity_and_Cultural_Identity_The_Role_of_Library_Pro grams_Services_and_Collections_in_Creating_Community.

19. "Strengthening Communities through Libraries: Librarian Toolkit for Developing STEAM Learning Opportunities during Out-of-School Time," Association for Library Services to Children, 2017, http://www.ala.org/alsc/sites/ala.org.alsc/files/content/externalrelationships/170823%20ALSC%20 toolkit-%20single%20page.pdf; STEM Resources Taskforce, "STEAM Programming Toolkit," Young Adult Library Services Association, December 14, 2016, http://www.ala.org/yalsa/sites/ala.org.yalsa/files/content/YALSA_ STEAMToolkit_WEB_Dec2016.pdf.

20. Rudine Sims Bishop, "Mirrors, Windows, and Sliding Glass Doors," *Perspectives: Choosing and Using Books for the Classroom* 6, no. 3 (1990), accessed February 12, 2021, https://www.readingrockets.org/sites/default/files/Mirrors -Windows-and-Sliding-Glass-Doors.pdf.

21. Sims Bishop, "Mirrors, Windows, and Sliding Doors."

22. "Competencies for Librarians Serving Children in Libraries," Association for Library Services to Children, accessed February 12, 2021, http://www .ala.org/alsc/edcareeers/alsccorecomps.

23. George M. Eberhart, "The Greenville Eight," *American Libraries* (June 1, 2017), https://americanlibrariesmagazine.org/2017/06/01/greenville-eight-library-sit-in/; George M. Eberhart, "Desegregating Public Libraries," *American Libraries* (June 25, 2018), https://americanlibrariesmagazine.org/blogs/the-scoop/desegregating-public-libraries; Wayne A. Wiegand, "Desegregating Libraries in the American South," *American Libraries* (June 1, 2017), https://americanlibrariesmagazine.org/blogs/the-scoop/desegregating-public-libraries.

24. Keith Curry Lance, "Racial and Ethnic Diversity of US Library Workers," *American Libraries* (May 2005): 41–43, https://www.lrs.org/documents/workforce/Racial_and_Ethnic.pdf?lrspdfmetric=no; "Library Professionals: Facts and Figures, 2021 Fact Sheet," AFL-CIO, Department for Professional Employees, June 2021, https://www.dpeaflcio.org/factsheets/library-profession als-facts-and-figures.

25. "Accreditation Frequently Asked Questions," American Library Association, accessed February 17, 2021, http://www.ala.org/educationcareers/accreditedprograms/faq#unaccredited_degree.

26. Kaetrena Davis Kendrick, "Considering: Deauthenticity in the Workplace," *The Ink on the Page* (blog), February 5, 2019, https://theinkonthepageblog.wordpress.com/2018/02/05/considering-deauthenticity-in-the-workplace/.

27. Kaetrena Davis Kendrick, "Tweet-Dux: Stereotype Threat and Deauthenticity in the PoC Low-Morale Experience," *The Ink on the Page* (blog), February 18, 2019, https://theinkonthepageblog.wordpress.com/2019/02/18/tweet-dux-stereotype-threat-and-deauthenticity-in-the-poc-low-morale-experience/.

28. "About BCALA"; Alma Dawson, "Celebrating African-American Librarians and Librarianship," University of Illinois, accessed February 5, 2021, https://www.ideals.illinois.edu/bitstream/handle/2142/8328/librarytrendsv49i1d_opt.pdf?sequence=1; Smith, "Thirteen Pioneering Black American Librarians."

29. Ana Ndumu and R. Chancellor, "DuMont, 35 Years Later: HBCUs, LIS Education, and Institutional Discrimination," *Journal of Education for Library and Information Science* 62, no. 2 (2021): 162–181; Ana Ndumu, "Shifts: How Changes in the U.S. Black Population Impact Racial Inclusion and Representation in LIS Education," *Journal for Education in Library and Information Science* 62, no. 2 (2021): 137–161.

30. "About BCALA."

31. "About," Joint Council of Librarians of Color (JCLC), accessed February 7, 2021, http://www.jclcinc.org/about/.

32. National Academies of Sciences, Engineering, and Medicine, *Communities in Action: Pathways to Health Equity* (Washington, DC: National Academies Press, 2017).

33. Melba Newsome, "Vaccinations in Black and White: Hesitancy or Exclusion?" *North Carolina Health News*, March 8, 2021, https://www.northcarolinahealthnews.org/2021/03/08/vaccines-in-black-and-white-hesitancy-or-exclusion/; Russ Bynum et al., "Playing Favorites?: Hospital Boards, Donors Get COVID Shots," Associated Press, January 30, 2021, https://www.abc27.com/news/us-world/national/playing-favorites-hospital-boards-donors-get-covid-shots/.

34. News 4 Staff, "Buffalo and Erie County Public Libraries Assisting with Vaccine Appointment Scheduling," WIVB4, March 20, 2021, https://www.wivb.com/news/local-news/erie-county/buffalo-and-erie-county-public-libraries-assisting-with-vaccine-appointment-scheduling/; Darian Benson, "In this Midwest State, Libraries Help with Vaccine Outreach," WKSU, February 5, 2021, https://www.wksu.org/health-science/2021-02-05/in-this-midwest-state-libraries-help-with-vaccine-outreach.

35. "About," The Connectory, accessed February 12, 2021, https://theconnectory.org/about-connectory; "National Education Technology Plan," US Department of Education, Office of Educational Technology, https://tech.ed.gov/netp/; "Science, Technology, Engineering, and Math, Including Computer Science," US Department of Education, accessed February 15, 2021, https://www.ed.gov/stem.

36. "Science, Technology, Engineering, and Math."

37. "Libraries Respond: Black Lives Matter, Equity, Diversity, and Inclusion," American Library Association, accessed February 12, 2020, http://www.ala.org/advocacy/diversity/librariesrespond/black-lives-matter; Gary Price, "Statements from Libraries and Library Organizations Re: Racism, Black Lives Matter, and Increased Violence," InfoDocket, June 1, 2020, https://www.infodocket.com/2020/06/01/statements-from-library-organizations-re-racism-and-increased-violence/.

Bibliography

AFL-CIO, Department for Professional Employees. "Library Professionals: Facts and Figures, 2021 Fact Sheet." June 2021. https://www.dpeaflcio.org/factsheets/library-professionals-facts-and-figures.

Alliance for Excellent Education. "Students of Color Caught in the Homework Gap." July 21, 2020. https://futureready.org/homework-gap/.

American Library Association. "Accreditation Frequently Asked Questions," accessed February 17, 2021, http://www.ala.org/educationcareers/accreditedprograms/faq#unaccredited_degree.

American Library Association. "ALA and US Library Associations Affirm Commitment to Equity, Diversity and Inclusion." June 17, 2019. http://www.ala.org/news/press-releases/2019/06/ala-and-us-library-associations-affirm-commitment.

American Library Association. "Libraries Respond: Black Lives Matter, Equity, Diversity, and Inclusion." Accessed February 12, 2020. http://www.ala.org/advocacy/diversity/librariesrespond/black-lives-matter.

Association for Library Services to Children. "Competencies for Librarians Serving Children in Libraries." Accessed February 12, 2021. http://www.ala.org/alsc/edcareeers/alsccorecomps.

Association for Library Services to Children. "Strengthening Communities through Libraries: Librarian Toolkit for Developing STEAM Learning Opportunities during Out-of-School Time." 2017. http://www.ala.org/alsc/sites/ala.org.alsc/files/content/externalrelationships/170823%20ALSC%20toolkit-%20single%20page.pdf.

Association of American Publishers. "Book Publisher Revenue Estimated at $25.8 Billion in 2018." June 21, 2019. https://publishers.org/news/book-publisher-revenue-estimated-at-25-8-billion-in-2018/#:~:text=Washington%2C%20DC%3B%20June%2021%2C,revenue%2C%20representing%202.71%20billion%20units.

Baek, John Y. "Public Libraries as Places for STEM Learning: An Exploratory Interview Study with Eight Librarians." National Center for Interactive Learning. October 2013. http://www.nc4il.org/images/papers/Baek_Public%20Libraries%20as%20Places%20for%20STEM%20Learning.pdf.

Bambra, Clare. "The COVID-19 Pandemic and Health Inequalities." *Journal of Epidemiology and Community Health* 74, no. 11 (2020): 964–68.

Benson, Darian. "In This Midwest State, Libraries Help with Vaccine Outreach." WKSU. February 5, 2021. https://www.wksu.org/health-science/2021-02-05/in-this-midwest-state-libraries-help-with-vaccine-outreach.

Black Caucus of the American Library Association. "About BCALA." Accessed February 7, 2021. https://www.bcala.org/about-bcala.

Bynum, Russ, Michelle R. Smith, and Rachel La Corte. "Playing Favorites?: Hospital Boards, Donors Get COVID Shots." Associated Press. January 30, 2021. https://www.abc27.com/news/us-world/national/playing-favorites-hospital-boards-donors-get-covid-shots/.

Carnegie Corporation of New York. "Andrew Carnegie: A Legacy of Support for Public Libraries." Accessed February 12, 2021. https://www.carnegie.org/news/articles/andrew-carnegie-legacy-support-public-libraries/.

The Connectory. "About." Accessed February 12, 2021. https://theconnectory.org/about-connectory.

Curry Lance, Keith. "Racial and Ethnic Diversity of US Library Workers." *American Libraries* (May 2005): 41–43. https://www.lrs.org/documents/workforce/Racial_and_Ethnic.pdf?lrspdfmetric=no.

Davis Kendrick, Kaetrena. "Considering: Deauthenticity in the Workplace." *The Ink on the Page* (blog). February 5, 2019. https://theinkonthepageblog.wordpress.com/2018/02/05/considering-deauthenticity-in-the-workplace/.

Davis Kendrick, Kaetrena. "Tweet-Dux: Stereotype Threat and Deauthenticity in the PoC Low-Morale Experience." *The Ink on the Page* (blog). February 18, 2019. https://theinkonthepageblog.wordpress.com/2019/02/18/tweet-dux-stereotype-threat-and-deauthenticity-in-the-poc-low-morale-experience/.

Dawson, Alma. "Celebrating African-American Librarians and Librarianship." University of Illinois. Accessed February 5, 2021. https://www.ideals.illinois.edu/bitstream/handle/2142/8328/librarytrendsv49i1d_opt.pdf?sequence=1.

Eberhart, George M. "Desegregating Public Libraries." *American Libraries* (June 25, 2018). https://americanlibrariesmagazine.org/blogs/the-scoop/desegregating-public-libraries.

Eberhart, George M. "The Greenville Eight." *American Libraries* (June 1, 2017). https://americanlibrariesmagazine.org/2017/06/01/greenville-eight-library-sit-in/.

Joint Council of Librarians of Color (JCLC). "About." Accessed February 7, 2021. http://www.jclcinc.org/about/.

Khan, Beethika. "The State of US Science and Engineering 2020: Executive Summary." National Center for Science and Engineering Statistics. Accessed January 10, 2021. https://ncses.nsf.gov/pubs/nsb20201/executive-summary.

Lee and Low Books. "Where Is the Diversity in Publishing? The 2019 Diversity Baseline Results." *The Open Book* (blog). January 28, 2020. https://blog.leeandlow.com/2020/01/28/2019diversitybaselinesurvey/.

Morgan, Thad. "Eight Black Inventors Who Made Daily Life Easier." The History Channel. Updated February 15, 2021. https://www.history.com/news/8-black-inventors-african-american?li_source=LI&li_medium=m2m-rcw-biography.

National Academies of Sciences, Engineering, and Medicine. *Communities in Action: Pathways to Health Equity*. Washington, DC: National Academies Press, 2017.

Ndumu, Ana. "Shifts: How Changes in the U.S. Black Population Impact Racial Inclusion and Representation in LIS Education" *Journal for Education in Library and Information Science* 62, no. 2 (2021): 137–161.

Ndumu, Ana, and Renate Chancellor. "DuMont, 35 Years Later: HBCUs, LIS Education, and Institutional Discrimination." *Journal of Education for Library and Information Science* 62, no. 2 (2021): 162–181.

News 4 Staff. "Buffalo and Erie County Public Libraries Assisting with Vaccine Appointment Scheduling." WIVB4. March 20, 2021. https://www.wivb.com/news/local-news/erie-county/buffalo-and-erie-county-public-libraries-assisting-with-vaccine-appointment-scheduling/.

Newsome, Melba. "Vaccinations in Black and White: Hesitancy or Exclusion?" *North Carolina Health News*. March 8, 2021. https://www.northcarolinahealthnews.org/2021/03/08/vaccines-in-black-and-white-hesitancy-or-exclusion/.

NPD Group. "Home Life and Educational Books on the Rise as Americans Shelter at Home, The NPD Group Says." March 23, 2020. https://www

.npd.com/wps/portal/npd/us/news/press-releases/2020/home-life-and-educational-books-on-the-rise-as-americans-shelter-at-home/.

Oldenburg, Ray. *Celebrating the Third Place: Inspiring Stories about "Great Good Places" at the Heart of Our Communities.* New York: Harlowe and Company, 2001.

Park Dahlen, Sarah. "Picture This: Diversity in Children's Books 2018 Infographic." *Sarah Park Dahlen PhD* (blog). June 19, 2019. https://readingspark.wordpress.com/2019/06/19/picture-this-diversity-in-childrens-books-2018-infographic.

Price, Gary. "Statements from Libraries and Library Organizations Re: Racism, Black Lives Matter, and Increased Violence." InfoDocket. June 1, 2020. https://www.infodocket.com/2020/06/01/statements-from-library-organizations-re-racism-and-increased-violence/.

Shtivelband, Annette, Kimberly S. Spahr, Robert Jakubowski, Keliann LaConte and Anne Holland. "Exploring 'STEM-Readiness' in Public Libraries." *Journal of Library Administration* 59, no. 8 (2019): 854–72.

Sims Bishop, Rudine. "Mirrors, Windows, and Sliding Glass Doors." *Perspectives: Choosing and Using Books for the Classroom* 6, no. 3 (1990). Accessed February 12, 2021. https://www.readingrockets.org/sites/default/files/Mirrors-Windows-and-Sliding-Glass-Doors.pdf.

Smith, Katisha. "Thirteen Pioneering Black American Librarians You Oughta Know." *Book Riot.* May 8, 2020. https://bookriot.com/pioneering-black-american-librarians/.

STEM Resources Taskforce. "STEAM Programming Toolkit." Young Adult Library Services Association. December 14, 2016. http://www.ala.org/yalsa/sites/ala.org.yalsa/files/content/YALSA_STEAMToolkit_WEB_Dec2016.pdf.

US Department of Education. "Science, Technology, Engineering, and Math, Including Computer Science." Accessed February 15, 2021. https://www.ed.gov/stem.

US Department of Education. "White House Initiative on Education Excellence for African Americans." Accessed February 12, 2021. https://sites.ed.gov/whieeaa/.

US Department of Education, Office of Educational Technology. "National Education Technology Plan." https://tech.ed.gov/netp/.

Welburn, William, et al. "Memory, Authenticity and Cultural Identity: The Role of Library Programs, Services and Collections in Creating Community." Presentation, 75th World Library and Information Conference, Milan,

Italy, August 2009. https://www.researchgate.net/publication/237431413_Memory_Authenticity_and_Cultural_Identity_The_Role_of_Library_Programs_Services_and_Collections_in_Creating_Community.

Wiegand, Wayne A. "Desegregating Libraries in the American South." *American Libraries* (June 1, 2017). https://americanlibrariesmagazine.org/blogs/the-scoop/desegregating-public-libraries.

CHAPTER TWELVE

Leading in Health Sciences Librarianship

Perspectives from Black Library Leaders

Bethany McGowan and Jahala Simuel

In this chapter, we capture the perspectives of ten Black academic health sciences librarian leaders, providing insights into their backgrounds, notable achievements, and professional and leadership development and recommendations for emerging leaders. These ten participants represent a combined total of more than 287 years of experience as health sciences librarians. Beverly Murphy, the first African American president of the Medical Library Association, describes the importance of Black leaders in health sciences librarianship as follows:

> Having Black librarian leaders in health sciences librarianship is critical because diversity makes us smarter and is necessary to help us survive and thrive in this profession. The melding of many different minds, thoughts, activities, feelings, and interactions produces a plethora of healthy, productive experiences that we all can gain from if we remain open and flexible. Having people of color in leadership is especially important because this is one of the domains where librarians can impact and affect the most change while serving as proactive examples for those who seek similar positions. Black librarians in leadership can champion for minority recruitment and retention, opportunities for inclusion, and cultural competency and humility, while proactively dealing with the challenges of bias, privilege, microaggressions, racism, white fragility,

and more. This is extremely important in creating an open, welcoming, and inclusive environment for patrons and staff.[1]

We interviewed directors and deans of health sciences libraries and one former leader of a health sciences library professional association to compile a cohort with a range of experiences. We envision that, though this chapter will capture the interests of many library professionals, it will be most relevant to emerging leaders, new professionals, health sciences librarians, academic librarians, and library and information school students.

Methodology

This study was granted an exemption by the Purdue University Institutional Review Board, IRB No. 2021-39. The authors collaborated with leaders of the African American Medical Library Association (AAMLA) to identify Black leaders of Association of Academic Health Sciences Libraries (AAHSL) member libraries. Twelve potential participants were identified and contacted via email, and ten participants responded and agreed to be included in the study. After signing a consent form, each participant was interviewed virtually, using recorded WebEx video conference calls. Each interview recording was transcribed by one of the authors. The interview transcriptions were manually coded by one of the authors using Excel, and Voyant Tools was used to conduct an automated text analysis. The corpus for the Voyant Tools analysis consisted of the text from the ten transcriptions combined into a single document.

The interview questions were as follows:

Professional Background
1. What is your current position and institution? How long have you held the position?
2. Have you held any previous positions? If yes, at which institutions and how long did you hold the position?
3. What degrees have you obtained and which universities did you attend?

4. What is your proudest or most notable professional achievement?

Participation in Professional Development Programs
5. Have you participated in any formal professional development programs?
6. Have you participated in any informal or ad hoc professional development programs?

Participation in Leadership Development Programs
7. Have you participated in any formal leadership development programs?
8. Have you participated in any informal or ad hoc leadership development programs?

Participation in Mentoring Programs
9. Have you participated in any formal or informal mentoring programs? Please describe your experiences as a mentee, mentor, or both.

Recommendations for Emerging Leaders
10. What practices or resources best prepared you for leadership?
11. What key challenges have you faced?
12. What current or future shifts in the profession might influence one's preparedness to enter a leadership position in health science libraries?
13. How has the COVID-19 pandemic changed your work? What long-term impact do you think it will have on the profession?

Results

Background Demographics
Most participants held the title of director of a health sciences library ($n = 7$). Other represented titles included assistant dean and director ($n = 1$), interim director ($n = 1$), and former president of a health sciences library professional association ($n = 1$).

The Network of the National Library of Medicine categorization of regional medical libraries was used to define regional locations. The Southeastern Atlantic region was best represented (n = 5), followed by the South Central region (n = 2), the Greater Midwest (n = 2), and the Pacific Southwest (n = 1).

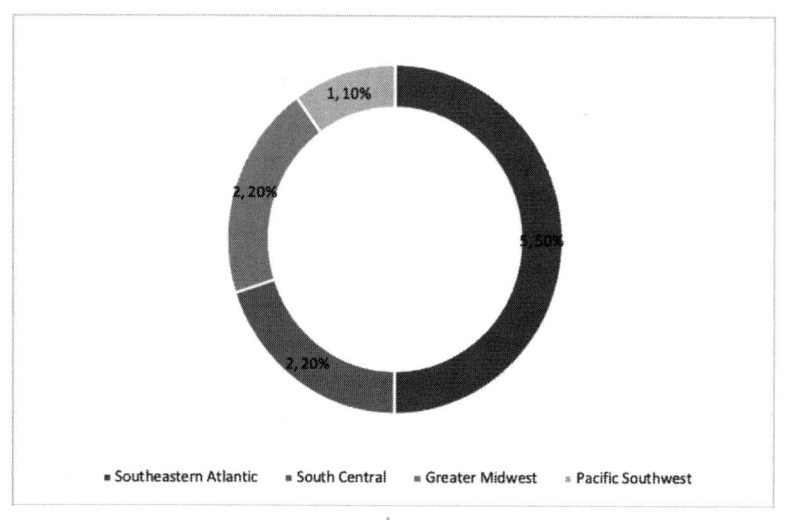

Figure 12.1. Regional Representation. Bethany McGowan and Jahala Simuel.

The average time spent in leadership was 5.6 years. Of the ten participants, five had three years or less of leadership experience, three had five to ten years of experience, and two had more than ten years of experience.

Years of experience in librarianship varied widely, with an average of 28.7 years. Of the ten participants, three participants had over thirty years of experience, and another three had forty or more years of experience.

Three participants had spent their entire career at the same institution, four participants held positions at one previous institution, one participant held positions at two previous institutions, and two participants held positions at three or more previous institutions. Three participants held a bachelor of science degree, and seven held

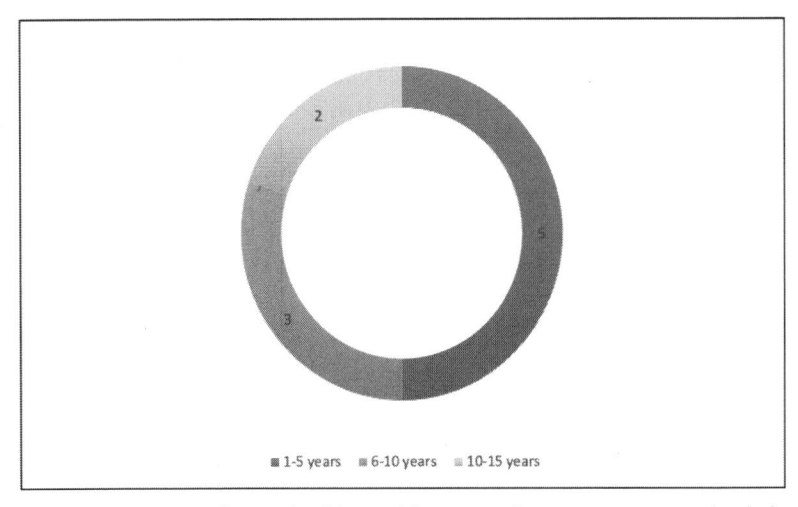

Figure 12.2. Years in Leadership Position(s). Bethany McGowan and Jahala Simuel.

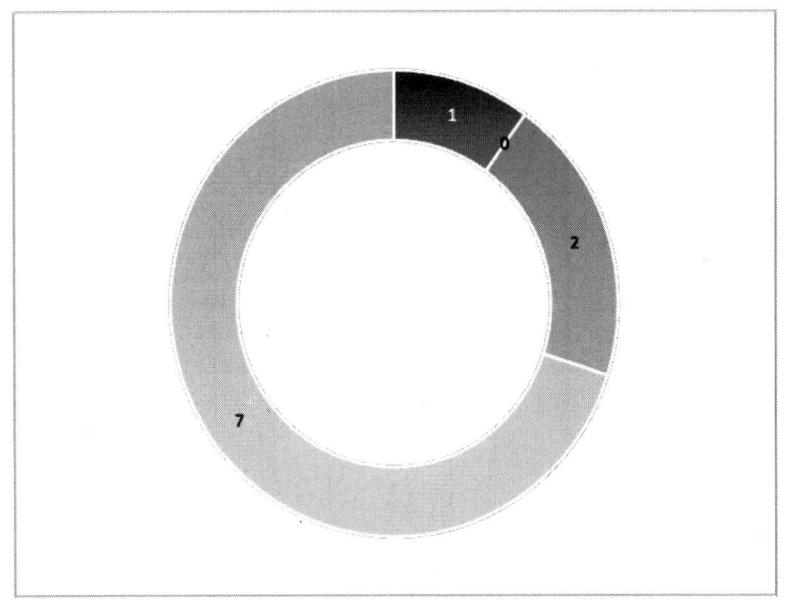

Figure 12.3. Total Years in Librarianship. Bethany McGowan and Jahala Simuel.

a bachelor of arts degree. All ten participants held some version of a master of library and/or information science degree, with MS, MLS, MIS, MLIS, and MSLS degrees being represented. Two participants held second master's degrees, and two participants held specialized graduate certificates. One participant held an EdD, and one participant is currently working to complete an EdD. Six participants were alumni of a Historically Black College or University (HBCU), at either the undergraduate or graduate level, with Clark-Atlanta University, North Carolina Central University, Fisk University, Southern University, Talladega College, and Morehouse University represented.

Notable Achievements
Seven categories emerged after a manual coding of responses related to participants' most notable achievements:

Publications
   Two participants mentioned specific scholarly publications as their proudest achievements.

Vision
   Five participants mentioned reenvisioning or reinventing the library and library services. For two participants, this meant changes to the physical library space including building a new building. For the other three, this meant changing perceptions about the work that librarians did or establishing new collaborations between the library and other partners.

Awards
   Three participants listed receiving a specific award as their proudest achievement. These included receiving academic awards as students and receiving awards that recognized them as library leaders and innovators.

Position
   Four librarians listed position-related achievements as their most notable. These included becoming a librarian and achieving specific leadership positions.

Community Influence
Three participants were most proud of their patient advocacy or community engagement efforts.

Mentoring
Three participants listed seeing their mentees go to library school and/or enter and thrive in the field of health science librarianship as their most notable achievement.

Other
One participant said that their most notable moment is yet to be determined.

Professional and Leadership Development

Formal Professional Development
Participation in formal professional development programs appears to correspond to total years of experience. More experienced leaders noted that no formal professional leadership development opportunities were available during their early career development. Others referenced opportunities from the National Library of Medicine (NLM), including the NLM Associate Fellows Program (*n* = 2), the NLM Woods Hole Informatics Program (*n* = 1), and the NLM Oak Ridge Training Program (*n* = 1). The Minnesota Institute for Early Career Librarians (*n* = 1) and the National Archives Special Collections and Record Management Training (*n* = 1) were also mentioned.

Informal Professional Development
The four most experienced leaders reported that they were less likely to participate in formal professional development programs but were more likely to participate in informal professional development. Specifically, these individuals received intense, structured training in their first librarian position. Other popular responses related to the completion of continuing education opportunities and certifications from professional associations, namely, opportunities from the Medical Library Association and the NLM regional medical library network. Other responses

included strategies such as observing professionals, picking up information in library school, and immersion in the field.

Formal Leadership Development
Four participants matriculated through the AAHSL Leadership Fellows Program, the most referenced formal leadership development opportunity among the participants. Also popular was the ARL Leadership Career Development Program, attended by three participants. The HBCU Library Alliance Leadership Program, the Harvard Leadership Institute for Librarians, the Triangle Research Libraries Network Leadership Program, the ACE Women's Network Leadership Program, and the Academic Impression Women's Leadership Program were also mentioned.

Informal Leadership Development
Based on this study's results, Black health sciences library leaders are most likely to receive informal leadership development by completing continuing education courses from the Medical Library Association at the regional and national level or from attending workshops at their universities. Other strategies included executive coaching, continuing education courses from the American Management Association, and participation on the university library council.

Mentorship Experience
All ten attendees noted the importance of mentoring as a mutually beneficial partnership, and each has benefited as a mentee and served as a mentor. Strategies for establishing a mentee-mentorship relationship are presented in the following section.

Recommendations for Emerging Leaders

Finally, we have synthesized participants' free-form responses as follows:

Advice to Mentees for Identifying and Vetting Mentors

- Look for opportunities to be mentored—consider supervisors, library school faculty, nonlibrarians, and people you feel a *strong*

connection with. Plan to be a lifetime mentee and have multiple mentors, and look for a new mentor at every career stage. Be discerning and be careful of barriers posed by people who you *think* should be mentors.
- Set a regular schedule to meet with your mentor—go to lunch or set up a similar type of regularly scheduled experience.
- Observe how your mentor tackles challenges and discuss issues such as assessment, budgeting, and fund-raising strategies.

Advice to Mentors for Identifying and Mentoring Mentees

- Seek out opportunities to be a mentor—mentor library school students; coauthor publications with early-career librarians, library staff, and paraprofessionals; seek mentoring connections through professional association mentoring programs; and reach out to people you feel a strong connection with. Library leaders should encourage their staff to participate in professional association mentoring programs.
- Be a lifelong mentor and all in when making mentoring commitments. Consider mentoring a mutually beneficial two-way exchange. Mentoring experiences should be informative, enlightening, consistent, cross-cultural, and cross-racial.

Leadership Best Practices

- Be able to look at the big picture—create a strategic plan for yourself and your organization, be aware of what the professional associations are doing and changing, and look at job descriptions from other libraries. But also, be able to boldly and concisely ask for what you need.
- Leaders should be team players—get involved with team projects with your staff and let them see you working with them. Be an example to the people around you and someone they want to follow. Master active listening and learn to ask relevant follow-up questions. Be open and welcome to a diverse group of people and allow them to teach you to observe and learn from multiple angles. Bring someone along and help the people around you shine.

- Learn the language of your stakeholder audience—join university committees and use your voice, befriend the student body, and read scholarly journals that cover library science, health sciences, and higher education.
- For those who want to move into health sciences librarianship leadership roles, plan your leadership trajectory. Consider discussing your future plans with your supervisor and, together, draft a plan to reach your goals. Find a strong mentor in your area of interest—for example, reach out to and collaborate with members of the African American Medical Library Association (AAMLA). Develop a passion for and become an expert in library leadership and management issues. Learn everything you can about leadership principles and understand how to apply them under the right circumstances. Look for leadership development opportunities externally if no internal opportunities are available. Craft and regularly update an elevator speech that accurately and concisely explains the value of your work. Be well rounded—try to know a little about everything and look for experiences that expand your comfort zone. Examine job descriptions to see what skills are being asked for and scour the AAHSL website for a synopsis of what is going on in library leadership, including interview tips and salary data.
- Know who you are and be confident in your own skin. Work to improve yourself but don't let others change you into something that makes you uncomfortable. Practice self-care, eliminate negative speech, be open to new opportunities, understand your strengths, and build collaborations with people you feel a connection to. Be at the top of your game and prepared to effect change!

Advice for Black Library Leaders

- Be prepared to experience budget and financial issues, including operating with a small or reduced staff. Understand the needs of your whole institution. Find out what makes your boss tick and what makes your boss's boss tick; then develop a few key initiatives the library can lead to meet those needs.

- Be prepared to experience communication issues, for example, finding out that people perceived what you said differently than what was intended. Be prepared for individuals and systems to push back and for people not to like you or support you, and know that not everyone will agree with or support your vision.
- Learn to manage the *-isms*, such as racism, nepotism, sexism, and ageism, and white fragility, jealousy, sabotage, microaggressions, cultural taxation, teams that don't work, and the perceived need to constantly prove oneself. Be prepared to be the only African American in a space. Don't take criticism too personally, try to turn challenges into opportunities, and know that you may receive the best support from outside your library or institution.

Notable Shifts in Profession

- Thanks to advances in technology, the ability to develop and grow relationships is no longer bound by time or place. This allows for more robust opportunities for collaboration and for being better connected to a more diverse community.
- The continued shift to and growth of online and digital resources requires more technical expertise but also allows librarians to work remotely while maintaining a high level of service.
- Health sciences libraries are being merged or combined with the university library system, resulting in fewer leadership opportunities.
- More people of color are entering librarianship and assuming leadership roles, and there is an increased awareness around equity, diversity, and inclusion issues. Organizations like AAMLA are also offering leadership development opportunities. This greater cultural awareness could lead to improved recruitment and retention of Black librarians.

Long-Term Impacts of the COVID-19 Pandemic

- Librarians have been highlighted as providers of timely information, with the library viewed as a vital and necessary institution.

Librarians have learned to work smarter *and* harder—they better understand user needs and the provision of virtual services, are protecting and reclaiming their time, have learned to say no, are working smarter with a smaller staff, and are thinking outside the box.

- A focus on radical self-care has emerged, along with a greater awareness of and sensitivity to toxic work environments.
- Some institutions and organizations will permanently move to hybrid models for work, professional conferences, and meetings.
- Library leaders will need to manage ongoing budget cuts, resource cuts, and staff cuts for years to come.
- An increased competition for the library's physical space has emerged, with other departments temporarily or permanently acquiring library space.
- Library stakeholders will continue to expect digital information delivery services and remote learning opportunities.

Discussion

Perhaps the strongest recurring theme heard across the ten interviews is that library leaders must understand and respond to their institutions' changing needs. Leaders should understand engagement strategies and be prepared to advocate for the library with an elevator speech or an ask practiced and ready. Many leaders also highlighted their efforts to repurpose the library's physical space to best suit patron needs, while others fought efforts by other university departments to have library space reallocated or managed their library through its merging with the university library system. When satisfactorily navigated, these efforts were a career highlight.

Black health science library leaders are optimistic as more people of color enter careers in libraries and enter leadership positions. In fact, half (five out of ten) of this study's participants are new leaders with one to five years of experience. However, our findings show that Black health sciences librarians are often very experienced before entering leadership positions. Though the average time spent in librarianship was 28.7 years, the average time of leadership experience was only 5.6 years. Organizations like AAMLA are helping to prepare new and midcareer librarians for leadership positions, efforts that are especially crucial as many highly experienced Black library leaders prepare to retire. Access to library-centered professional development and leadership development programs has also improved significantly over the past years, better preparing early- and midcareer professionals for leadership.

Study participants noted shrinking library staff and budgets as key challenges, and leaders anticipate that staff numbers and budgets will be further reduced as a result of the COVID-19 pandemic. This trend, paired with concerns related to the consolidation of health sciences libraries into the broader university library system, could drastically reduce the number of leadership positions available in health sciences libraries and should be closely monitored. HBCUs have played an important role in preparing Black librarians for leadership positions. Sixty percent of this study's participants are HBCU alumni. And, the Southeast Atlantic region boasts the majority of Black health sciences library leaders, with half of this study's participants being from that region.

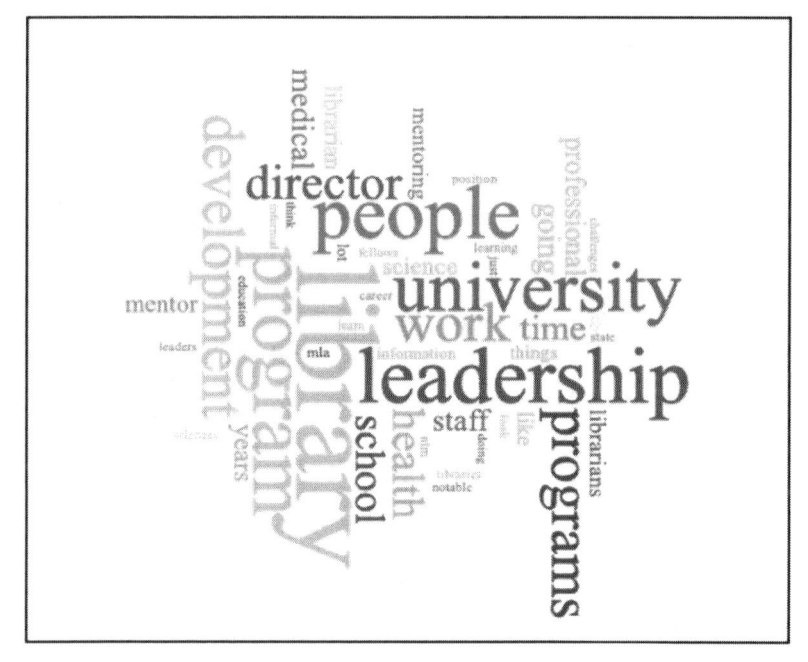

Figure 12.4. Most Frequent Words. Bethany McGowan and Jahala Simuel.

Conclusion

Seven of this study's ten participants have worked in academic health sciences libraries for more than twenty years. As they prepare for retirement, they are optimistic that greater cultural awareness and improved access to formal professional development and leadership development programs will improve the recruitment and retention of Black health sciences librarians. Organizations like the African American Medical Library Association (AAMLA) are developing resources and opportunities that will help the next generation of Black health sciences librarians prepare for leadership opportunities. Of great concern are the shrinking budgets and staff numbers faced by many academic health sciences libraries, the consolidation of independent health sciences libraries into the broader university library system, and the reallocation of library space to other university departments. These issues should be closely monitored by those seeking leadership opportunities in health sciences libraries.

Note

1. Beverly Murphy, email message to the authors, February 2021.

CHAPTER THIRTEEN

The HBCU Librarians' Experience

Doing More with Your Time and Talent for Less Treasure

Jamillah Scott-Branch, Vernice Riddick Faison, and Danielle Colbert-Lewis

North Carolina Central University (NCCU) is a state-supported Historically Black University (HBCU) within the University of North Carolina System. Our university is the only remaining HBCU that is accredited by the American Library Association to offer the master of library science. NCCU "was the third school in the country to educate African American library professionals."[1] NCCU'S legacy of developing and providing employment opportunities to librarians of color also extends to its campus libraries, the School of Library and Information Science (SLIS), and NCCU's five libraries: James E. Shepard Memorial Library (Shepard Library), School of Library and Information Sciences Library, Curriculum Materials Center Library, Music Library, and the School of Law Library. HBCU librarians' work at NCCU libraries is rewarding in many regards but also challenging when one fully understands the magnitude of librarians' many work responsibilities. NCCU librarians working within Shepard Library, the main undergraduate library, are cross-trained to perform in all respective library departments. Librarians working at NCCU must be adaptable and have an arsenal of skills that make them multidimensional leaders.

In this chapter, we share our experiences as HBCU librarians to demonstrate workforce disparities rooted in higher education inequities. We argue that our experiences at NCCU are shaped by our commitment to a collective HBCU institutional mission of accessibility, equality, and opportunity. We will thus describe how we are required to be resilient and resourceful.

Doing More with Less

HBCUs have always done more with less. As a result of historical biases in higher education funding and federal or state support, HBCU libraries tend to occupy a complicated space that spans academic affairs, student support, and community relations. The HBCU library often responds to unmet campus and municipal needs. Historically, HBCU libraries were some of the first public spaces to offer access to modest reading collections for African American communities, particularly through investments from sources such as the Carnegie and Rosenwald funds.[2]

HBCU librarians are often overstretched and expected to fulfill multiple roles. Furthermore, at some HBCUs, librarians' status varies depending on the individual campus. Some librarians are tenure-track faculty with the same promotional path as research faculty. At other institutions, librarians serve in nonteaching faculty roles with the same promotion path as staff. Additionally, some HBCU librarians are in hybrid positions with a combination of faculty and staff promotion paths, a duality that induces stress for many.

At NCCU, the librarians are expected to satisfy their position requirements and many other duties that lead to being inundated and challenged with the responsibility of wearing many hats and assuming a plentitude of other tasks. We have ten librarians on staff, each serving as a liaison to at least three or more different campus disciplines. Every librarian is responsible for collection development, particularly building and maintaining designated subject areas. This involves assessing the collection, weeding out outdated resources, and ordering from vendors. The librarians' responsibilities include serving as each of the department's primary contact persons in the library for collection development issues and working in conjunction with faculty to select library resources that are adequate and relevant to support the department's curriculum.

The librarians at Shepard Library also serve as librarian liaisons to the departments and schools at the university. Indeed, these "liaisons effectively support teaching, learning, and research; identify opportunities for further development of tools and services; and connect students, staff, and faculty to deeper expertise when needed."[3] The librarians at NCCU Shepard Library are intentional in their interactions with faculty, staff, department, schools, and students. Each connection with the aforementioned communities is an opportunity for continued collaborations for years to come, which Shepard Library does not take for granted. This includes programming, classes, and individual consultations. According to the Ithaka S+R publication "Leveraging the Liaison Model," "Much liaison work can be labor intensive and viewed as an add-on to an already full plate. And most liaisons are responsible for supporting many faculty and students, precluding a lot of individual attention."[4] Thus, the concept of labor representation continues with librarians and their interactions with faculty. Furthermore, librarians teach library instruction classes to these departments, provide individual consultations, attend departmental meetings, and market new resources and services. Unlike other universities where instruction is a dedicated department, these same librarians are also tasked with providing information literacy instruction to first-year learners. The library instruction requests can range from a general overview of library resources to more details or specific requests. Some of these librarians are in administrative, management, supervisory, or leadership positions, despite having management responsibilities and duties, including leading students, support staff, or other librarians. These librarians are continuously tasked with fulfilling other obligations. Two librarians manage branch libraries, supervise staff, and provide service to patrons. They are responsible for cataloging, classifying, and organizing resources; processing library resources; and making the resources accessible for patrons in the two branch libraries that fall under Shepard Library's umbrella.

Within the last ten years, the library's staff size has decreased due to retirements, library cuts, and lost positions. Meanwhile, the different functions in the other areas of the library still have to be carried out. Librarians whose primary job is in technical services, public services, and branch managers have been thrust into being cross-trained in the Research and Instructional Services Department, Access Services, and staffing the Information Desk to keep these areas operational. All librarians have to be versatile and able to shift from one role to another. Every weekend a librarian from one of the library's departments works an eight-hour shift at the Research and Instructional Service Department and sometimes may also have to provide coverage to the Access Services Department. With the increasing duties of library staff, the need to form meaningful partnerships with other departments outside of the library has led to developing a culture of collaboration.

Culture of Collaboration

The process of establishing meaningful campus alliances between the library and other campus entities was birthed out of the realization that our library staff could accomplish more by intentionally and consistently reaching out to our campus colleagues to streamline overlapping services. We thoughtfully made efforts to develop pertinent and relevant programming for our students, faculty, staff, and the community at large. With a flat library budget and fewer staff, we strategically sought partnerships with campus departments to expand our footprint. Moreover, librarians directed their attention to departments responsible for creating cocurricular, extracurricular, and specific professional development opportunities geared toward knowledge transfer. These campus collaborations brought about extra help in planning and executing events, assistance with marketing library services and programs, and additional funding provided in support of library collaborative programming from our campus partners. Some of our partners include the Office of Faculty Professional Development, the Office of Diversity and Inclusion, NCCU-TV Studio, Department of Residential Life, the Office of Community Engagement and Service, the Department of Music, the NCCU Art Museum, Information Technology Services, Office of Transfer Services, University Honors Programs, Tutoring, and Supplemental Instruction, Writing and Speaking Studio. Forming these strategic alliances proved to be invaluable for our small library. We have yielded substantial returns because of cross-departmental efforts, which afforded us the ability to sufficiently support and empower our community of users.

Labor Representation

The James E. Shepard Library currently employs ten librarians who serve a student population size of more than 8,011. Librarians are expected to collaborate, interact, and actively engage with faculty, students, and staff. We volunteer for and are placed on committees throughout the campus, community, and local and national library organizations. According to the National Education Association (NEA), HBCU faculty earn on average $18,000 less than their counterparts at non-HBCU institutions.[5] This also includes librarians at HBCUs with faculty rank.[6] While HBCU faculty earnings are a little more than half of their counterparts, expectations and workload experience feel doubled. Salaries at HBCUs and budgets can remain stagnant or have no significant increase for long periods while the cost of living and resource costs rise. All the while, positions go unfilled. Faculty, including librarians, are left to fill in the gap.

The experience of librarians at HBCUs is one that is distinctive and scant in the research. There is a growing body of literature and research about HBCUs; however, research focused on the day-to-day workload of librarians at HBCUs, research activities, and committee work is not represented in the literature at length. Ndumu and Rollins researched HBCU-LIS pipeline partnerships.[7] Research substantiates the University of Pennsylvania report that mentions that most students who attend HBCUs are first-generation students; therefore, faculty spend additional time mentoring students outside of the classroom.[8] The same can be stated for librarians. We find ourselves mentoring students in research and technology skills to ensure they are successful in college.

When it comes to scholarly and research activities, librarians at HBCUs are active on multiple university and community committees. This overrepresentation, defined as having representatives in a proportion higher than average,[9] coupled with the intense workloads and expectations of mentoring students, causes many to wish they had doppelgängers at times. Indeed, these circumstances lead to overextension. As such, the same librarians at HBCUs show up to multiple committee meetings year after year. In some cases, committee responsibilities increase, and so do the meetings. Campus and community involvement plays an essential role for libraries and librarians; however, labor representation at HBCUs is a topic that is worth further exploration.

First-Generation College Students at HBCUs

HBCUs have historically enrolled first-generation students (FGS) in record numbers.[10] FGS present unique needs on college campuses and opportunities in college libraries. Research states FGS may have lower incomes, be less academically prepared, and have less family or social support.[11] Arch and Gilman, in a study conducted in 2019, found that library programs should be more "student ready" "instead of expecting first-generation students (or any students) to be "college-ready." Specifically, they found that library programming can assist FGS by focusing on academic support and tutoring (liaison program to academic departments), social and cultural (social and cultural environment on campus), home and family (provide a welcoming environment), financial (financial concerns), and mentoring and advising ("Librarians should seek to be mentors or become involved in student life and academic affairs programming").[12]

The librarians at Shepard Library have executed all the above programmatic strategies to create a welcoming and student-ready environment. Collaborative cultural and social programs are a hallmark of Shepard Library's programming mission. Holistic and mindful programming was implemented to forge multigenerational community engagement. For example, these events included International Game Nights, the Fashion and Art Exhibition, Shepard Library's Author's Club, Voter Education, Faculty Staff Publication Showcase and Financial Literacy, and other Money Smart Week activities. The librarians at Shepard Library also consider mentoring a part of student success, "focusing on relationship-building in order to more successfully teach information literacy concepts and skills."[13]

Furthermore, to ensure the success of FGS and all students, librarians at the Shepard Library are instructors and embedded librarians for the UNIV 1100 First-Year Seminar. The First-Year Seminar course's goal is to ensure that students are presented with all the resources on campus to teach them effective learning strategies to succeed in college. Barbara Dewey describes embedding librarianship as the following: "Embedding requires more direct and purposeful interaction than acting in parallel with another person, group or activity. Overt purposefulness makes embedding an appropriate definition of the most comprehensive collaborations for librarians in the higher education community."[14] The First-Year Seminar course is an example of how librarians engage first-year students with campus resources, scavenger hunts for library resources, and research sessions. This ensures that students see the connection between what they are learning in the classroom and how the library is crucial to lifelong learning.

Generalist versus Specialist

The librarians at James E. Shepard Memorial Library and its branches have always found a way to accommodate the students and faculty and provide efficacious outcomes and amicable and satisfactory services. In reviewing websites of predominantly white institutions (PWIs) libraries in the Research Triangle Park (RTP) area in North Carolina, we found that PWI libraries generally comprise a combination of generalist and specialist librarians. These libraries have more librarians and staff and larger budgets and serve a significantly larger student and faculty population. The specialists in libraries usually have an advanced degree and/or more advanced training and a specific area or concentration, including geographical information systems (GIS), human resources, web development, grant writing, data management, marketing, scholarly communications, and institutional repository. At the NCCU James E. Shepard Memorial Library, the librarians are tasked with performing many of these duties performed by one and sometimes several individuals at PWIs. There is a significant emphasis on professional development at our library. The librarians at Shepard Library equip themselves with the necessary skills and tools by participating in professional development via workshops, webinars, classes, conferences, self-paced courses, and so forth. The reason for this disparity is often due to a lack of funding, the difference in philanthropic donations and alumni giving, and a significant endowment gap. Frequently, HBCUs are working toward financial sustainability. HBCUs rely heavily on philanthropic fund-raising. Yet the reality is that:

> Generally, Black Americans tend to give a larger share of their discretionary income to charity than whites do. But "wealth begets wealth." ... "This same thing happens with HBCUs." African Americans tend to have less built-up wealth than whites, even at similar levels of education. Besides alumni, schools can get donations from philanthropists, and there's a history of HBCUs being at a disadvantage in this regard as well. "There's racism involved in acquiring funds," says Gasman. In the

past, "funders did not trust African Americans to manage their money, so they didn't give. That's left the schools with bigger gaps to close."[15]

Conclusion

Overextension, pay disparities, doing more with less, and wearing many hats are common themes that we as librarians often hear during conversations with our counterparts at other HBCUs. HBCU librarians' firsthand accounts are essential, and more needs to be written to highlight the strides made at these historically rich institutions. HBCU librarians play a significant role in support of student success, teaching, learning, and research. Their ingenuity often leads to dynamic programmatic efforts, scholarship, and innovative ways of offering unique services on shoestring budgets. HBCU librarians have learned to persist despite having less support staff and less treasure, so to speak. Our reward is in advancing information access for underserved communities. Our desire is for more HBCU collaborative efforts to transfer knowledge and share our contributions to the field of library science.

Notes

1. "About SLIS," North Carolina Central School of Library and Information Science, 2021, https://www.nccu.edu/slis/about-slis.

2. Shaundra Walker, "A Revisionist History of Andrew Carnegie's Library Grants to Black Colleges," in *Topographies of Whiteness: Mapping Whiteness in Library and Information Science*, edited by Gina Schlesselman-Tarango, 23–33 (Library Juice Press, 2017); Aisha Johnson-Jones, *The African American Struggle for Library Equality: The Untold Story of Rosenwald Library Program* (Rowman & Littlefield, 2019).

3. Janice M. Jaguszewski and Karen Williams, *New Roles for New Times: Transforming Liaison Roles in Research Libraries* (Association of Research Libraries, 2013).

4. Anne R. Kenney, "Leveraging the Liaison Model: From Defining 21st Century Research Libraries to Implementing 21st Century Research Universities," Ithaka S+R, March 25, 2014.

5. "Faculty Pay: The HBCU Penalty and the Gender Gap," NEA News, National Education Association, April 25, 2021, accessed October 13, 2021, https://www.nea.org/advocating-for-change/new-from-nea/faculty-pay-hbcu-penalty-and-gender-gap.

6. "ACRL Standards for Faculty Status for Academic Librarians," Association of College and Research Libraries, 2021, http://www.ala.org/acrl/standards/standardsfaculty.

7. Ana Ndumu and Tina Rollins, "Envisioning Reciprocal and Sustainable HBCU-LIS Pipeline Partnerships: What HBCU Librarians Have to Say," *Information and Learning Sciences* 121, no. 3–4 (2020): 155–74.

8. Marybeth Gasman, "The Changing Face of Historically Black Colleges and Universities," Penn Center for Minority Serving Institutions, 2013, https://repository.upenn.edu/cgi/viewcontent.cgi?article=1396&context=gse_pubs.

9. "Overrepresentation," *Merriam-Webster's*, 2021.

10. "About HBCUs," Thurgood Marshall College Fund, 2019, https://www.tmcf.org/about-us/member-schools/about-hbcus/.

11. Arch, Xan and Gilman, Isaac. "First Principles: Designing Services for First-Generation Students," *College & Research Libraries*, 80, no. 7, 996–1012, 2019.

12. Ibid.

13. Adriana Parker. "Academic Libraries and Vulnerable Student Populations: A New Model of Embedded Librarianship for First-Generation University Students." *The Political Librarian* 3, no. 1 (2017): 9.

14. Barbara I. Dewey, "The Embedded Librarian: Strategic Campus Collaborations," *Resource Sharing and Information Networks* 17, no. 1–2 (2004): 5–17.

15. Kate Smith, "Historically Black Colleges Try to Catch Up as Rich Schools Get Richer," *Bloomberg*, July 18, 2017, https://www.bloomberg.com/news/articles/2017-07-18/historically-black-colleges-try-to-catch-up-as-rich-schools-get-richer.

Bibliography

Arch, Xan and Gilman, Isaac. "First Principles: Designing Services for First-Generation Students," *College & Research Libraries*, 80, no. 7, 996–1012, 2019.

Association of College and Research Libraries. "ACRL Standards for Faculty Status for Academic Librarians." April 2021. http://www.ala.org/acrl/standards/standardsfaculty.

Dewey, Barbara I. "The Embedded Librarian: Strategic Campus Collaborations." *Resource Sharing and Information Networks* 17, no. 1–2 (2005): 5–17.

Gasman, Marybeth. "The Changing Face of Historically Black Colleges and Universities." Center for Minority Serving Institutions. 2013. https://repository.upenn.edu/cgi/viewcontent.cgi?article=1396&context=gse_pubs.

Jaguszewski, Janice, and Karen Williams. *New Roles for New Times: Transforming Liaison Roles in Research Libraries.* Association for Research Libraries, 2013.

Johnson-Jones, Aisha. *The African American Struggle for Library Equality: The Untold Story of Rosenwald Library Program.* Lanham, MD: Rowman & Littlefield, 2019.

Kenney, Anne R. "Leveraging the Liaison Model: From Defining 21st Century Research Libraries to Implementing 21st Century Research Universities." Ithaka S+R. March 25, 2014.

National Education Association. "Faculty Pay: The HBCU Penalty and the Gender Gap." NEA News. National Education Association, April 25, 2021. Accessed October 13, 2021. https://www.nea.org/advocating-for-change/new-from-nea/faculty-pay-hbcu-penalty-and-gender-gap.

Ndumu, Ana, and Tina Rollins. "Envisioning Reciprocal and Sustainable HBCU-LIS Pipeline Partnerships: What HBCU Librarians Have to Say." *Information and Learning Sciences* 121 no. 3–4 (2020): 155–74.

North Carolina Central School of Library and Information Science. "About SLIS." 2021. https://www.nccu.edu/slis/about-slis.

Parker, Adriana, "Academic Libraries and Vulnerable Student Populations: A New Model of Embedded Librarianship for First-Generation University Students." *The Political Librarian* 3, no. 1 (2017): 9.

Smith, Kate. "Historically Black Colleges Try to Catch Up as Rich Schools Get Richer." *Bloomberg.* July 19, 2017. https://www.bloomberg.com/news/articles/2017-07-18/historically-black-colleges-try-to-catch-up-as-rich-schools-get-richer.

Thurgood Marshall College Fund. "About HBCUs." 2019. https://www.tmcf.org/about-us/member-schools/about-hbcus/.

Walker, Shaundra. "A Revisionist History of Andrew Carnegie's Library Grants to Black Colleges." In *Topographies of Whiteness: Mapping Whiteness in Library and Information Science,* edited by Gina Schlesselman-Tarango, 23–33. Library Juice Press, 2017.

CHAPTER FOURTEEN

Leading While Black

Are We Up for the Challenge?

Deloice Holliday and Michele Fenton

African Americans in leadership roles have historically faced resistance.[1] These challenges have been especially egregious in librarianship. Racism, sexism, ageism, and ableism can not only hinder an individual's entry into positions of leadership but also hasten their exit. Individuals starting out as leaders may wonder, "Do I really have what it takes to be a leader, or am I just kidding myself?" Those who have been leaders in libraries for some time can feel like imposters and often ask themselves, "Do I really have a right to be in this position?" and "Am I here by accident?"[2] Going further, some African American librarians know they are qualified leaders but often find themselves defending their actions to their white superiors and subordinates. Sadly, the same is true when it comes to superiors and subordinates of color—in other words, people who Black librarians may assume would stand in solidarity with them may behave in just the opposite manner. As a result, some African American librarians walk away from positions of leadership altogether, not willing to suffer damage to their mental, spiritual, and physical health.[3]

This phenomenon is not limited to just one type of library. On the contrary, hostility to Black/African American leadership occurs in all types of libraries—academic, school, public, and special—and at all levels of leadership, from team leader to department head to director or dean. Furthermore, African Americans employed by library-related organizations, associations, and vendors are not immune from resistance received from individuals who do not acknowledge people of color as capable leaders.[4]

Despite all the successes and achievements that people of color have made in the library profession, bias still occurs. We must ponder what to do about it and whether the field is adequately preparing African American leaders. We should also contemplate the role of library associations in advocating for people of color in leadership roles. The reality is that library associations and organizations are complicit in the lack of respect, acceptance, support, and recruitment of Black/African American library leaders. Regardless of education, skill set, or time in position, African American librarians are passed over for leadership roles. Too often, African American librarians stagnate in rank while recruits are hired from outside the organization. This disparity leads to discouragement and disillusion.[5]

These persistent inequities are contradictory to our professional ethos. A main tenet of the American Library Association (ALA) is "to provide leadership for the development, promotion, and improvement of library and information services and the profession of librarianship."[6] It is unclear, however, whether African Americans are receiving adequate support to become library leaders, which begs several questions: Is training and mentoring enough? Who are the current mentors and trainers? More importantly, who *should* serve as mentors and trainers? How should the training and mentoring be carried out? It is time for a review of the methods and tools used in the education, training, mentoring, and coaching librarians of color receive in preparation for leadership roles. Thus, in this chapter, we seek to answer the question: What challenges do African American library leaders face, and how can we intervene? Here, we address, dissect, and provide possible solutions to the lack of representation of African Americans within library leadership ranks.

What Is Leadership?

Leaders are defined by how well they can pull groups of people together to attain a specific goal. An old adage states, "If no one is following you, you are taking a walk by yourself."[7] A good leader has the ability to formulate a plan of action and mobilize a diverse group to work cohesively to effect or implement the action. This includes providing oversight and motivation without alienation or favoritism, making sure to include their staff who may feel like outliers. One thing that most agree on is that leaders are made not born. A leader can be corrected if group dynamics go awry. It takes time, education, and experience to become a good leader.[8] Attributes of good leaders include empathy, charisma, good communication skills, respect, patience, and integrity. Leaders "often come from where you least expect and less from where you predict."[9] However, we must recognize that leadership and being a leader are two different things. Leadership is the act of leading, whereas leaders are developed as a result of deep experience and strength.

Leadership in Libraries

We must also distinguish administrators from leaders. Leaders set goals, priorities, direction, and the overall framework for an organization. A leader sets the standards by which success is to be achieved, measured, or realized. Administrators carry out the objectives of the leader by acquiring the needed workforce or assets, establishing policies, and detailing the steps by which the objectives are to be accomplished. In the field of librarianship, obtaining a leadership role usually involves a long journey of education, experience, and excellent professional and personal references. Those with the right skills, knowledge, and abilities can supervise library workers in the day-to-day functions of the library. Some are elevated to "title" roles but are not leaders. They simply have assigned roles that have more to do with position description than the essence of leadership. For example, they follow guidelines for readiness and/or compliance. Some may seek out ways to improve processes and performance, but simply following instructions does not make one a leader. Leaders have an innate quality, evident in their demeanor and character. Leaders also have to be empathetic.[10]

Leadership Challenges

The most challenging part of leadership is obtaining buy-in from those you lead. Leaders establish policy. Sometimes, those policies run counter to established norms. Change is often very difficult to implement because of resistance. A leader has to figure out how to overcome any resistance within the team. The leader often gains agreement by showing change to be in the best interest of the group or organization; engaging the group or organization in the change process; addressing fears or concerns; and welcoming feedback regarding the change. Many library workers have these abilities, yet it is still difficult for librarians of color to achieve advancement. Many are stuck in department head positions with limited ability to transition. This is the case particularly when it comes to dean or directorship positions. It is even more difficult for workers to be promoted internally. Often, an external candidate is brought in or recruited.

Challenges like macroaggressions, microaggressions, race-based pay inequality, and a lack of opportunities for advancement also contribute to librarians of color being passed over when it comes to leadership attainment.[11] Daily, constant exposure to hostility, racism, and bullying can take a mental, spiritual, and, in some cases, a physical toll on a person, making it difficult to function fully and efficiently on the job. This leaves librarians of color vulnerable to poor performance reviews, probation, and/or termination—although some leave on their own before things get that far.[12]

Additional challenges include the lack of personal, professional, and career development opportunities for librarians of color. Librarians of color may need mentoring, coaching, or instruction in taking the next steps to move through the ranks to upper-level library administration. With many library workplaces or organizations no longer able (or willing) to sponsor conferences and workshops, librarians increasingly pay out of pocket. Many seek free training or just forgo training altogether to remain free of debt. In light of economic disparities in US society, African American librarians and other librarians of color are more likely to be impacted by astronomically higher education costs, difficulty obtaining entry-level positions, and lower wages when compared to white counterparts. Going through the job application and interview process can bring about discouragement and disappointment.

With all the above to deal with, what can African American librarians and other librarians of color do to overcome these challenges? What can administrators and leadership instructors do to help? What role can library associations play?[13]

A Call to Action

The road to leadership is hardly straightforward. However, having a solid action plan is helpful in navigating the many roadblocks encountered along the journey. A solid action plan should include professional development, mentoring, service to the profession, and having a strong support network.

When it comes to professional development, prospective leaders should look for institutes, workshops, webinars, and conferences. These venues offer librarians a chance to gain leadership skills and hands-on experience through group activities, team discussions, and special projects. In dealing with the cost of attendance, prospective leaders can take advantage of scholarships, grants, early-bird registration discounts, and any financial assistance provided by employers. They should consider taking advantage of free training opportunities; in some cases, these opportunities are better than some paid trainings. In addition, prospective leaders should be mindful that professional development includes ongoing learning, especially reading. They should familiarize themselves with professional journals, books, newsletters, and blogs targeted to librarianship. Prospective librarians may also consider contributing to the professional librarian literature by writing articles, books, chapters, and blog posts.

Prospective leaders should not overlook mentorship. A mentor can guide librarians in terms of professional service, navigating the job search process, and conducting conference presentations. When choosing a mentor (or two, or three, or thirty—you do not have to settle for just one), it is recommended to connect with veterans in the profession who remain passionate about the profession and are willing to school a mentee on the ins and outs of the profession. When mentors are not available within the local setting or organization, it is vital to look beyond.[14] Some library associations and library schools have mentor/mentee matching programs. One must also realize that there are different types of mentoring. Traditional mentoring and micromentoring are two examples. Traditional mentoring is a long-term fellowship and can be formal or informal. Micromentoring is a form of mentoring in which mentors and mentees establish a brief fellowship.[15] Whatever type of mentoring route is chosen, prospective leaders must ensure that they take full advantage of the advice, assistance, and lessons offered by mentors.

Service to the profession is another path to leadership and includes committee work, special projects, advocacy, teaching, and serving in an elected/appointed office. Many library associations and library schools have numerous committees, roundtables, and special interest groups devoted to specific areas of the library profession. Prospective leaders should find one or several venues that meet their interests and where they can hone their skills.

Most importantly, one must find a support network. Many try to make the journey to leadership on their own and find themselves overwhelmed, depressed, and disillusioned. A support network keeps one grounded, focused, and empowered. In addition, members of one's support networks may be in a position to hire for administrative positions or can provide leads and serve as references. When establishing a support network, it is key to choose people with a proven record of being loyal, steadfast, caring, and willing to give constructive feedback and stand with you in times of trouble and in times of good.

Notwithstanding, transforming the experiences of African American librarians with leadership aspirations is not just the responsibility of librarians who hope to be leaders. Library administrators and other decision-makers need to do their parts as well. They should use their authority, power, and influence to help African Americans and other people of color who wish to advance within the profession. Recruitment coupled with ongoing support is crucial. Most importantly, administrators need to show caring and appreciation—indeed, a key aspect of retention.

Administrators must take an honest look at their institutions and staff. Administrators must ask whether African Americans and other people of color feel welcomed and supported. Are staff open to diversity or against it? If the work environment is not welcoming, then administrators should take action to enact change. If there are staff members whose modus operandi is the disruption and destruction of any plans for diversity, equity, and inclusion in the workplace, then administrators should not tolerate, cave into, or, heaven forbid, allow them to hold leadership positions. Until library administrators start challenging the status quo and deliberately make change happen in their institutions, things will remain the same.[16]

Library associations, whether at the local, state, national, or international level, need to do more than collect membership dues and add names to their membership rosters. Library associations need to do more to recruit, encourage, and support African American librarians and other librarians of color by encouraging, nominating, and appointing librarians of color to serve on boards, committees, councils, focus groups, task forces, and special interest groups. They must also inspire librarians of color to run for the association president, treasurer, secretary, and other administrative roles within the organization. Other mechanisms include establishing scholarships and grants for people of color to attend library school, leadership institutes, and conferences or conduct research and community projects. The time has come to be deliberate and sincere about supporting and implementing racial representation and equality in LIS. Mediocrity, apathy, and indifference must not be tolerated if African American librarians and other librarians of color are to have a fair shot at leadership.

Looking Ahead
As the future population of the United States continues to trend upward to a majority minority society, it's imperative that libraries mirror the populations they serve. Libraries and library-affiliated organizations should invest in developing, recruiting, supporting, and retaining a diverse workforce. A diverse workforce provides numerous benefits to libraries: an increased understanding and appreciation of the cultures within the communities they serve, more user engagement and connection with libraries, more thought and sensitivity in collection development and subject analysis, and more collaboration and cooperation among staff. In addition, a diverse workforce brings variety and innovation to the marketplace of ideas and solutions for improving and expanding library services and programming, which is crucial to the survival and relevancy of libraries in the decades to come. Finally, a diverse workforce makes a library more attractive to potential employees and aids in retention, especially when the leadership is also diverse and committed to promoting diversity, equity, and inclusion and sees to it that everyone has an equal shot at success and advancement.[17]

Conclusion

"Leading While Black" seeks to add to the existing body of work describing the difficulties of African Americans in all areas of librarianship. Many have left the profession due to macro- and microaggressions. Librarians must learn to persevere when navigating such prejudices. Through perseverance, prospective leaders can become library executives. Library leaders, on the other hand, must be mentored, cultivated, coached, educated, and trained with care and humanity as well. Hopefully, what was shared in this chapter will motivate, encourage, and inspire African American librarians and other librarians of color to continue in their efforts to become leaders in the library profession.

Notes

1. Herb Boyd, "Black Leadership Imperiled," *New York Amsterdam News* 100, no. 34 (August 19, 2010): 13–28.
2. Erin Collier-Plummer, "Managing Imposter Syndrome," *Public Libraries* 59, no. 6 (2020): 23–26.
3. Twanna Hodge et al., "Why I Left the Library Profession—A DEI Perspective: Part I," Association of Southern Research Libraries, December 10, 2020, https://vimeo.com/489791999; Carole Smallwood and Linda Burkey Wade, eds., *Job Stress and the Librarian: Coping Strategies from the Professional* (New York: McFarland, 2013).
4. Steven O. Roberts et al., "God as a White Man: A Psychological Barrier to Conceptualizing Black People and Women as Leadership Worthy," *Journal of Personality and Social Psychology* 119, no. 6 (2020): 1290–315; Ashanti White, *Not Your Ordinary Librarian: Debunking the Popular Perceptions of Librarians* (Amsterdam: Chandos Publishing, 2012).
5. Deborah A. Curry, "Your Worries Ain't Like Mine: African American Librarians and the Pervasiveness of Racism, Prejudice, and Discrimination in Academe," *The Reference Librarian* 21, no. 45/46 (1994): 299–311.
6. "Mission and Priorities," American Library Association, June 9, 2008, http://ww.ala.org/aboutala/missionpriorities.
7. Benjamin L. Hooks, "Speech at Gustavus Adolphus College, St. Peter, MN, April 3, 1978," American Public Media, accessed April 11, 2021, http://americanradioworks.publicradio.org/features/sayitplain/blhooks.html.
8. N. M. Richardson, "What True Leadership Means," *Black Enterprise* 36, no. 1 (2005): 146.

9. Paul Okum, *Leadership DNA* (Bloomington, IN: iUniverse, 2012), 14.

10. Shin Freedman and James M. Freedman, *Becoming a Library Leader: Seven Stages of Leadership Development for Academic Librarians* (Chicago: ALA Editions, 2020); Maha Kumaran, *Leadership in Libraries: A Focus on Ethnic-Minority Librarians* (Amsterdam: Chandos, 2012).

11. Donna M. Druery, Jemimah L. Young, and Chanda Elbert, "Macroaggressions and Civil Discourse," *Women, Gender, and Families of Color* 6, no. 1 (2018): 73–78.

12. Twanna Hodge et al., "Why I Left the Library Profession—A DEI Perspective: Part II," Association of Southern Research Libraries, February 11, 2021, https://vimeo.com/511328271.

13. Alex H. Poole, "Pinkett's Charges: Recruiting, Retaining, and Mentoring Archivists of Color in the Twenty-First Century," *The American Archivist* 80, no. 1 (2017): 103–34.

14. Dawn Lowe-Wincentsen, *Beyond Mentoring: A Guide for Librarians and Information Professionals* (Amsterdam: Chandos, 2017); Carol Smallwood and Rebecca Tolley-Stokes, eds., *Mentoring in Librarianship: Essays on Working with Adults and Students to Further the Professions* (Jefferson, NC: MacFarland, 2012).

15. Linda W. Braun, "Targeted Micro-Mentoring Helps Librarians Advance and Problem Solve," *School Library Journal*, November 24, 2020, https://www.slj.com/?detailStory=targeted-micro-mentoring-helps-librarians-advance-and-problem-solve-professional-development.

16. Robert I. Sutton, *The No Asshole Rule: Building a Civilized Workplace and Surviving One That Isn't* (New York: Warner Business Books, 2007); Roosevelt Weeks and Katie Dover-Taylor, "Lessons in Diversity, Equity and Inclusion from Public Libraries: Managing Change from Where You Are," Association of College and Research Libraries, January 28, 2021, https://www.youtube.com/watch?v=hjxOWy7R2hI.

17. Gregory L. Reese and Ernestine L. Hawkins, *Stop Talking, Start Doing!: Attracting People of Color to the Library Profession* (Washington, DC: American Library Association, 1999).

Bibliography

American Library Association. "Mission and Priorities," June 9, 2008, http://ww.ala.org/aboutala/missionpriorities.

Boyd, Herbert. "Black Leadership Imperiled," *New York Amsterdam News* 100, no. 34 (August 19, 2010): 13–28.

Braun, Linda W. "Targeted Micro-Mentoring Helps Librarians Advance and Problem Solve," School Library Journal, November 24, 2020, https://www.slj.com/?detailStory=targeted-micro-mentoring-helps-librarians-advance-and-problem-solve-professional-development.

Collier-Plummer. "Managing Imposter Syndrome," Public Libraries 59, no. 6 (2020): 23–26.

Curry, Deborah A. "Your Worries Ain't Like Mine: African American Librarians and the Pervasiveness of Racism, Prejudice, and Discrimination in Academe," The Reference Librarian 21, no. 45/46 (1994): 299–311.

Druery, Donna, Jemimah L. Young, and Chanda Elbert. "Macroaggressions and Civil Discourse," Women, Gender, and Families of Color 6, no. 1 (2018): 73–78.

Freedman, Shin and James M. Freedman. *Becoming a Library Leader: Seven Stages of Leadership Development for Academic Librarians* (Chicago: ALA Editions, 2020).

Hodge, Twanna et al. "Why I Left the Library Profession—A DEI Perspective:Part I," Association of Southern Research Libraries, December 10, 2020, https://vimeo.com/489791999

Hooks, Benjamin L. "Speech at Gustavus Adolphus College, St. Peter, MN, April 3, 1978," American Public Media, accessed April 11, 2021, http://americanradioworks.publicradio.org/features/sayitplain/blhooks.html.

Kumaran, Maha. *Leadership in Libraries: A Focus on Ethnic-Minority Librarians* (Amsterdam: Chandos, 2012).

Lowe-Wincentsen, Dawn. *Beyond Mentoring: A Guide for Librarians and Information Professionals* (Amsterdam: Chandos, 2017).

Okum, Paul. *Leadership DNA* (Bloomington, IN: iUniverse, 2012), 14.

Poole, Alex H. "Pinkett's Charges: Recruiting, Retaining, and Mentoring Archivists of Color in the Twenty-First Century," *The American Archivist* 80, no. 1 (2017): 103–34.

Richardson, N.M. "What True Leadership Means," *Black Enterprise*, 36, no. 1 (2005): 146.

Reese, Gregory L. and Ernestine L. Hawkins. *Stop Talking, Start Doing!: Attracting People of Color to the Library Profession* (Washington, DC: American Library Association, 1999).

Roberts, Steven et al. "God as a White Man: A Psychological Barrier to Conceptualizing Black People and Women as Leadership Worthy," *Journal of Personality and Social Psychology* 119, no. 6 (2020): 1290–315.

Smallwood, Carole and Rebecca Tolley-Stokes, eds. *Mentoring in Librarianship: Essays on Working with Adults and Students to Further the Professions* (Jefferson, NC: MacFarland, 2012).

Smallwood, Carole, and Linda Burkey Wade, eds. *Job Stress and the Librarian: Coping Strategies from the Professional* (New York: McFarland, 2013).

Sutton, Robert I. *The No Asshole Rule: Building a Civilized Workplace and Surviving One That Isn't* (New York: Warner Business Books, 2007)

Weeks, Roosevelt and Katie Dover-Taylor. "Lessons in Diversity, Equity and Inclusion from Public Libraries: Managing Change from Where You Are," *Association of College and Research Libraries*, January 28, 2021, https://www.youtube.com/watch?v=hjxOWy7R2hI.

White, Ashanti. *Not Your Ordinary Librarian: Debunking the Popular Perceptions of Librarians* (Amsterdam: Chandos Publishing, 2012).

PART IV

MOVING FORWARD: ANTIRACISM, ACTIVISM, AND ALLYSHIP

CHAPTER FIFTEEN

Passing the Torch

The Tradition of Mentorship among Black Librarians

Satia M. Orange and Tracie D. Hall

In this chapter, Tracie D. Hall, the first African American female and tenth executive director of the American Library Association (ALA) and her longtime mentor, Satia Marshall Orange, a second-generation librarian and former director of ALA's Office for Literacy and Outreach Services (now Office for Diversity, Literacy and Outreach Services) explore the dynamics of their own relationship and experiences being mentored by some of the profession's most heralded Black librarians, including nationally renowned scholars, civil rights leaders, administrators, and academicians, all change makers in their professional circles and communities, leaders such as Anwar Ahmad, Pauletta Bracy, Jon Cawthorne, Sylvia Sprinkle-Hamlin, Carla Hayden, Andrew Jackson, E. J. Josey, A. P. Marshall, Effie Lee Morris, Greg Reese, Spencer Shaw, Lorelle Swader, Andrew Venable, and Barbara Williams.

Collectively, the careers of Hall and Orange span a variety of institutional settings (school, public, special libraries, graduate library school programs, and nonprofits) and roles (front line, middle management, and executive administration) and the American Library Association, where they eventually worked as colleagues. Their reflections cover the merits of formal and informal mentorship, when and why they have chosen to seek out mentoring, how mentorship has supported their individual career trajectories, the role and responsibility of mentoring for Black librarians, and the dialogical nature of successful intergenerational mentoring relationships.

The interview between Hall and Orange provides insight into the importance of mentoring to library and information service career development and resilience and gives visibility to the mentoring contributions that some of the field's most noted Black library leaders have made, even while managing their own high-level positions. As well, this conversation suggests traditions, patterns, and key themes that emerge in collegial relationships, with mentoring as key to the cultural continuity and preservation of Black librarianship, both as a profession and a unique form of activism.

Name some Black librarians you personally identify as mentors. What common threads exemplify the support received from each of these mentors?

Satia Orange: I am fortunate to have welcomed many different mentors of many races and backgrounds into my life at different stages. When it comes to Black librarians who have mentored me, the first was my father, Albert Prince (A. P.) Marshall, who was an academic library director. From my first after-school job in the alumni office on the campus of Lincoln University [Missouri], where my father led the library, to moving into ALA management, my father was always advising me about library-related realities. Virginia Lacy Jones, who was my dean at Atlanta University's School of Library Sciences, widened my vision as a young library professional. She had high expectations of us as new librarians, and she made that known. Sylvia Sprinkle-Hamlin was also extremely influential. She was the first library director [Forsyth County Library System] I worked for, and I learned so much watching her navigate the role of public servant and lead professional initiatives. Sylvia made me feel comfortable going to her for advice and instruction at a pivotal time in my career development. Something that all of my mentors have had in common throughout my career is the willingness to support me as well as to call me out respectfully, knowing that I welcome their perspectives, and that they respect my expertise. Having that kind of support has been invaluable.

Tracie Hall: When it comes to the mentorship I have received from Black librarians, I definitely count the relationship you and I have built as among the most influential. You were the first person to encourage me to go to library school. Even though I had been working at the Seattle Public Library for over two years, you were the first person to tell me that librarianship was deep and wide enough to hold my interests and aspirations. You were at ALA by then, and when you talked about your own career—setting up daycare programs in low-income communities, heading TransAfrica's library, and public library management—everything you talked about having done was something that I dreamed of doing. I applied for a Spectrum Scholarship [a program of the ALA] the same week you told me about it and was eventually accepted at the University of Washington Information School. You have always been a role model for me, but I think our mentoring relationship really started when I came to ALA in 2003 to head the Office for Diversity.

Watching how you built relationships with ALA members and forged partnerships to advance practice and policy was like a master class. I count several other Black librarians as mentors as well. Dr. Spencer Shaw, who helped to integrate the professional ranks of the Hartford Public Library and was a lauded children's librarian, was my professor at the University of Washington at the end of his career. He was a consummate professional, always unruffled, always prepared. I learned so much from him. Ironically, I later ended up managing the same branch he had at Hartford PL several decades earlier. Another Black librarian, Anwar Ahmad oversaw HPL's community libraries and recruited me to head the Upper Albany branch. Anwar deserves so much credit for the work that he did recruiting and inspiring young Black and Latino library staff. I remember him telling me that running a branch library was like running a small business and that we had to work to be worthy of residents' time and investment rather than take it for granted. I took that to heart. It is because of Anwar that I spend so much time thinking about the people that libraries are not serving and how we can reach them.

At what points over your career have you determined the need for a mentor?

Orange: Early in my career I thought I knew everything, so the mentoring I received was mostly unsolicited. As my career grew and required more strategy and vision, I felt the need to seek out support, primarily with dealing with my managers and with learning to manage others. Unsolicited mentorship, informal membership—whatever we call the casual relationships that can develop between people with different levels of experience—is also really valuable. I am one of those people who is always ready to help, ready to jump in. I remember that another manager I worked with once gave me advice that I didn't ask for. It made me upset at first, but it really helped. He told me, people don't always want to hear your opinion or what "you" would do. They don't always want you to fix it. Sometimes, they just want to be heard. And of course, he was right. My need for formal mentoring became more evident as my responsibilities increased and as the expectations placed on my leadership grew. My moving into new settings from a public library to a library in a private cultural institution to an association have all called for me to operate and manage staff more strategically, and I have turned to mentors and also to friends in leadership roles for guidance.

Hall: I don't know that I have ever consciously thought, "I need a mentor." Rather, whenever I have felt the need to grow in a particular way, I have subconsciously gravitated toward people who modeled those skills. When I first started working in libraries, I heard so much about the ALA Annual Conference that a colleague and I—both of us were support staff as are the majority of Black people working in libraries—wanted to see what the buzz was about. We decided to go together, paid our own way, and ended up sharing a room with a few other people. It didn't matter. We wanted to be there so bad. It was all worth it because I met so many Black librarians who would become role models. Andrew Venable was then director of Cleveland Public Library and really heralded in the field. He was very much a statesman and took time to speak with early-career library workers. His generosity stood out. It was at that same conference that I met Carla Hayden, who is now Librarian of Congress. She was the director of Enoch Pratt Free Library then. She had the unmistakable bearing of a leader but was completely down to earth. I remember she had a great sense of style. When we talked, I could feel her genuine interest. From that first ALA conference in 1996 or 1997—this is before I met you, Satia—Andrew and Carla became early examples of what was possible in the field. And Carla has remained an incredibly important mentor throughout my career in and outside of libraries. This is why it is so important to me that Black, Indigenous, and People of Color (BIPOC) library staff get to experience an ALA conference and get engaged in the association. Even though our numbers are small, the opportunity to become proximate to Black library leaders doing field-changing work and to establish a strong peer network that can serve as pacesetters for your career development is critical.

Is there an ethos of Black librarianship that your mentors passed on to you? How is it the same or different from what you've strived to pass on to others?

Orange: There was a visible sense of responsibility for paying it forward in my father's generation. They were committed to cultivating their successors, to passing on the baton. One of my foremost mentors, pioneering San Francisco children's librarian, Effie Lee Morris, who became the first Black librarian to be elected president of the Public Library Association division and the first female chairperson of the Library of Congress, modeled that dedication. Effie insisted on excellence and constantly expanded her leadership capacity by becoming deeply engaged in professional initiatives. I've tried to pass that on by sharing the resources that I have sought to support my own professional development with my mentees. Transferring my dependence from what I would call the "perks of my personality" to learned experience to help me navigate leadership roles and workplace decision-making was a difficult transition for me. I've always been a people person, and I have taken for granted that I can go into a room and hold my own. However, the mentors that I have found most effective relied on observation, research, professional activity and publications to build their leadership credibility. In turn, I encourage the younger people that I mentor to similarly explore all of the professional resources and avenues they can to broaden their experiences. I tell them not to wait on a boss or an institution. Broadening one's professionalism and career opportunity is a personal responsibility.

Hall: I completely agree. Black librarianship is not a passive endeavor. The mentors I have most admired have also shared that deep service orientation you reference—to the field, to the tenets of information access—yes, but also an orientation to librarianship as a form of activism. That has been the primary denominator: a recognition that library services can be a tangible means of supporting BIPOC, low income, rural, people with disabilities, or communities dealing with barriers of any kind. Second, I have often observed an entrepreneurial bent in Black librarianship. I am always struck with how, even within institutional parameters, Black librarians have worked to innovate new programs and services and build new audiences—sometimes with limited budgets. I was recently researching the life of Bertha Pleasant Williams. Montgomery [Alabama] Public Library's first Black librarian. When she was denied a bookmobile to serve users of the segregated system's two "Colored" branches, she organized library supporters to create their own book transport system, and she installed microcollections in community agencies to bring materials directly to users. That ingenuity, that refusal to take no for an answer, is a hallmark of Black librarianship for me and something that I have observed in many of my mentors and that I try to model in my own work.

Can you identify some key considerations for mentoring relationships?

Orange: It's important to agree on the intent and terms of the mentorship relationship. In other words, make sure that both people in the relationship know what they want to achieve and how they are going to go about achieving it. Start with questions like, "When will we meet and what should we be working on?" As a mentor, I have had both formal and informal arrangements. I have been in situations that were very structured in terms of stated goals and even in terms of how long and how often we would meet. I have also had cases where a mentee would call me sporadically and only when they had a major crisis or question.

Both can work and be gratifying as long as both parties are clear. There are pluses and minuses to both. Someone may think they want formal mentoring but may not think they need help in an area where a mentor feels the need to coach them. When it comes to informal coaching, we may not consider ourselves a mentor to someone who sees us that way. I have been called a mentor by people I never suspected saw me that way, which places another layer of responsibility to be present, honest, and in integrity, and of course mindful of confidentiality. In any mentoring relationship confidentiality, creating a safe space though often unspoken, is essential.

Hall: I agree. I would just add that it shouldn't feel like an obligation or a sacrifice for either party. If the mentor is approaching the relationship as if they are paying some sort of penance, they are starting off on the wrong foot. If you look at some of the great mentoring relationships, there is always a spirit of mutuality and colearning. You've modeled that in our relationship as did Black Caucus of the American Library Association founder and educator Dr. E. J. Josey. I met him in the latter part of life when he was older and battling illness. I was at ALA working on an IMLS grant, a doctoral fellowship program, to create more racial diversity in the library and information services [LIS] professorate. Dr. Josey's books had been so inspirational to me in that regard. His writings advocated for more diversity in LIS education. One day, I found out how to reach him, and we would have these wonderful phone calls. I had a million questions, and he enthusiastically welcomed them. He must have been in his eighties then, but he was still intellectually curious and passionate about the field. He would reference books and articles from decades earlier, and I would search them out and reference them in the grant narrative. When we got the grant, I named it after him because he had been inspirational and generous with his expertise and experience, traits that are integral to effective mentorship.

What is the single most important piece of advice that a mentor has passed on to you?

Orange: My father used to tell me, "Don't take yourself too seriously." He was always warning me against being too quick to give what I thought was the right answer. He'd remind me to stop and listen and to pay attention. He'd say, "You don't know what someone needs until they tell you what they need." I loved to give advice. But my daddy would tell me, "Stop to listen." It was advice I have held on to. Because it is true that we need to be present, especially if we want to make a difference in someone else's life.

Hall: That's profound advice. It speaks to a leader's need to cultivate empathy. Empathy, the ability to see and understand the other, may actually be at the heart of Black librarianship. I have received stellar advice that I still draw on from leaders in the field. Jon Cawthorne, Dean of Libraries and the Library School at Wayne State University in Detroit, and I are basically the same age, but I still see him as a mentor because he has always been so invested in leadership development. He sent me an article years ago on establishing an "internal tenure clock," which means having a sense of what you want to accomplish in a particular role before assuming it and how much time that accomplishment might take. That article turned out to be life changing for me. A few years ago, a colleague made a comment that I seemed to work in "double-time," knocking out goals quickly. My mind went right back to that article and about the need to have a sense of clarity and mission going into a job. I thank Jon for introducing me to that and so many other leadership insights.

As a Black librarian do you feel a sense of responsibility to intentionally mentor the next generation? If so, why?

Orange: More than ever. There are so many BIPOC librarians who feel isolated and unsupported in their work environments. I have experienced that feeling and feel called to advocate for them. In my early career, I remember not feeling seen, heard, or empowered. Even when I'd gotten the proverbial seat at the table, my opinions would get limited responses. Someone would say a version of something I'd just said, and, all of a sudden, it would be received as a great idea. I remember how disheartening that was, and I want to encourage the next generation of librarians to see their value and understand their worth much earlier than I did. I'm trying to encourage newer BIPOC librarians to use their voices and to recognize that the reason that they are where they are—even if they are the only or one of the only Black librarians in their institutions—is because they have something to offer. I want them to look in the mirror and know they bring something important and valuable to the field.

Hall: That sense of value cannot be overstated. Especially today when not even a full 6 percent of professional librarians are Black. At this point I feel an urgency to mentor. That's why I am committed to improving the mentorship opportunities provided through ALA. I am concerned about the BIPOC librarians who may never otherwise be exposed to leaders like Barbara Williams, Pauletta Bracy, Lorelle Swader, or Andrew P. Jackson, some of the other Black librarians you've cited as exemplifying excellence. I'd add to that stellar lineup the late Lillian Lewis, with whom we worked at ALA, and Greg Reese, former director of the East Cleveland Library, both of whom were very intentional about discussing the library management journey. Lillian was one of the first people to speak to me openly about the "costs" of leadership, especially for a Black woman. Greg was similarly transparent in talking about navigating the hypervisibility that came with being a library director. When I speak to younger librarians, Black or otherwise, I always take time to discuss the trade-offs and mistakes I've made or areas of my life and leadership that are still works in progress. I want them to know that I am still learning every day.

What can the profession do to encourage the mentoring of Black librarians?

Orange: Institutions need to do a better job of investing in mentorship programs and holding managers responsible for developing their BIPOC staff. When we see the numbers of BIPOC librarians leaving the field year after year, it is because we aren't holding ourselves responsible for talent development. We should be looking across the field and outside the field for the best mentoring offerings for BIPOC and all library staff. If you don't know where to start, sit down with BIPOC employees and ask what they need. For example, after the murder of George Floyd in Minnesota shocked the world, my daughter, who works in human resources for a major automotive company, brought some suggestions to her colleagues for encouraging reflection and dialogue among the staff. They were actually relieved that someone had an idea of what some next steps could be. Similarly, we have to step up with concrete ideas when it comes to mentoring Black librarians. What shape can that take? How might someone like me, given my experience, help a library director bridge that gap?

Hall: Honestly, I think that libraries would do well to actually give Black librarians time to mentor. I think back to something my mentor Anwar Ahmad told me when I was a branch librarian in Hartford. He said that my effectiveness would be predicated on whether I was as visible in the community as I was in the library. I have the same philosophy about the mentoring of early- and midcareer Black librarians. It is not enough that they just know that we are here; we have to make ourselves accessible to them. Ultimately, whether or not Black librarianship is viable rests on whether we are actively engaged in nurturing future Black librarians. We have to make concerted efforts to pass the torch.

Oftentimes, mentoring is intergenerational. Are you learning from the next generation of Black librarians?

Orange: Now, as a retiree, I learn so much from my exchanges with younger Black librarians, and I try to incorporate what I learn in my current mentoring relationships. Professional contexts are always changing. Each new generation develops a new set of strategies. I am really learning from you, Tracie. That has always been true. I count you as a mentor too. When I read your columns in *American Libraries*, I often see things differently. For instance, when I read your article on "information redlining," I had never thought about the effect of information disparity in that way before. I admire, and have since I met you, your visionary perspective and your fearlessness, an attribute I am still trying to perfect. I think the mentoring relationship we have cultivated shows that essentially mentorship runs in both directions.

Hall: I am humbled to hear that. You have literally and figuratively epitomized the impact that mentoring can have on an emerging Black librarian. Having you to talk to and to see in action and your candor in revealing both the highs and lows of leadership has been invaluable. It is highly unlikely that I would be here, certainly in this position, if it had not been for you. I am realizing that what you have passed on to me is the result of the investment in you that earlier Black librarians made. I owe it to you and them to pay it forward to those coming after me.

CHAPTER SIXTEEN

Rethinking Black MLIS Student Recruitment

A Call to Action

Vivian Bordeaux and Jahala Simuel

What is it about the library profession that seeks out people who enjoy working with books, technology, and other information materials; engaging with people of all ages and backgrounds; and encouraging creativity and lifelong learning?[1] For many librarians, working in a library is rewarding and ever evolving. Libraries are doors to information, opportunities, challenges, and adventures. Why is it that few outside the library profession see its occupational potential? What if the librarian career were widely seen as an adventure for those who use its resources?

Recruitment and retention to the library field remains very important. Attracting, engaging, assessing, and onboarding a new workforce is vital for the future of the profession. The methods and tools that institutions use to recruit and retain diverse, creative, and enthusiastic professionals must be relevant to those they wish to attract into this profession.

Background

For the library profession to survive and to be able to attract intelligent, compassionate, and creative people from all backgrounds, the profession needs to be marketed. The use of social media in recruiting to Library and Information Science (LIS) programs and to library organizations is crucial in this age, especially with certain age groups. To attract potential students, it is essential that LIS programs use all types of social media and listservs to advertise their program.[2] Organizations need to do the same in advertising their open positions.[3] Using social media to recruit might be considered the newest and most popular method, but other familiar methods that have been used for recruiting in the past can be just as effective. Another method of recruiting to the profession is through professional conferences, webinars, workshops, and career or job fairs. Career and job fairs have in the past been very effective in recruiting. In the past, newspapers also have played a big role in advertising jobs and word of mouth. Social and civil organizations like sororities, fraternities, and civic clubs can play a part in recruiting. College and career fairs can attract potential students or those considering changing careers. A second master's sometimes is a benefit for those being recruited by an organization. MLIS program advisors can be instrumental in sharing information about the profession and actively reaching out to Black students and others of color.[4]

Foregrounding

The target audience for this article is Black LIS (Library and Information Science) students, potential students, LIS educators, and library administrators. The library profession faces challenges as it tries to bridge the gaps and barriers that face the community they serve. Some barriers that communities face are economic, environmental, physical, and mental, educational, and one's bias. Libraries have a responsibility to recruit people from various backgrounds to provide the best service to their community and to those they work with. Libraries, whether academic, public, or special, need people who see the world beyond, can think outside of the box, are flexible and motivated, and can embrace the mission and vision of the library they work in.

In marketing the profession, we should follow what other professions have done and find an opportunity to talk in the schools. Starting in elementary and middle schools would give an introduction to the profession to an audience who are younger and have not decided on their future career.[5] Just as schools invite fire, medical, and law enforcement personnel to talk about their profession to classes, those who work in libraries—professionals and paraprofessionals—should be invited to talk about the work they do. In marketing the library profession, we would need to enlist the support of all school administrators, teachers, guidance counselors, and coaches. These and other educators play an important part in providing information that will help young students plan their future. We know that the way information is shared is not the same for all communities, especially in the Black communities where education resources may be insufficient and the attitude of the teachers are indifferent toward Black students.

It is also important to market the library profession in every community, to be inclusive. We need to get the word out that libraries and the library profession are vital and a very important tool used to transform lives.[6] We need to work on ways to change the way society views this profession. Institutions need to change the way they reach out to potential Black students. Marketing strategies must be inclusive and appeal to everyone in all communities and not to just a selected few in selected communities.

Libraries have changed over the years and are not delivering services in the same manner that they were doing fifty, twenty-five, or even five years ago. Not only has technology played a vital role in changing the way the library delivers services, but the face of the profession is slowly changing. The profession is changing from only middle-aged white men and women in the forefront to young men and women from diverse backgrounds also providing services.

Historically, a Black person in America must deal with economic disparity, racism, bigotry, bias, disenfranchisement, feelings of powerlessness, and institutional racism. In reviewing literature, studies have been done on recruiting people to the library profession, especially people of African descent. As far back as twenty years ago, there was a great disparity in the number of Black male and female library professionals compared to the number of white male and female library professionals. Professional organizations and library schools across the nation acknowledge that there is a problem in recruiting Black students. Acknowledging that there are disparities in how students are recruited to the profession, especially in the Black community, can help in the process of moving forward in modifying recruitment methods, which must be diverse and inclusive. So often methods used in sharing information about the profession have been directed and marketed to a target audience in a selected community by white professionals. It is important that the Black community sees that the library profession is inclusive not only for the white community but also for Black professionals.

Methodology

The survey was distributed to various listservs and professional networks. The authors gathered the data from the survey via Google Survey.

Findings and Results

From the data compiled from the Association for Library and Information Science Education, we were able to see the number of Black students enrolled in library schools across America during a specific period of four years, between 2017 and 2020.

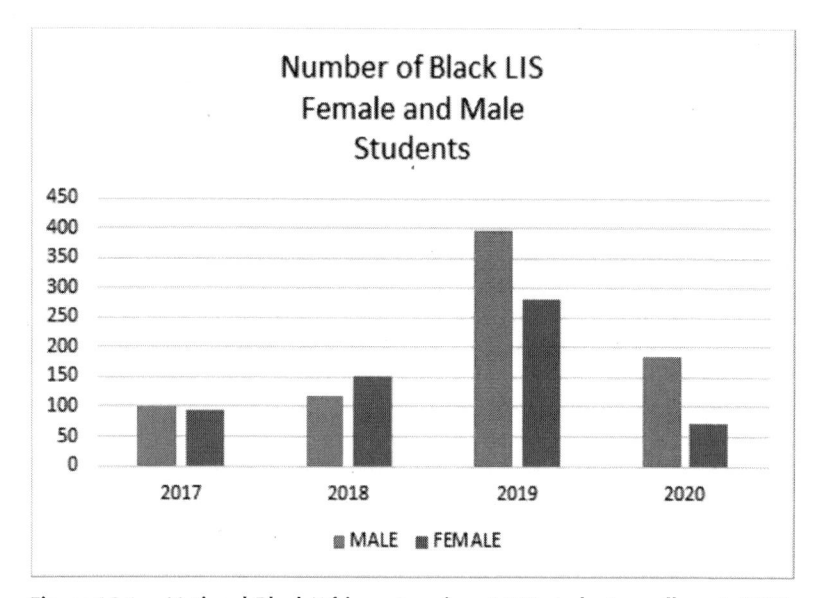

Figure 16.1. National Black/African American MLIS student enrollment, 2017–2020. Vivian Bordeaux and Jahala Simuel.

In 2020, 72 females and 185 males; 2019, 282 females and 397 males; 2018, 150 females and 119 males; and 2017, 95 females and 100 males were enrolled. As a result, you can see that there was a decrease in Black students attending library schools during 2017, 2018, and 2020, with 2019 representing the year with the highest number of Black students enrolled in MLIS programs. The survey can thus be considered a pilot study since it garnered few responses and cannot be said to be representative of the overall population of Black MLIS students.

We distributed a survey comprising eleven questions via social media and the BCALA listserv. We received only nine responses. The survey questions are as follows:

1. Name of library school you are attending or have attended?
2. Gender?
3. Age?
4. Demographics?
5. What events or people encouraged you to seek out information about the library profession?
6. What was it about your recruitment process that was encouraging, insightful, or totally discouraging? Explain what changes you would make.
7. Were you recruited to the field by another librarian? If yes, could you share their racial/ethnic background?
8. What field of librarianship do you plan to go into or are already in?
9. Is this your second career? If so, what made you decide or who influenced you to go into librarianship?
10. The recruitment process is different for every student, more so for Black students. Some might say their initial introduction to the profession was beneficial; others might say that it was a challenge. Why?

Discussion

Demographics
Of the nine responses, one person attended the only HBCU (Historically Black Colleges and Universities) MLIS program. Two males and

seven females completed the survey. Respondents' ages ranged from twenty-five to forty-three years of age. The data from questions 5 through 11 reflect the following:

Motivation for Pursuing Librarianship

Among the reasons for pursuing an MLIS, it was stated that a cousin happened to be a librarian; another respondent states that they were recruited by a teacher/professor who worked at the downtown public library. Another answered that the Black/African American librarians and staff explained and encouraged them to pursue an MLIS because they were finishing their BA in sociology. Others noted that a high school librarian encouraged them; a librarian encouraged them to seek out information about the library profession while attending their undergraduate studies. One respondent replied that they saw a clear lack of representation while working at predominantly white public libraries and noticed the systematic racism. A library director at a previous institution became a mentor and helped them throughout the process.

Entry into the Field

There were various insightful responses regarding entry points or pathways into the field. One person answered that their recruitment process was fueled by a diversity fellowship that required professional commitment for two years beyond completion of the degree. This opportunity was encouraging because it aligned with the person's life circumstances at the time. The respondent added, "What was encouraging was prior to being recruited by my current institution, I was rejected by another for a lesser position. Both interviews were held by white people, and yet I was accepted for the higher paid, more professional position. The color of my skin did not seem to impact either decision and that was encouraging for me." They went on to add, "I do not feel when applying and gathering more information that there was enough about diversity in general. I feel like people were friendly but [students like me] need to see more people like me, resources for people like me, and more courses (mandatory if possible) about the diversity aspect of librarianship would be helpful." Another respondent shared, "The open house at Rutgers was inviting and informative. The young age range of potential students in the orientation was discouraging, but online students were closer in age and had outside experiences like me. I was pleased that the GRE scores were eventually waived, opening the door to applicants like myself that do not test well, but had excellent grades in the classroom." Another shared, "There was a lack of mentorship because of limited options, though the mentors I had were extremely encouraging, and of course, were primarily Black women. I would say the support I had and still have is very encouraging to work in this field." Other responses reflect varied experiences.

"At times, working in libraries can be different but from my experience working in academic libraries, public libraries, and now working in an urban library allows you to have experience in all lanes." Five stated that they were recruited to this field by another librarian and four stated they were not recruited to this field by another librarian. Among those who stated they were welcomed to the field by another person, they each added that they were welcomed by a Black/African American person.

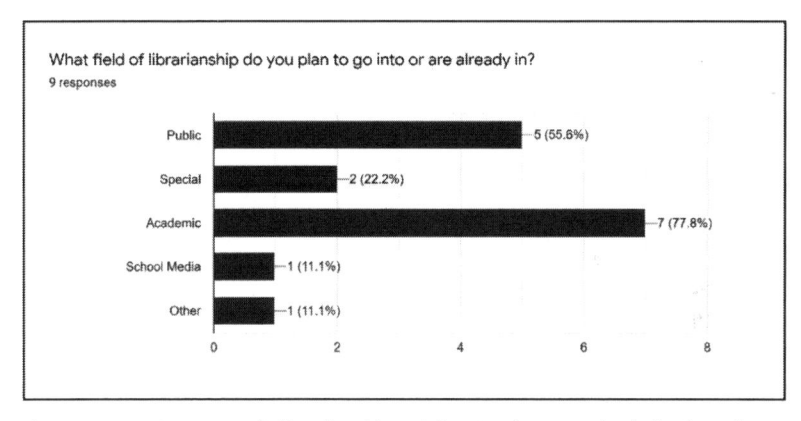

What field of librarianship do you plan to go into or are already in?
9 responses

- Public — 5 (55.6%)
- Special — 2 (22.2%)
- Academic — 7 (77.8%)
- School Media — 1 (11.1%)
- Other — 1 (11.1%)

Figure 16.2. Segment of Librarianship. Vivian Bordeaux and Jahala Simuel.

Librarianship as a Career Transition

Four people responded that being a librarian is their first career, and only one responded that this is their second career. Only five participants responded to this question.

Recruitment Barriers and Opportunities

The question on recruitment barriers and opportunities also led to rich and important feedback. The responses suggest that some Black students may feel pressure to find a profession that will produce larger salaries. One survey respondent stated, "My challenge was convincing my circle that there is value in a career librarianship. Also, that despite there not being hordes of Black librarians, I feel our community is comforted when they see themselves behind the circulation/reference desks in public and school libraries." Another shared, "My recruitment was not difficult at all, though I know that is not everyone's story. Going to Rutgers, diversity was celebrated, and there was even a center dedicated to offering programs for the African Diaspora. Prior to completing my program, I was recruited by my current institution. It was a very easy process, but I understand that this is not a normal occurrence." There were opposing viewpoints, however: "The lack of representation is the first issue. You don't see the potential to be a librarian and, depending on where you are, the librarians you do have access to must be willing to impart what they know and be encouraging. This is not always the case. There is also frustration when people do not listen if you point out what could be better to diversify the profession." Another participant shared, "There are roadblocks and the only way to move them is to have people already in the profession willing to do so. That would encourage more diverse populations to see themselves in these roles. I can speak to this personally. I was the ONLY male of color to graduate from the MLIS program at the University of Maryland this past year. I believe the reasons why it is so difficult to get people of color into the library and information science field are myriad: most people are unaware that the degrees are incredibly versatile and as such not restricted to librarianship. The field is stereotyped as being mainly a field for women, largely white women. This has not helped outside perceptions of the field even today. I believe people of color are not encouraged enough to pursue higher education in general, and certainly not into the library and information science field. The earning potential is not often high in this field, which can potentially turn away a lot of people looking to make certain kinds of living. These are just a few of my hypotheses, but I think they are valid, realistically, or historically."

Similarly, a respondent shared, "It was kind of challenging to enter this field. It was hard to get a chance as an undergraduate to gain experience. I begged the library dean to give me a chance, which allowed me to consider this path to get the library degree. My initial introduction was one that helped me understand the importance of racial and cultural representation within the field of librarianship. It was beneficial to me to understand that to see more librarians of color actively working in the field, people of color who are interested in the discipline must also accept that we are those professionals that we wish to see, and we simply need to take our place."

Though few, these insights corroborate that recruiting Blacks and other minorities into the profession is crucial for now that we are twenty-one years into the twenty-first century. It appears that library schools are slow to recruit more Black students to LIS programs and to be more inclusive in their recruiting process. Black librarians need to be given equal opportunity for promotion and leadership experiences as their white coworkers. Human Resource Departments and those who are responsible for hiring for organizations are changing their strategies and are (slowly) making a conscious effort to hire Black support and professional staff. To educate the community on the many resources that the libraries have to offer, more community programs should be organized for all communities, including the communities that serve the Black population. Libraries, in an effort to draw more Blacks and others of color to the profession, should realize the importance of doing more community programs and collaborating with other community agencies sharing information about the library's resources and services along with the profession more broadly. Working in the community by conducting outreach programs can also be helpful in recruiting potential Black students. Studies show that the Black community is more likely to frequent and support libraries that have Black staff at the public service desk and Black staff in leadership positions. A feeling of being seen and being able to relate to the person serving them is a feeling of empowerment.

Conclusion

After recruitment there needs to be criteria in place that are used to retain and support the motivated and creative Black librarian and library worker. Black librarians should be encouraged to ideate; they should be granted equal opportunity for staff development through clear planning, training, and mentoring. One approach is to have new librarians and perhaps even MLIS students shadow seasoned staff. We must also encourage new and emerging librarians to join professional organizations, attend conferences, express their ideas. Those who are entering the field or might be attracted to the profession can become cross-trained and invited to collaborations. In addition, equal opportunities for promotions and leadership opportunities are vital to keeping those who are assets to the profession same as their white coworkers. This is vital for the profession. Those who are responsible for hiring must establish strategic methods for onboarding new staff and make genuine efforts to increase the number of qualified Black professionals. Not only should strategic methods be created for organizations but also an ongoing collaborative effort between library schools established to recruit more Black students to the program and to the workforce.

Notes

1. Allyson Ard et al., "Why Library and Information Science? The Results of a Career Survey of MLIS Students along with Implications for Reference Librarians and Recruitment." *Reference & User Services Quarterly* (2006): 236–48.

2. Joseph A. Boissé and Connie V. Dowell, "Increasing Minority Librarians in Academic Research Libraries," *Library Journal* 112, no. 7 (1987): 52–54.

3. Don L. Bosseau and Susan K. Martin, "The Accidental Profession," *Journal of Academic Librarianship* 21, no. 3 (1995): 198–99.

4. Stephanie D. Taylor et al., "A Follow-Up Study of the Factors Shaping the Career Choices of Library School Students at the University of Alabama," *Reference & User Services Quarterly* (2010): 35–47.

5. Shannon Gordon, "Generation Y Not? The Rs of Millennial Librarians," *Feliciter* 57, no. 6 (2011): 218–19.

6. Kyung-Sun Kim and Sei-Ching Joanna Sin, "Recruiting and Retaining Students of Color in LIS Programs: Perspectives of Library and Information Professionals," *Journal of Education for Library and Information Science* (2006): 81–95.

Bibliography

Ard, Allyson, Susan Clemmons, Nathan Morgan, Patrick Sessions, Brett Spencer, Tracy Tidwell, and Patricia J. West. "Why Library and Information Science? The Results of a Career Survey of MLIS Students along with Implications for Reference Librarians and Recruitment." *Reference & User Services Quarterly* (2006): 236–48.

Boissé, Joseph A., and Connie V. Dowell. "Increasing Minority Librarians in Academic Research Libraries." *Library Journal* 112, no. 7 (1987): 52–54.

Bosseau, Don L., and Susan K. Martin. "The Accidental Profession." *Journal of Academic Librarianship* 21, no. 3 (1995): 198–99.

Gordon, Shannon. "Generation Y Not? The Rs of Millennial Librarians." *Feliciter* 57, no. 6 (2011): 218–19.

Kim, Kyung-Sun, and Sei-Ching Joanna Sin. "Recruiting and Retaining Students of Color in LIS Programs: Perspectives of Library and Information Professionals." *Journal of Education for Library and Information Science* (2006): 81–95.

Taylor, Stephanie D., R. Alexander Perry, Jessica L. Barton, and Brett Spencer. "A Follow-Up Study of the Factors Shaping the Career Choices of Library School Students at the University of Alabama." *Reference & User Services Quarterly* (2010): 35–47.

CHAPTER SEVENTEEN

Post-2020 Public Libraries

The Urgency of Community Dialogue and Healing

Taliah Abdullah, Hadiya Evans, and Regina Renee Ward

Libraries are community hubs. People of different ages, races, ethnicities, socioeconomic backgrounds, and experiences shape and share the space, giving the public library a unique position to engage people in civic and civil discourse, which can lead to healing. This discourse and healing is necessary action for both the library's external and internal communities. The summer of 2020, with both the pandemic and continued killings of unarmed Black folks by police and others, was both confirmation and opportunity for Black staff to acknowledge personal power and that regardless of positional power held in our library systems that it was essential to lead in the creation of spaces for us and by us, spaces to speak our truth and heal from the oppressive, inequitable systems that exist within libraries. John Lewis asked, "If not us, then who? If not now, then when?" The reality is that although libraries purport to be welcoming spaces to all, this has not always been the experience of Black staff and patrons. The chapter will discuss how Black library workers can and have created space to provide support and healing through programs and employee resource groups. This chapter explores public library programming that fosters external community building and internal community healing.

Walks and Talks

Walking to build community. Walking to increase engagement. Walking to encourage partnership and collaboration. Walking as a form of resistance. Walking as a library program for dialogue and healing. Library walking programs provide active opportunities for staff to step beyond the library walls and to facilitate walks that encourage dialogue and contribute to healing around injustice, isolation, and inactivity. At the center of these walk and talks is a podcast titled "GirlTrek's Black History Bootcamp."[1] Each episode of the podcast celebrates Black voices and stories, with lessons from the past that help guide us through the present, particularly timely as we build resistance and reckon with racial injustices. In advance of the meet-up, walk attendees are encouraged to listen to an assigned podcast episode, either a single episode or episode within a designated range. The walks begin with participant introductions and a summary of the walk route; then the walk facilitator provides a summary of the episode to begin the walking discussion. These walks provide many wellness benefits—social, intellectual, physical, and emotional—and discussions have centered on Audre Lorde, James Baldwin, Claudette Colvin, Bob Marley, Wangari Maathai, Octavia Butler, Malcolm X, Cori Bush, and more. During uncertain and challenging times, walk and talks provided information, inspiration, and healing conversations and engaged patrons with library resources, such as Hoopla and Kanopy, in addition to print materials for further learning and exploration. In recognizing the tremendous and disproportionate impact COVID-19 has had on Black, Indigenous, and People of Color (BIPOC), the walks were transitioned to virtual walk-and-talk options for participants to maintain connection, culture, and care. Walk participants were a resource to the library, as was the library to them, and were invited to community conversations for further engagement.

Community Conversations

To listen, learn from, and engage their community, a metro Denver, Colorado, area library system facilitated twenty-one community conversations with three hundred attendees. When asked to identify what they would like to see the library offer in terms of programming, the overwhelming response was "civic dialogue on topics that are relevant to the community." Participants were seeking a space that would welcome and encourage engagement in conversations of interest and relevance, about current events, issues, and topics that attendees may not otherwise find a way or place to be a part of a conversation. A similar initiative was established at a neighboring Denver library system conducting community conversations using the Harwood model of turning "outward." The model and the subsequent training that followed have created a shift in the institutional approach and philosophy regarding how libraries are reaching customers and what it means to be responsively turned outward. Rich Harwood, founder of this model, describes "libraries as 'change agents' that are ideal for getting to the root of what people want and need for their community."[2] Libraries are commonly considered "safe" and "trusted" institutions where people who work in libraries are more open to the turned outward approach as opposed to the one size fits all mentality creating the willingness needed to connect with the community.[3] For more than two years, multiple community conversations were conducted in neighborhoods throughout Denver that have informed and led to the continued evolution of R.A.D.A. (Read. Awareness. Dialogue. Action.).

Read. Awareness. Dialogue. Action. (R.A.D.A.)
R.A.D.A. is a majority BIPOC, staff-led committee and library program that centers BIPOC voices and uses deep listening methods to provide both internal and external spaces to the public and to the staff to discuss social justice issues in depth. The R.A.D.A. program origins stem directly from the rise in publicized police brutality and the ensuing response by the Black Lives Matter movement with marches and protests in Denver and all around the nation. Programs have been held in communities throughout Denver that have expressed and or demonstrated specific needs for meaningful dialogue on topics that range from black male identity, mass incarceration, and ageism. One of the most successful discussions took place in 2017 in the historic Five Points neighborhood to address increasing housing disparities and rampant gentrification. The National Community Reinvestment Coalition (NCRC)[2] found Denver to be the "second-most gentrified city in America," in a study conducted between 2013 and 2017. The lack

of affordable housing paired with widespread displacement resulted in many black and brown families with roots in the Five Points neighborhood to lose homes or be completely priced out of the rental market.[4] The dynamic between established residents and new residents (gentrifiers) caused a palpable tension and frustration for all involved parties. Using the title *How to Kill a City: Gentrification, Inequality, and the Fight for the Neighborhood*, by Peter Moskowitz, the discussion brought together a variety of stakeholders and was able to illuminate the sources of resentment and frustration and offer ways to find common ground and understanding using the parallel examples of gentrification that occurred in neighborhoods in New Orleans, Detroit, San Francisco, and New York. The program places high value on the awareness and action part of the name, especially action that is combined with intentionality. In the community conversations, the library heard a recurring theme from community members who expressed exasperation at being in open forum spaces that only paid lip service to community issues. At each of the discussions, resources are provided that allow participants to dive deeper into the selected topic, identify key individuals and organizations who are active in the topic, and invite participants to consider what action they will commit to take to provide an actionable list of activities that serve a variety of interests and commitment levels.

We've learned from hosting community conversations and discussion groups that a one-size-only approach for each and every community is ineffective and ultimately not what communities are interested in. The goal is not to promise the world and then not deliver but to take on challenges that are manageable and that the community deems important. Approximately 2.66 percent of the population in one southern Colorado city identifies as Black/African American. Library workers are majority white as is representative for the profession across the nation. However, unlike the library districts to the north, there is one Black librarian working in the district and one other Black library worker for a total of two Black employees in the district.

Internal Community Healing

Social Justice Interest Group

Following the murder of George Floyd and the subsequent uprisings in the summer of 2020, many organizations, including libraries, issued statements against state-sanctioned police violence and in support of Black lives. Some statements were written with unambiguous language and placed prominently on their respective websites. Other statements were written with vague, poetic language and were not highly visible to the public in the name of neutrality. It was after advocating for the former type of statement and being presented with the latter that staff in one southern Colorado library system realized anew that library workers are a community of their own and needed a space to engage in community dialogue, a space to explore the social justice issues confronting the United States of America and process them with colleagues in order to promote a work environment that is welcoming and supportive and promotes growth and development opportunities for all. This is how the Social Justice Interest Group began. A diverse group of library workers—staff of various racial identities, ages, and genders and holding various positions—gather for a monthly book discussion centered on transforming the library culture in regard to social justice issues.

During this time of the COVID-19 global pandemic and continued state-sanctioned violence against the Black community by the police, pundits have reminded the US population of the admonition to learn from history so that we are not doomed to repeat mistakes of the past. Conversely, critics argue that Say Their Name and other campaigns that call for the memorialization of Black lives hold us back as a society by focusing on the past. Similarly, some argue that openly discussing social justice issues in the workplace invites human resource complications. However, the library has found that intentionally holding space for civil discourse and raising awareness about injustice and racial inequality has empowered Black, Indigenous, and People of Color (BIPOC) staff by providing a venue in which they and their perspectives are seen, heard, respected, and valued.

Structure of Social Justice Interest Group Meetings

Each meeting begins with a brief sharing of current events around the book and social justice issue topic of the day. We observe a moment of silence for those who have died as a result of injustice. Next, community agreements along with I/we affirmations are shared by the group facilitator. Each member of the group, which can vary from meeting to meeting with a core group of regular attenders, agrees to the guidelines and is given the opportunity to add an agreement or affirmation that they would like to bring to the space. The discussion itself involves deep reflection on the book and themes related to the relevant issue. In addition to the engagement with the text is the engagement with the other participants. Each staff member is expected to share from their own experience and actively listen to others, particularly those who self-identify as BIPOC or another marginalized identity. Finally, the group addresses implications for library staff, patrons, and services. Directly addressing the topic of implications has resulted in a deeper understanding of our mission, the potential risks that staff members assume through participation, more meaningful allyship, and accountability. Additionally, discussing the implications that social justice has on the library has opened conversation on transforming library culture and improving library services for marginalized populations.

Questions to consider if a library system wants to assemble a social justice interest group:

1. Does the library have an official statement on equity, diversity, inclusion, and social justice?
2. Will a representative from Human Resources participate in the group and in what capacity?
3. What is the mission of the group?
4. How will conflicts be addressed?
5. What leadership model will be used?

Reminders for librarians of color doing this work:

1. Relax (physical exercise, breathing exercises).
2. Relate (find a support group).
3. Release (let it go).
4. Reflect. (Why are you doing this work? Why is it important?)
5. Reconnect with family, friends, hobbies, and activities.

African Diaspora Affinity Group

Amidst the global pandemic of COVID-19, while many were working at home, library staff and administrators watched videos detailing the murders of Breonna Taylor, Ahmaud Arbery, and George Floyd and recognized the continued absence of justice when systems value white supremacy and patriarchy over Black lives. What Black people have known, seen, and felt on a regular basis, others were recognizing—disbelief, anger, sadness, frustration, exhaustion, and continued injustice. However, even with these visual images, at many libraries it was business as usual. Libraries continued to serve patrons while failing to acknowledge the pain experienced by Black library staff. In another library system, Black library staff and allies also had to ask those in positional leadership roles to acknowledge Black lives, internally and via public-facing platforms. The statement was vague, with no actionable steps to intentionally affirm that Black lives matter. The time was momentous for Black staff to center us in work environments where we feel heard, valued, and respected. From the pain and trauma of summer 2020, a door that did not previously exist, opened to promote a culture of authenticity, courage, and inclusion that centered anti-Black racism. In this library system in Colorado, the African Diaspora Affinity Collective ("The Collective") was birthed by seven Black women, to foster dialogue and healing; to model connections where Black employees feel a sense of belonging, have opportunities to thrive, and can be authentically present; and to advocate, promote, and support the expansion of information, services, and resources between communities from the African diaspora and libraries. Armed with a plan, goals, and a budget, The Collective has taken the lead on advocating for and centering Black voices with programs, professional development, and staff recruitment and retention. The labor is significant for Black staff members who have committed to this work. We have to be the change we want to see and anticipate that the rewards will be greater for existing and future staff.

Sankofa

The concept of Sankofa, "go back and get it," is something Black women and women of color demonstrate in our tendency to support. As a white female–dominated profession, librarianship affords unique opportunities for Black women who are librarians to serve in solidarity. Having the visual representation of Black women as librarians has led many of us to this profession, and often Black women in leadership positions accept the role and acknowledge the opportunity to reach out and bring in additional qualified Black, Indigenous, and People of Color into the library and profession. Black women seek opportunities to mentor and engage other Black women already working in libraries and to also encourage those who may not have considered positions in the libraries. Black women bring unique perspectives to interviews and hiring teams and can ensure that qualified candidates who reflect the community are selected. Black women are brave and creative in building healing spaces to support Black staff who feel empowered to dismantle inequitable systems within libraries. In facilitating programs and conversations, women of color bring an inclusive lens. We know what we need to thrive and feel a sense of belonging and prioritize creating these spaces for others to be seen and heard in a way that encourages and embraces authenticity. In the words of Sonia Sanchez, "This is not a small voice you hear."[6] The voice of resistance has been amplified, and the reawakening is occurring. Libraries, as a trusted institution for many, should be at the forefront of the social justice movement and prioritize inclusivity and equity and provide opportunities for reflection and action both within the library and the larger community. What actions are you committed to taking to foster community dialogue and healing in your family, library, and community?

Notes

1. Dixon, Morgan, and Vanessa Garrison. "Girltrek's Black History Bootcamp Podcast." June–August 2020. https://www.buzzsprout.com/1127882.

2. Lisa Peet, "Rich Harwood on Libraries as Change Agents," *Library Journal* 140, no. 2 (2015): 22.

3. Peet, "Rich Harwood on Libraries as Change Agents."

4. Student Nonviolent Coordinating Committee (U.S.), John Lewis and Natalie Bullock Brown, 2011, *SNCC 50th Anniversary Conference, Volume 28*, http://www.aspresolver.com/aspresolver.asp?BLST;1833703.

5. Jason Richardson et al., *Shifting Neighborhoods: Gentrification and Cultural Displacement in American Cities*, National Community Reinvestment Coalition, 2019, https://ncrc.org/gentrification/.

6. Sonia Sanchez, "This Is Not a Small Voice," in *Wounded in the House of a Friend* (Beacon Press, 1995), 63–64.

Bibliography

Dixon, Morgan, and Vanessa Garrison. "Girltrek's Black History Bootcamp Podcast." June–August 2020. https://www.buzzsprout.com/1127882.

National Community Reinvestment Coalition. "Denver Deemed Second-Most Gentrifying City." *Colorado Politics*. July 10, 2020. https://ncrc.org/colorado-politics-report-denver-deemed-second-most-gentrifying-city/.

Peet, Lisa. "Rich Harwood on Libraries as Change Agents." *Library Journal* 140, no. 2 (2015): 22–23.

Richardson, J., B. Mitchell, and J. Franco. *Shifting Neighborhoods: Gentrification and Cultural Displacement in American Cities*. National Community Reinvestment Coalition. March 19, 2019.

Sanchez, Sonia. "This Is Not a Small Voice." In *Wounded in the House of a Friend*, 63–64. Beacon Press, 1995.

Student Nonviolent Coordinating Committee (U.S.). John Lewis and Natalie Bullock Brown. 2011. *SNCC 50th Anniversary Conference, Volume 28*. http://www.aspresolver.com/aspresolver.asp?BLST;1833703.

CHAPTER EIGHTEEN

Thoughts on Sustaining the Academic Library

Angiah L. Davis and Michelle E. Jones

The year 2020 opened our eyes to change. Indeed, the one constant in 2020 *was* change. This pivotal moment prompted us to ponder how the role of libraries has transformed and how, in order to be sustained, libraries must also be willing to quickly adapt. The disruption brought on by the pandemic, racial unrest, and political strife underscored the importance of finding innovative solutions for sustaining academic libraries. As library systems that are vulnerable to the direction and health of host institutions, academic libraries remain in precarious positions. In this chapter, we will first review traditional methods for sustaining academic libraries. We then share nontraditional methods to achieving academic library sustainability.

Traditional Methods of Sustaining Libraries

The academic library is an important piece of institutional culture in the higher education realm. In fact, it is a dynamic one that empowers students to move forward in scholastic pursuits as well as lifelong learning journeys. Academic librarians are responsible for providing diverse collections for patrons to utilize. This not only provides a broader perspective for research but also gives students the opportunity to become well-rounded, well-versed individuals beyond their specific major. Students should be gaining knowledge about many subjects during their college matriculation. The college experience provides familiarity in many areas otherwise not readily available to many. Upon graduation, employers will expect proficiency beyond the academic major as a result of exposure to a plethora of people and insight regarding a multiplicity of topics. This helps students become more successful in general while also developing better citizens. We show them the varying forms of items available beyond just print books. There are various ways to introduce patrons to other resources to use besides the tried-and-true journal articles and books. It shows that deep research was conducted when the reference list includes resources that take more time to find and/or review for useful gems. Such resources include personal interviews, documentaries, and archival materials.

Diverse programming provides a more engaged experience for students in reference to the library. Students need to be able to connect to the culture and people at the institution. This helps them to feel more comfortable and thereby form friendships. This sustains the need for the library. At the same time, it helps them enjoy the college experience. If the programming offered appeals to the student body, then the library will truly become the "hub" of the campus. Students will drop in just to see what lecture or activity might be of interest. Methods of advertising about these programs can also draw students who are not regular visitors into the building. Once they come to participate in a fun activity, they might become more interested in using the resources or getting help from the library staff.

Library instruction feeds directly into the academic part of the student's needs. Once they know how to find sources for their classes, they will excel. This leads to higher grades, targeted class selection, and increased retention. Library staff are able to make a compelling case to show the correlation between those who receive library instruction and/or visit the library and higher graduation rates. For example, Nevada State College found that students who used library resources had a higher semester GPA, greater semester retention rates, and higher rates of good academic standing than nonlibrary resource users.[1] When students gain expertise in how to conduct research, they become empowered. This benefits them individually but also extends to their peers. Professors will recognize the improvement contact with librarians has made on their students. Conversation among faculty members will accentuate the library's value prior to budget creation. Value must be shown before budgets are created. We must be proactive and not only reactive. Perhaps the next time the library is left out of funding or shortchanged, others will feel more compelled to speak up about it. Students hold great significance in decision-making by administration as it relates to fees and other items that directly affect the vitality of the library in years to come. Library administration tends to act faster upon the complaints and suggestions of students. Many times, students can use the influence of such structures as the Student Government Association to make sure their voices are heard. Library staff will not always be present in the influential meetings that determine the library's effectiveness. It is always helpful to have as many constituencies as possible underscore merit.

Nontraditional Methods to Sustain the Library
There are several ways to sustain the academic library. We refer to these as the three Cs: collaboration, communication, and community engagement (or, alternatively, connection).

Collaboration
No library is an island, and every interaction is important. Let's face it; most of our numbers are going down in terms of circulation, enrollment, and student traffic. Some of this is due to the pandemic, and some of it is due to other factors. So how can we reimagine the library? What can we improve upon? How can we deliver service in a safe and better way? The answer is through collaboration. Through collaboration you can achieve more with less. Academic libraries support the teaching and learning needs of their respective institutions. With that said, academic libraries must realize the importance of collaborative work. Potential partners for collaboration include, but are not limited to, student affairs, career services, communication department, academic departments, athletics, student success, financial aid, and counseling services. The library can work with any department on campus.

Communication

Libraries should be able to convey their story in sixty seconds or less. Think of it as an elevator speech. I was on the phone with a potential donor, and he asked what the library needs. Perhaps he was just asking to be nosey, but I took this time to tell him exactly what the library needed. Vulnerability can be an asset. Do not be afraid to ask for what you need. In fact, ask for more than what you need. So my question to you would be Do you know what your library needs? If you do not know, take some time to figure it out. Think of it as a business plan, a communication plan/tool.

Community Engagement

Host local events to engage the community and start a dialogue. This is one way to expand your network and develop relationships with people. Libraries must continue to meet a community need. Community engagement helps people know what the library is doing, and these people can help tell your library's story. If I needed to get something done and I may have experienced what I considered as a setback from administration, I knew the key players involved that I could trust to hear my story and help me make a stronger case or present it in a different way. Libraries will not be sustained without the community.

Retaining and Recruiting Black Librarians

Now that we have shared traditional and nontraditional methods of sustaining academic libraries, we will share ways to retain and recruit Black librarians. One way in which to recruit and retain Black librarians is by facilitating a workplace environment where diversity, equity, and inclusion are respected. Even though the profession is lacking in minority staff, it is possible to encourage everyone's opinion and personality without discouraging those who do not fit the "status quo." In fact, diversity makes the library culture more enriched. We serve diverse types of people, so we should nurture multiplicity in staff and not just in those we serve. This feat requires active participation and foresight instead of a passive hope that everyone will all get along. Small misunderstandings can lead to detrimental challenges in the future of the organization. Because we spend so much time at our place of employment, it is mandatory that we feel heard, understood, appreciated, and respected. If any of these are lacking or not supported by the administration, Black librarians are more likely to leave. Any individual might want to leave; however, minorities may feel more trepidation about filing complaints and retaliation within the department for reporting such issues. It can be a very unsatisfying experience if these tenets are not demonstrated and upheld without fail in every instance.

Recruiters can work with groups of color to recruit and retain Black librarians. Many already do this, but more of an effort should be made in the area. Libraries can reach out to their Human Resources Department, or libraries can forward the job announcement to the groups of color and/or post on social media. Some examples of groups to reach out to would be HBCUs, sororities, fraternities, and Black media groups. Libraries should invest in their own, and Black librarians must recruit our own. When I come across a Black person who has worked in the library for at least a year, I usually strike up a conversation with them to recruit them to librarianship no matter their age. Some people are not thinking about their future, and they may need a little push or someone to encourage them to give librarianship a try. Some employers offer tuition reimbursement plans. There are also scholarships to attend library school.

One way to retain Black librarians is by letting them create their own path. For example, some librarians may get bored with their jobs. Let the librarian try something new or participate in professional development for personal growth. I have been fortunate to be able to do this at my places of employment, but some places do not provide this flexibility. I also think that as an employee you must take the initiative to go after what you want. For example, tell your employer that you are interested in gaining more experience, which will help the library solve this problem. Develop a training program specifically for Black librarians. Black librarians have a different struggle than non–people of color. A training program that helps us create an immediate network for us to learn and grow and will be a safe space for us to discuss, share, and support and motivate each other.

Personal Reflections

During my sixteen years in the profession, I have noticed that library staff are expected to be the "first responders" of the institution or community. It is great to know that when faculty, staff, and students do not know where else to turn, they come to the library. It took a long time for the library to reach this status, so we do not want to return to negative stigmas about the library. In this day and age, many still think everything is available on the internet even though it is not. The library can be sustained by providing library staff the tools they need to assist others and reasonable expectations about what services can be offered when there are obviously limited resources available. You cannot do more with less. The hearts of library staff to provide the best for patrons have not changed. What has changed is the dwindling amount of finances devoted to support the important work of the library. Other areas reduce their services while most libraries try to keep adding more services. We need to choose what we can do best in order to provide those specific services. We cannot be everything to all people. However, the library is an integral part of the campus and can be used as a referral service to campus departments. The library should choose a specific niche or suite of services that serve its users well.

As a librarian I am an advocate, a community leader, an educator, a change agent. If you are working in the field, it is your duty to help someone else along the way. I have had the privilege of working at an HBCU library. It was one of the most culturally rich experiences that I have had as a librarian. There, I had mentors who ended up becoming great friends. Through these experiences, however, I have realized that we must develop and nurture our own. While I did have mentors who did not look like me, it was also important for me to have mentors who did look like me.

Moving Forward

So how do we deal with the next pandemic? How can we be prepared for remote work on the academic and public side? Libraries and librarians must continue their work through collaboration, building a connection. No one person or agency can sustain libraries and the profession. We must do so with the help of others. While we want to preserve our heritage and grow within ourselves and in our own communities, the truth of the matter is we can get more accomplished by working with other groups. This may mean working with groups that are not Black. How do we work with other groups? First, we must empower ourselves. Create a vision for ourselves and then find the resources to help us accomplish the goal. Once we do that, then we can go to other groups and advocate. Tap into your network. We must keep honing our skills. Technology skills are everything, and customer service will always be in demand.

Librarians are social influencers of the community. We have the potential to help shape our communities from K–12, college, and beyond. By partnering with community groups and working across agency and department lines, we are able to create sustainability since we are serving the same people within our community. Public librarians are great at partnering with agencies in their communities. However, we encourage academic librarians to step outside their campus and get into the community. This type of work is also a way to help with enrollment. Many agencies want to partner with you because it makes them look good but also because it's a great idea and most times does not cost anything.

Note

1. Tiffany LeMaistre et al., "Connecting Library Use to Student Success," *portal: Libraries and the Academy* 18, no. 1 (2018): 129.

Bibliography

LeMaistre, Tiffany, Qingmin Shi, and Sandip Thanki. "Connecting Library Use to Student Success." *portal: Libraries and the Academy* 18, no. 1 (2018): 117–40.

CHAPTER NINETEEN

Expanding the Black Archival Imagination

Digital Content Creators and the Movement to Liberate Black Narratives from Institutional Violence

keondra bills freemyn

Over the past decade, social media has not only shaped the societal norms around communication; it has indelibly shaped the current and future use and understanding of archival materials. Traditional archival and digital curation practices have become more accessible to a noninstitutional audience, making way for anyone with interest and an internet connection to contribute to the extensive body of work within Black archives and digital humanities. Digital content creators employ archival and curatorial practices to engage and inform their audience using digital surrogates of primary source material. Many creators have no formal training in archives and digital curation, yet their work affirms the importance and significance of independent and institution-based Black archives while disrupting the legacy of violence and symbolic annihilation[1] enacted by them.

Though some of the recent increase in social media–based archival projects can be attributed to accessibility of technology, it is perhaps equally, if not more, a reflection of the vibrant legacy of the storytelling traditions and historical stewardship practices foundational to Black memory work. For digital content creators focused on the Black experience, social media platforms broaden opportunities for reclamation of erased histories, allow greater agency in defining and redefining dominant narratives, allow for community-accountable archival practice,[2] and disrupt the history of institutional violence within traditional archives through the democratization of information. Archivists and special collections librarians have an opportunity to support Black digital memory workers in this work while improving discovery of archival collections and expanding the use of primary source material among the general public. The profession also has much to gain from developing and sustaining relationships with members of the community, allowing for richer relationships that move beyond community-based metadata initiatives into a reimagining of the archive itself in a digital age.

Independent Black digital memory workers are part of an established lineage of memory workers stewarding diasporic and family histories outside of archival institutions. Many of us recognize members within our own families who are the keepers of the traditions, family history, and artifacts of several generations. Many notable Black institutional collections including the Schomburg Center for Research in Black Culture and Moorland-Spingarn Research Center at Howard University were established and significantly expanded by contributions from the personal collections of Arturo Schomburg and Jesse E. Moorland, respectively. Digital content creators, more specifically Black digital memory workers, continue this legacy, with less emphasis on building independent collections[3] and more on curating the broad array of objects publicly available in digital collections globally.

The curatorial creativity inherent in their work not only connects the dots between disparate digital collections but also expands the reach of archival material to traditionally excluded and underserved information seekers. Black digital memory workers with social media–based practices rely heavily on easily accessible digital surrogates of original images yet are able to avoid direct interaction with institutions and repositories that have historically enacted archival violence against Black communities. However, the absence of reference interactions means that archivists and special collections librarians miss the opportunity to directly engage Black digital memory workers and build meaningful relationships for outreach. Archival practice in the digital era requires that we as a profession find new ways to engage with our collections and support the work of our digital users, not merely to meet outreach goals but to aid in the disruption of legacies of archival violence and systemic marginalization.

Disrupting Legacies of Archival Violence within Archives

The curatorial approach of social media–based Black digital memory workers not only supports greater access to and awareness of Black collections within institutional repositories but also recontextualizes archival records to reflect a broader historical interpretation. Continuing the tradition of family historians and noninstitutional Black memory workers, this interpretive work is as much an intentional desire to center the rich contributions of Black people in a community-focused digital space as it is a direct response to the violence and erasure of traditional archives. Black digital memory workers subvert racist and narrowly conceived notions of Black diasporic history by moving it from margin to center.

Looking specifically at Facebook's image-based social media platform Instagram, digital memory workers are building online communities that center the brilliance and breadth of Black life outside of traditional institutions. Using the image-based platform, digital memory workers are able to reimagine special collections in digital form. Focusing on specific facets of Black cultural production and history, accounts like Black Women Radicals, The Free Black Women's Library, and Black Archives create a hybrid educational experience for the information seeker by blending digital humanities approaches with that of the archive. Individual image posts are often accompanied by captions providing historical context for the images, while the collective content of the account pages provide a curatorial experience for users. In this practice, memory workers are not concerned with archival notions of *respect des fonds* and instead are able to reenvision the contextualization of digital objects in relationship to each other.

Functioning similar to open metadata, hashtags allow digital memory workers to link their content to that of other users on the platform. Instagram has no controlled vocabularies, giving digital memory workers the freedom to select culturally relevant keywords for their content that would not likely be possible within traditional archival structures. Digital memory workers are thus able to reconstruct meaning through arrangement of images and dynamic vocabularies in a way that supports culturally relevant interpretation of digital objects.

As Sharpe suggests, making sense of the absences within the archive, we must become "undisciplined."[4] That is to say, to move toward a reparative archive,[5] we will need to reimagine our concept of the digital archive, examine our responsibilities as stewards of the historical record, and make room for a more expansive definition that includes memory workers operating outside of the very institutions that have and continue to cause us harm. Dismantling the divide created by the professionalization of our work is one way we can move closer to archives that honor our collective epistemologies and legacies of independent cultural stewardship.

Memory Work in the Age of Misinformation: Bridging the Divide between Institutional Archivists and Black Digital Memory Workers

Creating connections between independent digital memory workers and institution-based archivists and librarians is imperative to further liberate the Black historical record from archival violence while also meeting the information needs of digital-only users. Though Black digital memory workers engage with core tenets of archival practice like arrangement and outreach, their work differs from that of traditional archivists due to their work being largely ephemeral and particularly susceptible to loss.[6] Independent Black digital memory workers could benefit from the experiences of institutional archivists in understanding the more technical aspects of the work, including appropriate application of fair use, web archiving options, proper citation and source attribution methods, and the development of right-sized due diligence processes in determining the integrity of information shared on their platforms.

Use of digital platforms like Instagram comes with its own challenges, including navigating copyright infringement,[7] potential for dissemination of misinformation, incorrect attribution, bias in algorithms affecting audience engagement,[8] and the commodification of user information and content for financial gain that is foundational to the operation of social media platforms. Institutional archivists do not have solutions for every challenge independent digital memory workers face, but they can readily share insight on potential solutions when available. Greater exchange of information can help protect social media–based Black digital memory workers from account suspension, termination, and algorithmic censorship[9] or *shadow banning*.[10]

Copyright and Attribution

One of the most significant contributions institutional archivists can make in support of Black digital memory workers engaging with their collections is to encourage a basic understanding of US copyright law and the necessity of good attribution practices. Many Instagram-based Black archival accounts primarily reproduce copyrighted content for informational and educational purposes, which may qualify for dissemination under the fair use section of US copyright law. Institutional archivists need not provide legal consultations but can connect independent Black digital memory workers with public copyright information from the Library of Congress to promote a basic understanding of the risks associated with copyright infringement.

Instagram explicitly states in its community guidelines that users should post only original content or content for which they have express permission to disseminate but that exceptions are made in the interest of the public good.[11] Sharing information on creating takedown policies, explaining the institution's permissions request process, and promoting proper attribution practices are all useful foundational principles. It is important to note that some digital memory workers may be hesitant to properly attribute their sources as a strategy to deter the replication of their content by similar accounts.

Information Literacy and Combating Misinformation

The internet is rife with improper attribution of quotes and images on the internet, and the development of advanced technological techniques like "deep fakes" makes the web a challenging place to find trustworthy information. Providing training and resources on determining reputable sources can help reduce the risk of spreading misinformation to vulnerable users. Many academic libraries have this information readily available for teaching and learning purposes, but incorporating information literacy principles into digital archival work will grow in importance as users engage less with repository staff.

Highlighting Black Digital Collections

Institution-based archivists and special collections librarians can improve visibility and accessibility of their digital collections by using institutional social media accounts to highlight Black collections and catalog items. By researching and using relevant hashtags, institutions can reach new audiences and tap into robust communities of people looking for Black archival content. For institutions with limited outreach resources, hashtag optimization is one way to create greater visibility of Black collections and connect with digital memory workers and Instagram archives. Some accounts also use location tagging to attribute their posts to the repository where the information was found. Ensuring that staff responsible for social media engagement are tracking these metrics can help understand how off-site digital collections are being accessed.

Outreach and Collaboration Opportunities

Black digital memory workers on Instagram often have an intimate understanding of how to nurture strong audience engagement and provide specialized content to their community of followers. Many libraries and cultural institutions lack this level of understanding and can benefit from relationships with content creators who access their digital collections. Including digital communities in program marketing and promotion strategies supports outreach and access goals for repositories while recognizing the unique role Black digital memory workers play in expanding audience engagement and community building. Whenever possible, partnerships and requests for participation in sponsored events should offer equitable compensation.

Building Trust

For partnerships and outreach to be successful, institution-based archivists and special collections librarians must find ways to restore trust among the community of Black digital memory workers. Not all

Black digital memory workers will be interested in working closely with institutions that have histories of exclusion and archival violence. Archivists and special collections librarians affiliated with institutions with a history of harm may have a difficult time navigating the effects of this multigenerational breach of trust. Extra care will need to be taken in ensuring that the legacies of erasure and marginalization are not perpetuated in an effort to increase outreach and that engagement is based in mutual respect and not merely extractive.

Conclusion

Independent Black digital memory workers have proven that it is possible to engage wide audiences in cultural heritage and archival work and remain innovators in audience engagement, outreach strategies, and creative curatorial practices. As archivists and librarians with institutional ties and access to resources and professional networks, we have an opportunity to leverage our privilege in support of digital memory workers who engage with our collections in both our professional and personal capacities.[12] Improving engagement with Black digital memory workers as an integral part of our outreach strategies allows us to interrogate our own methods for expanding access, improving arrangement and description practices for Black collections, and pushes us past the current tendency to engage communities solely in late-stage description and metadata processes. Above all, supporting the labor of independent Black digital memory workers is a necessary strategy in challenging the legacies of harm enacted by many institutions toward Black communities.

Much like our long-standing relationships with research communities, we must value the contributions of independent Black digital memory workers to the digital humanities and archival disciplines and resist our tendency to delegitimize the work of nonprofessional memory workers. This is particularly important as it relates to Black collections, as the work to undo generations of erasure and archival violence will require a wide array of committed advocates who not only understand the significance of preservation but also have the lived experience to properly contextualize the records that exist and identify remaining gaps.

A Selection of Black Archival Instagram Accounts

Many Instagram-based archival projects utilize multiple digital platforms to engage with their audiences. This list includes accounts that either exclusively function on the platform or have a strong presence. The list is by no means inclusive but is included to provide current examples of the range of Black digital memory workers active at the intersection of digital humanities and memory work.

Black Archives (@blackarchives.co)
The mission of Black Archives is to give voice to those stories undertold while providing authentic representation and inspiration to transformative growth of Black people everywhere.[13] Black Archives provides an array of historical content across several disciplines, including community documentary history, arts, and culture, engaging an audience of over 400,000. Black Archives collaborates with a diverse range of partners to produce multimedia archival projects.

The Black Lesbian Archives (@blacklesbianarchives)
Created in 2017, the Black Lesbian Archives creates awareness, fosters community, and preserves Black lesbian culture. Launched in response to the lack of digital representation of Black lesbian archival materials in institutional repositories, BLA operates a community archive and uses its digital presence to highlight relevant items in institutional and private collections. With a community of over nine thousand followers, BLA partners with organizations to highlight Black lesbian collections as well as providing training on personal digital archival practice.

Black Women Radicals (@blackwomenradicals)
Black Women Radicals is a Black feminist advocacy organization dedicated to uplifting and centering Black women and gender-expansive people's radical political activism.[14] BWR's work expressly looks to disrupt erasure of the contributions of Black women and gender-expansive people's political activism. Focused on the African continent and the diaspora, the organization operates a digital database of women's transnational activism and hosts web-based educational programming. Operational on Twitter and Facebook, in addition to a 160,000+ fol-

lowing on Instagram, the accounts source materials from commercial, public, and private archives to support their educational efforts and build community.
www.blackwomenradicals.com

Caribbean Archive (@caribbeanarchive)
Caribbean Archive focuses on digital documentation of Black Caribbean women artists, educators, poets, dancers, anthropologists, and change makers. Focused on providing educational content, Caribbean Archive centers accessibility of information with the purpose of highlighting legacies of resistance among Black Caribbean women. With an audience of over two thousand followers, the account was launched in 2019 to address the absence of Black women's role in rebellions and protests within the Caribbean diaspora from the larger discourse.

The Free Black Women's Library (@thefreeblackwomenslibrary)
A social art project, interactive installation, and book collection, the Free Black Women's Library celebrates the brilliance, diversity, and imagination of Black women writers. The monthly pop-up library consists of over three thousand titles, and the Instagram account shares archival material by Black women writers with its community of over sixty thousand followers.

Notes

1. For more on symbolic annihilation within archives, see Michelle Caswell, "Seeing Yourself in History: Community Archives and the Fight against Symbolic Annihilation," *The Public Historian* 36, no. 4 (2014): 26–37.

2. For an exploration of the concept of community-accountable archival practice as a tenet of Black feminist practice, see Alexis Pauline Gumbs, "Seek the Roots: An Immersive and Interactive Archive of Black Feminist Practice," *Feminist Collections: A Quarterly of Women's Studies Resources* 32, no. 1 (2011): 17–20.

3. There are a number of projects that collect born-digital and digitized materials for archival projects beyond Instagram, including Black Archives and the Black Lesbian Archive.

4. Christina Sharpe, *In the Wake: On Blackness and Being* (Durham, NC: Duke University Press, 2016), 13.

5. Lae'l Hughes-Watkins, "Moving toward a Reparative Archive: A Roadmap for a Holistic Approach to Disrupting Homogeneous Histories in Academic Repositories and Creating Inclusive Spaces for Marginalized Voices," *Journal of Contemporary Archival Studies* 5 (2018).

6. For more on the challenges and opportunities of Instagram archives, see Zakiya Collier, "Archival Activism: Community-Centred Approaches to Archives," Digital Repository of Ireland, October 22, 2020.

7. For further insights on copyright and social media, see Hayleigh Bosher and Sevil Yeşiloğlu, "An Analysis of the Fundamental Tensions between Copyright and Social Media: The Legal Implications of Sharing Images on Instagram," *International Review of Law, Computers & Technology* 33, no. 2 (2019): 164–86.

8. For more on racial bias in algorithms, see Safiya Umoja Noble, *Algorithms of Oppression: How Search Engines Reinforce Racism* (New York: New York University Press, 2018).

9. For more, see Jennifer Cobbe, "Algorithmic Censorship by Social Platforms: Power and Resistance," *Philosophy & Technology* (2020).

10. Shadow banning is the limitation of visibility of user content without their awareness. The algorithm is designed to reduce hate speech and other harmful content, but many users believe it targets accounts unevenly. For more, see Erwan Le Merrer et al., "Setting the Record Straighter on Shadow Banning," 2020, arXiv, preprint arXiv:2012.05101.

11. Facebook, "Instagram Community Guidelines, 2021, https://www.facebook.com/help/instagram/477434105621119.

12. For a recent example of institution-based Black memory workers acting in their personal capacity in service of Black people, see Zakiya Collier, "Call to Action: Archiving State-Sanctioned Violence against Black People," *Medium*, June 6, 2020, https://medium.com/community-archives/call-to-action-archiving-state-sanctioned-violence-against-black-people-d629c956689a.

13. "About," Black Archives, https://www.blackarchives.co/about.

14. "About," Black Women Radicals, https://www.blackwomenradicals.com/about.

Bibliography

Bosher, Hayleigh, and Sevil Yeşiloğlu. "An Analysis of the Fundamental Tensions between Copyright and Social Media: The Legal Implications of Sharing Images on Instagram." *International Review of Law, Computers & Technology* 33, no. 2 (2019): 164–86.

Caswell, Michelle. "Seeing Yourself in History: Community Archives and the Fight against Symbolic Annihilation." *The Public Historian* 36, no. 4 (2014): 26–37.

Cobbe, Jennifer. "Algorithmic Censorship by Social Platforms: Power and Resistance." *Philosophy & Technology* (2020).

Collier, Zakiya. "Archival Activism: Community-Centred Approaches to Archives." Digital Repository of Ireland, October 22, 2020.

———. "Call to Action: Archiving State-Sanctioned Violence against Black People." *Medium*. June 6, 2020. https://medium.com/community-archives/call-to-action-archiving-state-sanctioned-violence-against-black-people-d629c956689a.

Gumbs, Alexis Pauline. "Seek the Roots: An Immersive and Interactive Archive of Black Feminist Practice." *Feminist Collections: A Quarterly of Women's Studies Resources* 32, no. 1 (2011): 17–20.

Hughes-Watkins, Lae'l. "Moving toward a Reparative Archive: A Roadmap for a Holistic Approach to Disrupting Homogeneous Histories in Academic Repositories and Creating Inclusive Spaces for Marginalized Voices." *Journal of Contemporary Archival Studies* 5 (2018).

Le Merrer, Erwan, Benoit Morgan, and Gilles Trédan. "Setting the Record Straighter on Shadow Banning." 2020. *arXiv*, preprint arXiv:2012.05101.

Noble, Safiya Umoja. *Algorithms of Oppression: How Search Engines Reinforce Racism*. New York: New York University Press, 2018.

Sharpe, Christina. *In the Wake: On Blackness and Being*. Durham, NC: Duke University Press, 2016.

Afterword

State of Black Librarianship

Julius C. Jefferson Jr.

Take advantage of every opportunity; where there is none, make it for yourself.

—Marcus Garvey[1]

Five decades after E. J. Josey first chronicled the state of Black librarianship and almost a decade since the last narrative of African American librarians was documented in the *21st Century African American Librarian in America*, we are taking the temperature of Black librarianship as we begin the third decade of the twenty-first century. In short, the state of Black librarianship is tied to the state of the Black community.

During the past year, Americans experienced a global health crisis that took the lives of hundreds of thousands of Americans and millions worldwide, with Black Americans twice as likely to contract the novel COVID-19 virus and twice as likely to die. The health crisis led to the worst economic downturn since the 1930s, and again Blacks were disproportionately affected. Add to this unkindly mix racial justice protests triggered by the unarmed killings of Black and Brown people at the hands of the police. Combine that with the fallout from a contested presidential election fueled by a disinformation campaign that led to a full-out insurrection at the US Capitol and efforts to roll back access to the ballot particularly targeting the voting rights of Black Americans under the guise of fighting false accusations of massive voter fraud. If it were winter in America, then it would be a blizzard in the Black community.

As institutions, libraries can be equalizers helping us understand our past and our current condition or institutions of inequality providing a one-sided view of information and knowledge. The fact is that ten years after publishing *The 21st-Century Black Librarian in America: Issues and Challenges*, Black librarians are still fighting implicit bias with the right to not only have a seat at the table but to lead. Black librarians still have to work twice as hard and have the best education and résumé to be considered for an entry-level position. We often get much less pay and acknowledgment for our work and are judged by a separate and unequal set of standards. We endure microaggressions or blatant discrimination and racism and are often told that our complaint or allegation does not meet the standard for discrimination.

Yet there are those who point to significant progress for Black people in LIS leadership positions. Today, the Librarian of Congress is a Black woman. We currently have back-to-back African American presidents of ALA and an African American executive director of ALA.

The Black activists who founded the Black Caucus would be very proud of the response and activism of BCALA leadership and members over the past year. The Black Caucus has and should continue to be the training ground for leaders in the profession and in ALA. With active BCALA members elected to lead ALA and many more members elected to ALA division leadership and the ALA governing body and appointed to lead ALA committees, we are sitting at the table and making a difference. In fact, 2020 saw three Black ALA division presidents, from AASL, ALSC, and ACRL, three of whom previously served on the BCALA Executive Board.

Even with a Black woman Librarian of Congress, the racial climate at our nation's library rivals that of fifty years ago.[2] BCALA was moved to release a statement to the ALA Council addressing racism and microaggressions as a Black ALA president and executive director confronted open microaggressions.³

As Black librarians, we must remain active in our communities and libraries, being civically engaged and advocating for policies that lead to inclusion. In the words of W. E. B. Du Bois "Now is the accepted time, not tomorrow, not some more convenient season. It is today that our best work can be done and not some future day or future year."⁴ But we cannot act in isolation. Coalition building is the way forward for advancing an inclusive ALA and advocating for services in our communities. BCALA must be a leading voice for librarians of color working with the National Librarians of Color (NALCO).

Moving forward, Black librarians must connect with and find strength in our Black librarian lineage heeding the wisdom of those who have gone before us. Ancestors like Clara Stanton Jones, E. J. Josey, Alma Jacobs, Joseph Henry Reason, A. P. Marshall, and so many others provided the blueprint to organize and advocate for Black librarians and library service to Black communities. Fredrick Douglass reminds us that the efforts and struggles of our ancestors "may be a moral one, or it may be a physical one, and it may be both moral and physical, but it must be a struggle. Power concedes nothing without a demand. It never did and it never will."⁵

Our trailblazers paved the way for those who follow, and we must continue to demand better treatment. We must center ourselves in the narrative of America's past, present, and future and reject the current narrative that does not center us. I know it is and has always been exhausting to be a Black librarian and work in spaces that do not want to include us; however, we must continue to fight for a brighter future for Black librarianship and library service to Black people. After all, this is the debt we owe our ancestors and the price we pay for our space on earth.

Notes

1. Amy Jacques Garvey, *Garvey and Garveyism* (Garvey Press, 1963).
2. See *Ringer v. Mumford*, 355 F. Supp. 749 (D.D.C. 1973); *Cook v. Billington*, C.A. No. 82-0400.
3. "Press Release: BCALA Statement to ALA Council against Racism." Black Caucus of the American Library Association, March 17, 2021.

4. W.E.B. Du Bois, Frederick Douglass, and Booker T. Washington. *Three African-American Classics: Up from Slavery, The Souls of Black Folk and Narrative of the Life of Frederick Douglass.* (Courier Corporation, 2012.)
5. Ibid.

Bibliography

Black Caucus of the American Library Association. "Press Release: BCALA Statement to ALA Council against Racism." March 17, 2021.

Du Bois, W. E. B., Frederick Douglass, and Booker T. Washington. *Three African-American Classics: Up from Slavery, The Souls of Black Folk and Narrative of the Life of Frederick Douglass.* (Courier Corporation, 2012.)

Garvey, Amy Jacques. *Garvey and Garveyism.* Garvey Press, 1963.

Index

@Blacklibrarians network, 5, 141–151
#Blackdisabledlivesmatter, 109

135th Street Branch Library (NYPL), 10, 11–13, 96
2020 election, 264

Abdullah, Taliah, 6, 231–240
ableism, 4, 103–121, 197
academic library, 241–247, 187–196
African American male librarian, 91–102, 123–139
African American Medical Librarians Association (AAMLA), 80, 174, 182, 184
African Diaspora Affinity Collective, 239
African Progressive Library & Information Activist Group (PALIAct), 131

Afro-American Historical and Genealogical Society (AAHGS), 134
ageism, 183, 197
Ahmad, Anwar, 211, 213
Alabama Slave Code of 1833, 91
ALA Bill of Rights and Code of Ethics, 99
ALA Spectrum Scholarship, 76, 80
Alford Sr., Thomas, x
algorithmic censorship/bias, 255
Allen, Minta B., 12
Alston, Jason, 129
American Association of School Librarians (AASL), 264
American Disabilities Act, 113
American Library Association, ix–x, 2, 3, 25, 42, 47, 146, 155, 198
American Missionary Association, 56
Andrew W. Mellon Foundation, 45

Andrews, Regina Anderson, 11, 15, 53
Anthony, Susan B., 54, 57
anti-oppression, 4
Association of Research Libraries Career Enhancement Program, 76
Association of College & Research Libraries (ACRL), 145, 264
Association for Library Services to Children (ALSC), 264
Association for LIS Education (ALISE), 47
Association of Academic Health Sciences Libraries (AAHSL), 182
Atlanta University. *See* Clark Atlanta University

Baek, John, 156
Baldwin, James, 234
Barksdale-Hall, Roland, 4, 123–139
barrel children, 82
Bartley, Kelsa, 4, 73–90
BCALA Reading is Grand!, 130, 133
Bell, Gladys Smiley, 125, 128
Berne, Patricia, 111, 113
bias, 80, 103, 134, 159, 162, 164, 173, 188, 198, 222–223, 254, 264; bibliotherapy, 110
Biddle, Stanton, 130
bigotry, 223
BIPOC in LIS Mental Health Summit, 106
Black Archives, 6, 253, 258
Black Classic Press, 130
Black cybercultures, 4–5, 6
Black Lesbian Archive, 258
Black Librarian Pioneers Oral History Project, 127
Black Lives Matter, 109, 235

Black Panther Party, 108
Black Women Radicals, 6, 253, 258–259
Black-ish, 67
Bland, Shannon, 4, 141–152
Bland, Sandra, 103
Bogle, Paul, 81
Bordeaux, Vivian, 5, 221–230
Bracy, Pauletta, 211
Breedlove, Sarah. *See* Madame C.J. Walker
Brown, Jennifer, 109
Brown v. Board of Education, 107
Bureau of Labor Statistics, 161
Bustamante, Sir Alexander, 81
Butler, Amalia, 5, 153–171
Butler, Octavia, 234

Cabrera, Jaena Rae, 145
Caribbean Archive, 259
Carnegie, Andrew, 59, 155; Carnegie corporation, 37–38, 41; Carnegie libraries, 10, 92, 127, 188
Carver, George Washington, 54
Cawthorne, Jon, 211, 218
Center for Disease Control, 112
Center for Independent Living, 108
Chestnutt, Charles W., 60
Chicago Public Library, 14
Chicano/a, 113
civil rights, 27, 107
Clare, Eli, 111
Clark Atlanta University, 10 40, 42–43, 47, 56, 178
Coates, W. Paul, 130
Colbert-Lewis, Danielle, 5, 187–194
collaboration, 245
Collins, Stacy, 109

Collins, Jazzie, 109
Colorado Black Librarians Association (CBLA), 98
colorism, 77, 79
Columbia University, 13, 26, 34, 40
Colvin, Claudette, 234
community engagement, 246
Corbett, Kizzmekia, 163
Costa, Karen, 112
Council on Library and Information Resources, 28, 45
COVID-19 pandemic, 1, 5, 106, 112–113, 142, 154, 185, 234, 237, 263
Cullen, Countee, 11
Curtis, Florence, 43

Davis, Angiah L., 6, 243–249
Davis Jr., James Allen, 4, 91–102
Dean, Mark, 153
Delaney, Sadie Peterson, 110
Denver, Colorado, 4, 91–102, 234–235
DH+Lib, 144
digital humanities, 251
disability/disability justice, 4, 16, 103–121, 216
diversity in books, 157
diversity residence, 75, 83
Dixon, Amanda America, 54
Douglas, Aaron, 11
Douglass, Frederick, 265
DuBois, W.E.B., 3, 9–24, 54, 57, 59, 265
Dunbar, Paul Lawrence, 60
DuVernay, Jina, 3, 68–72, 150

Emmett Till Memorial Project, 47
emotional labor, 77, 84
Enoch Pratt Free Library, 214

equity, diversity, and inclusion (EDI), 99, 155, 161, 183, 238, 246
Ettarh, Fobazi, 106, 109
Evans, Rhonda, 3, 9–24
Evans, Hadiya, 5, 233–240

Faison, Vernice Reddick, 5, 187–194
Fenton, Michele, 5, 197–204
Farrell Public Library, 123
first-generation college student, 192
Fisk University, 12, 42, 178
Flash, Kenya, 4, 73–90
Floyd, George, 80, 147, 219, 236, 239
Ford, Justina, 93
Free Black Women's Library, 10–11
Free Library of Philadelphia, 113
Freeman's Bureau, 56
freemyn, keondra bills, 5, 251–259

Galleries, Libraries, Archives, and Museums (GLAM), 143
Galloway, Donald, 107, 109
Garland-Thomson, Rosemarie, 108
Garner, Eric, 103
Garvey, Marcus 81, 263
Gelobter, Lisa, 154
General Education Fund, 42
gentrification, 100, 235–236
Georgia Conference on Information Literacy, 130
GirlTrek's Black History Bootcamp, 234
Gordon, George William, 81
Government Alliance for Race and Equality, 99
Gray, Freddie, 103
Gray, Keri, 109
Green, Bella de Costa, 53

270 ~ Index

Greenville (South Carolina) Eight, 92

Hagelin, Karina, 106
Hall, Tracie D., 2, 5, 130, 211–220
Hall, Malikkah, 146
Hamer, Fannie Lou, 109
Hampton (Institute) University, 40, 42–43, 47
Harlem (New York), 9–24, 41, 94, 96
Harlem Book Fair, 133
Harlem Renaissance, 11–12, 54
Harriet Tubman Collection, 105
Harwood, Rich, 235
Harwood Training Program, 93
Haskins, Narcissa, 150
Hayden, Carla, 2, 80, 153, 211, 214
HBCU Library Alliance, 45, 178
HBCU Library Alliance Leadership Institute, 180
health sciences, 173
heteropatriarchy, 106
Historically Black Colleges and Universities (HBCUs), 3, 30, 39, 53–63, 187–196, 225, 247–248
HIV/AIDS, 129
Hodge, Twanna, 4, 73–90
Holliday, Deloice, 5, 197–204
homework gap, 154
Hopper, Franklin, 13
Howard University, 42, 129
Hughes, Langston, 133
Hurston, Zora Neale, 11
Hurst, Bishop John, 60

Imes, William, Lloyd, 16
immigrants, 4, 11, 73–89, 134
imposter syndrome, 77

incarceration, 99, 100, 235
information redlining, 220
Imad, Mays, 112
Institute of Museum and Library Services (IMLS), 46–47, 217
International Federation of Library Associations, 26, 31, 36–37
international librarianship, 31
intersectionality, 101, 106, 109, 111, 113, 148, 149
iSchool, 36

Jackson, Andrew (Sekou Molefi Baako), 133, 134, 211
Jackson, Lorin K., 143
Jacobs, Alma, 265
Jamaica, 74, 81–83
James E. Shepherd Memorial Library, 193
Jarrett, Shancia, 107
Jefferson Jr., Julius, 263–265
Jim Crow, 9
Johnson, Aisha, 3, 39–52
Johnson, James Weldon, 11
Johnson, Lonnie, 153
Joint Conference of Librarians of Color (JCLC), 98, 162
Jones, Barbara, 109
Jones, Virginia Lacey, 30, 162
Jones, Clara Stanton, 2, 25, 265
Jones, Michelle, 6, 243–250
Josey, E. J., 10, 12, 25, 45, 125, 128, 124, 162, 215, 263, 265
Journal of the Medical Library Association, 148
Juneteenth, 128

Kendrick, Kaetrena Davis, 113
Kumbier, Alana, 106, 108, 113–114
Kwaanza, 124, 127

Lacy, Johnnie, 107, 109
Larsen, Nella, 11, 61
Latimer, Catherine, 11
Latinx/Latin America, 44, 78
leadership, 33, 80, 197
Lewis, Ida Mary, 127, 134
Lewis, John, 233
Library Institute for Negro Librarians, 42
Library of Congress, 110, 255; Librarian of Congress, 215
Locke, Alain, 11
Logan, Adella Hunt, 3, 53–63
Lorde, Audre, 53, 106, 109, 234
Louisville Public Library for Colored People, 10
Louisville, Kentucky, 10
low-income, 110, 213, 216
Lukin, John, 108
Lyells, Ruby Stutts, 3

Maathai, Wangari, 234
Madhubuti, Haki, 130
Manley, Norman Washington, 81
Marbury, Nathaniel, 109
Margaret, Sebastian, 111
Marley, Bob, 234
Marshall, A. P., 30, 211, 265
Masutha, Michael, 114
McGowan, Bethany, 5, 173–186
Medical Library Association (MLA), 80, 173, 179
mental health, 103, 106, 111, 163
mentorship, 5, 146, 159, 162, 164, 180, 201, 211–220
microaggressions, 80, 113, 149, 173, 183, 200, 204, 264
Milbern, Stacey, 111
Mingus, Mia, 111
Minnesota Institute, 179

misinformation, 162
Mississippi, 3
MLIS students, 221–230
Montgomery, Benjamin T., 153
Moore, LeRoy, 109, 111
Moorland, Jesse E., 6, 252
Moorland-Spingarn Research Center (Howard University), 252
Morehouse, 178
Morgan, Garrett, 153
Morris, Effie Lee, 110, 211, 215
Moskowitz, Peter 236
Murphy, Beverly, 80, 173
Murray, Stewart A. P., 92

National American Women's Suffrage Association (N-AWSA), 57
Nanny of the Maroons, 81
National Alliance of Multicultural Disabled Advocates, 109
National Archives and Records Administration (NARA), 179
National Association for the Advancement of Colored People (NCAAP), 13–16, 53, 77
National Associations of Librarians of Color (NALCO), 265
National Black Disability Coalition, 109
National Braille Association, 110
National Center for Trauma-Informed Care, 112
National Community Reinvestment Coalition (NCRC), 235
National Conference for African American Librarians (NCAAL), 124–134
National Defense Education Act, 46
National Library of Medicine (NLM), 179

National Library Week, 25
National Science Foundation, 155
National Trust for Historic Preservation, 44, 47
Native Son, 124
Ndumu, Ana, 3, 25–38, 191
Negro Teacher-Librarian Training Program, 42
Nelson, Terry, 92
neutrality, 100, 237
New York Public Library (NYPL), 3, 9, 11, 35
Nkabinde, Bongiwe, 127
North Carolina Central University (NCCU), 44, 47, 178, 187

Obama, Barack, 154
Oliver, Mike, 108
Onyemeh, LaQuanda, 4, 141–152
Orange, Satia, x, 2, 5, 211–220

Pan-African diaspora, 85
Parham, Loretta, 128
Pionke, J. J., 106
Pleasant, Bertha, 216
police brutality, 1, 13, 80, 100, 104, 233, 235, 237, 263
Porter, Dorothy B., 162
Potvin, Sarah, 144
Powell, Adam Clayton, 16
Prairie View A&M University, 42
predominantly white institution (PWI), 193
professional development, 9, 17, 45, 144, 155, 162, 175–186, 190, 193, 201, 215, 239, 247
ProLiteracy Worldwide, 26
Public Library Association (PLA), 110
Pun, Raymond, 150

Quick, Teresa A., 5, 153–171

racism, 1, 5, 77, 79, 80, 98–99, 103, 106, 111–113, 125, 145, 173, 183, 190, 197, 202, 223, 226 239 264; racial battle fatigue, 77
Read. Awareness. Dialogue. Action. (R.A.D.A.), 99, 235–236
Reason, Joseph Henry, 265
Reese, Greg, 211
remittances, 82
retention, 47, 70, 72, 109, 156, 164, 173, 183, 186, 202, 203, 221, 239, 244, 246–247
Rios-Alvarado, Eva, 150
Roberts, Jasmine, 111
Robinson, Carrie, 30
Robinson, Pauline, 93
Rollins, Charlamae, 162
Rollins, Tina, 191
Roots (Alex Haley), 133
Rose, Ernestine, 11, 96
Rose, Tony, 128
Rose, Stephanie, 150
Rosenwald, Julius, 40, 188
Rowland, William, 114
rural, 54, 216

San Francisco Public Library, 110
Sanchez, Sonia, 240
Sankofa, 239
Savage, Augusta, 11
Say Their Name, 237
Schomburg, Arturo, 6
Schomburg Library, 10, 11, 252
school-to-prison pipeline, 100
schools, 153–172
Schuyler, George, 16
science, technology, engineering, mathematics (STEM), 5, 153–171

Scott-Branch, Jamillah, 5, 187–194
Services to People with Disabilities, 114
sexism, 183
shadow banning, 255
Sharpe, Sam, 81
Shaw, Spencer, 211
Simuel, Jahala, 5, 173–186, 221–230
Singer, Judy, 105
Small, Cheryl, 5, 153–171
Smith, Kai Alexis, 4, 103–122
Social Justice Interest Group, 236–237
social model of disability, 108
Social Responsibility Roundtable (SRRT,) 27, 28, 33
Society of American Archivists (SAA), 44, 47
Southeastern Library Association (SELA), 41
Southern University, 178
Sprinkle-Hamlin, Sylvia, 211
Starkey, Julia, 108, 113–114
Stokes Medical Library, 128
Substance Abuse & Mental Health Services Administration (SAMHSA), 111
Swader, Lorelle, 211
Swahili, 4, 124

Talladega, 178
Terrell, Mary Church, 54, 60
Thacker, Juanita, 146
The 21st Century Black Librarian in America, 264
The Handbook of Black Librarianship, 124
third space, 156
Tingling, Jessica, 150

Title II-B Higher Education Act, 46
Title XI, 46
Toomer, Jean, 54
Tougaloo (Mississippi) Nine, 92
TransAfrica, 211
trauma-informed violence, 112
Trinidad and Tobago, 74, 77–81
Tubman, Harriet 133
Tulsa massacre, 91; Tulsa, Oklahoma, 91
Tuskegee University, 42, 53–63, 110, 163; Tuskegee Women's Club, 59; Tuskegee, Alabama, 59

U.S. Congress, 31
U.S. Virgin Islands, 74–77
U.S. West, 4, 91
Uhuru, 4, 123–139
Universal Design for Learning Guidelines (UDL), 110
University of Illinois Urbana-Champaign, 26
University of Pittsburgh, 127
Urban League, 11
Urban Librarians Council, 98

Venable, Andrew, 211, 214
voter suppression, 1

Walcott, Bess Bolden, 57
Walker, Shaundra, 3, 53–65
Walker, Sylvia, 109
Walker, (a.k.a. Sarah Breedlove), Madame C.J., 153
Waller, Salvador 128
Ward, Regina Renee, 5, 233–240
Warren, Henry White, 93
Warren Library, 92
Washington, Booker T., 53–63

Watson, Kelvin, 124
Wedgeworth, Robert, 25–37
WeHere, 106
Welbourne, James, 128
white fragility, 173, 183
white supremacy, 1 77, 114
Williams, Barbara Ann, 128, 211
Williams, Edward Christopher, 41, 162
WOC+Lib, 5, 141–151

Work with Negroes Roundtable, 14, 96
Wray, Wendell, 124
Wright, Louis T., 16

X, Malcolm, 234

Young Men's Christian Association (YMCA), 16
youth, 5, 77–81, 109, 153–172

About the Editors and Contributors

About the Editors

Shauntee Burns-Simpson (MLIS) currently serves as the 2020–2022 president of BCALA. She is the associate director of school outreach for the New York Public Library. An ambassador for libraries and youth librarians, President Burns-Simpson enjoys connecting people to the public library and its resources. She works closely with at-risk teens and fosters a love of reading and learning with her innovative programs. In addition to leading BCALA, she chairs the American Library Association Office of Diversity, Literacy, and Outreach Services (ODLOS) Committee on Diversity.

Nichelle M. Hayes (MPA, MLS) is the BCALA president elect and current vice president. She leads the Center for Black Literature and Culture (CBLC) at the Indianapolis Public Library. Hayes graduated from Indiana University's School of Library and Information Science (SLIS) and began her library career as a library media specialist at an elementary school in Indianapolis. Later, she worked as an adult reference librarian specializing in business. She serves on a number of organizational boards throughout the state of Indiana, including the Indiana Black Librarians Network (IBLN) as immediate past president and the NAACP Greater Indianapolis Branch. She is also a member of Delta Sigma Theta Sorority Inc., a public service organization. Vice President Hayes blogs at https://thetiesthatbind.blog/, where she discusses genealogy and keeping families connected.

Dr. Ana Ndumu (MLIS, PhD) is an assistant professor at the University of Maryland College Park's College of Information Studies who primarily researches and teaches on library services to immigrants—particularly, Black diasporic immigrants—along with methods for promoting representation and inclusion in LIS. A former HBCU (Historically Black Colleges and Universities) librarian, she is interested in the cross between Black identity, information access, and social inclusion. Dr. Ndumu is a BCALA Executive Board member and cochair of the Professional Development and Recruitment Committee.

Dr. Shaundra Walker (MSLS, PhD) is library director at Georgia College. She holds a BA in history from Spelman College, a master's in library and information studies from Clark Atlanta University, and PhD in educational leadership with a concentration in higher education administration from Mercer University. Dr. Walker has over twenty years of experience working in libraries and higher education. Her work and research in libraries and education are deeply influenced by her experience attending and working in HBCUs. Her scholarly interests include the recruitment and retention of diverse librarians and organizational development within the library.

About the Contributors

Taliah Abdullah (MLIS) is a library manager at Arapahoe Libraries in Colorado, has been intrigued with libraries from a young age, and has worked in diverse library settings for nearly thirty years. Librarianship as a career was realized for Taliah when she met a Black librarian for the first time. Since that introduction, Taliah has worked as a school librarian in Illinois, at the Denver Public Library in Colorado, and at the South San Francisco Public Library in California. Taliah is passionate about equity in libraries and community engagement and is an advocate for Black staff thriving and feeling a sense of belonging in libraries.

Kelsa Bartley (MLIS) is the education and outreach librarian in the Learning, Research and Clinical Information Services Department at the University of Miami Miller School of Medicine. Kelsa earned her MS in information at Florida State University in December 2018. She migrated from Trinidad and Tobago to pursue a BFA in photography from Barry University, graduating in 2010. She is a 2016 Spectrum Scholar and received the 2017 Medical Library Association (MLA) Scholarship for Underrepresented Students. As the 2020–2021 chair of the African American Medical Librarians Alliance Caucus (AAMLA), she can speak to her experiences being Afro-Caribbean in an African American librarian space.

Roland Barksdale-Hall (MLIS) is a library director at the Roland, the library director at the Quinby Street Resource Center. He received valuable mentorship, mentored others, presented at NCAAL, published in proceedings, received valuable Reading Is Grand! grants for initiatives at a school library and public housing library, and served as editor of the *BCALA News* and as a contributing writer and interviewed publishers and authors. He is author of *African American Guide to Tracing Our Roots: Healing, Understanding and Restoring Our Families* and *Leadership under Fire: Advancing Progress, Communicating, Teaching and Setting Communities at Liberty*.

Shannon Bland (MLIS) is currently a branch manager for Charles County Public Library. Shannon was a part of ALA's Spectrum Scholar cohort of 2018 and was a finalist for Gwinnett County Public Library and San Jose State University's joint Innovative Librarian Award in 2018. She founded @BlackLibrarians in January 2018. Shannon obtained her MLIS in 2018 from the University of Maryland and holds a bachelor's degree in fine arts from Bowie State University in 2013.

Vivian Bordeaux, MLS, MSW, is a Librarian III at the Bridgeport Public Library, main branch, in Bridgeport, Connecticut. She is currently head of the Circulation and Technical Services Departments. She received her undergraduate and graduate degrees from Southern Connecticut State University, in New Haven, Connecticut.

In her library career, she has held positions as a support staff in an academic library, a manager in a medical library and a professional librarian in a public library, learning valuable skills about people and library concepts and practices.

What she enjoys about the library profession is how it can transform the lives of people of all ages. One of her passions is working with others in the United States and abroad to set up community libraries. She holds professional memberships in the American Library Association, Black Caucus of the American Library Association, Connecticut Library Association, and the National Association of Social Workers.

Amalia E. Butler (MSLIS) is a senior children's librarian in the New York metro area who works with families, educators, and community partners. She earned national recognition for award-winning public library programming, including workshops for workers' rights and childcare skills for nonparental caregivers; a partnership for a series of conversations on gender with families, educators, and health care professionals; and a school-age summer writing program. Amalia served as a peer trainer for a statewide early literacy initiative focused on empowering caregivers through intentionality and engagement. She is a member of BCALA, APALA, the Association for Library Services to Children, and the 2023 (John) Newbery Award Selection Committee.

Danielle Colbert-Lewis (MLIS, MEd) is the head of research and instructional services at the North Carolina Central University (NCCU) James E. Shepard Memorial Library. Previously, she held the research and instructional services librarian position at NC Central University and reference and instruction librarian at the University Library System, the University of Pittsburgh, with faculty ranking. Librarian expertise includes the following areas: reference, information literacy, and utilizing legal resources; first-year experience instructor; institutional repository; government documents; and programming. Prior higher education professional student affairs experience includes serving the University of Pittsburgh's Office of Cross-Cultural and Leadership Development and the Office of Student Life as a coordinator and advisor. Prior to serving the University of Pittsburgh, professional experience includes the following: assistant director of reunions and class activities at the University of Virginia Alumni Association, area coordinator at the University of Richmond Westhampton College, and assistant resident director at Virginia Tech Residence Life. She holds a Master of Library and Information Science from the University of Pittsburgh, a Master of Arts in Education from Virginia Tech, and Bachelor of Arts in Anthropology from the University of Virginia.

Angiah L. Davis (MLIS) is the director of library services at Gordon State College in Barnesville, Georgia. She brings academic and public library experience from the perspective of youth services, reference and instruction, outreach, and collection development. She is currently the chair of the Black Caucus Interest Group of the Georgia Library Association and worked at an HBCU library for over five years. Angiah obtained an MLIS degree from Florida State University. She has authored a chapter in the forthcoming book *Hope and a Future: Perspectives on the Impact That Librarians and Libraries Have on Our World* (2021). Her research interests include library leadership and management, organizational culture, and the information needs and information access of diverse groups.

James Allen Davis Jr. (MLIS) is a senior librarian for the Bear Valley Library, a branch of the Denver Public Library. He sits on the BCALA Executive Board and is a charter member of the Colorado Black Library Association. He is currently serving on the Steering Committee of JCLC and is cochair of the BCALA Professional Development Committee. James has worked in public libraries for over seventeen years and has developed programs and outreach to several communities. He's an advocate for the professional development and advancement of black librarians and actively works to mentor and assist in recruiting and retention of librarians of color. James is a member of the EDI (equity, diversity, and inclusion) team for the Denver Public Library and is the cofounder of the R.A.D.A. book group, which stands for Read. Awareness. Dialogue. Action., and advocates for intellectual freedom by working collectively with several DPL staff to host social book clubs in several communities by addressing current disparities among marginalized groups.

Jina DuVernay (MLIS) is the coordinator for African American studies and primary source literacy at Atlanta University Center's Robert W. Woodruff Library. She also held previous positions as a collection development archivist for African American collections at the Stuart A. Rose Manuscript, Archives, and Rare Book Library at Emory University (where she curates acquisitions for the African American collecting area; DuVernay worked as processing archivist for a year and a half at the same institution) and a special collections librarian at Alabama State University (where she collected the books and periodicals that pertained to African American history and culture). DuVernay, a 2018 ALA Emerging Leader and 2018–2020 BCALA Board Member, is involved in various aspects of librarianship and is currently on the 2021 ballot for ALA councilor-at-large. She serves on the ALA Committee on Diversity and as editor of the online publication WOC+Lib and the *Library Diversity and Residency Studies* journal.

Hadiya I. Evans (MA, MLIS) is a reference librarian at the Blair-Caldwell African American Research Library and Museum of the Denver Public Library. Her professional trajectory hasn't been a sprint but a marathon, with pit stops that have enriched her career due to the inspiration and guidance of unofficial mentorship. Having built a reputation in the community as a trusted representative of the library, she spends her time nurturing collaborative partnerships and creating relevant and community-focused programming. She is the 2021–2023 president of the Colorado Black Library Association, an affiliate of the Black Caucus of the American Library Association.

Rhonda Evans is the assistant chief librarian of the Jean Blackwell Hutson Research and Reference Division at the Schomburg Center for Research in Black Culture and a visiting assistant professor at Pratt Institute School of Library and Information Science. At the Schomburg Center, she supports the management of the Research and Reference Division's diverse collections that focus on people of African descent throughout the world. She also holds an MFA from Columbia University and a JD from the University of North Carolina at Chapel Hill. Prior to entering librarianship, she was a practicing attorney specializing in tort law. She is an American Library Association's Emerging

Leader for 2019–2020 and a proud former American Libraries Association Spectrum Scholar and Association of Research Libraries Initiative to Recruit a Diverse Workforce Scholar.

Vernice Riddick Faison (MLIS) is head music librarian at North Carolina Central University and manages the music library's daily operations, including reference, information literacy, cataloging, marketing, and outreach. She was instrumental in establishing the James E. Shepard Memorial Library's Marketing Committee and has served as chair since its inception in 2007. Faison was a member of NCCU's School of Library and Information Sciences (SLIS) first digital library class and helped produce (SLIS) library's first digital collection and, in turn, the first digital collection on NCCU's campus. In addition, she also served as project coordinator and spearheaded James E. Shepard Memorial Library's first digital collection, called the NCCU Digital Collection, and created Shepard Library's latest digital anthology entitled NCCU: The Early Years. Furthermore, Faison, along with several colleagues, authored a chapter in several books.

Michele T. Fenton is a monographs catalog librarian at the Indiana State Library in Indianapolis, Indiana. Ms. Fenton received her MLIS from the University of North Carolina-Greensboro in Greensboro, North Carolina. She was a 2016 International Federation of Library Associations and Institutions (IFLA) National Committee Fellow and is a member of the IFLA Library History Special Interest Group. Ms. Fenton is also a member of ALA's International Relations Round Table, Library History Round Table, and Ethnic and Multicultural Information Exchange Round Table. In addition, she is a member of the American Library Association, the Indiana Black Librarians Network, the Black Caucus of the American Library Association, and the Association for the Study of African American Life and History. Ms. Fenton has written several articles, encyclopedia entries, and book chapters for several publications and serves on the editorial board for the journal *Libraries: Culture, History and Society*. She is the creator of the blog *Little Known Black Librarian Facts*, where she explores the history of African Americans and libraries.

Kenya Flash (MLIS) is the librarian for political science, global affairs, and government information at Yale University. She also supports the Ethnicity, Race, and Migration and the Ethics, Politics, and Economics majors. Prior to working at Yale, Kenya was one of two diversity residents at the University of Tennessee, Knoxville, as well as one of their social sciences librarians. Kenya earned her MLIS from Drexel University and her MA in political science from East Stroudsburg University. Born in Kingston, Jamaica, but as an émigré to the United States at a young age, she feels she can bring a unique perspective to this chapter.

keondra bills freemyn is a writer, archivist, and digital memory worker. She has worked on archival projects across the humanities, including collections within the Library of Congress, Smithsonian National Museum of African American History and Culture, New York Public Library, and the People's Archive at the DC Public Library. She is a seasoned Wikipedia editor and founder of the Black Women Writers Project, highlighting the contributions of Black women writers to the literary canon. keondra is an alumna of Fordham University and Columbia University and holds a Graduate Certificate in Museum Studies from Harvard University. She is completing her Master of Library and Information Science at University of Maryland College Park. She lives with her wife and child in Maryland.

Tracie D. Hall (MA International Studies, MLIS) is an American librarian, author, curator, and advocate for the arts who serves as the executive director of the American Library Association since 2020, succeeding Mary Ghikas. Hall is the first African American woman to lead the association since its founding in 1876. Prior to her appointment as ALA director, Hall served as the director of the Joyce Foundation Culture Program. She also served as Chicago's Deputy Commissioner of the Department of Cultural Affairs and Special Events. In libraries, Hall was vice president of the Queens Public Library and assistant dean of Dominican University Graduate School of Library and Information Science. She was the director of the Office for Diversity for the American Library Association from 2003 to 2006. Earlier in her career, she had worked at the Seattle Public Library and Hartford Public Library and run a homeless shelter in Santa Monica.

In the private sector, she worked as a community investment strategist at Boeing's Global Corporate Citizenship Division.

Carla Hayden (MLIS, PhD) was sworn in as the fourteenth Librarian of Congress on September 14, 2016. Hayden, the first woman and the first African American to lead the national library, was nominated to the position by President Barack Obama on February 24, 2016, and her nomination was confirmed by the US Senate on July 13.

Prior to her latest post, she served since 1993 as CEO of the Enoch Pratt Free Library in Baltimore, Maryland. Hayden was nominated by President Obama to be a member of the National Museum and Library Services Board in January 2010 and was confirmed to that post by the Senate in June 2010. Prior to joining the Pratt Library, Hayden was deputy commissioner and chief librarian of the Chicago Public Library from 1991 to 1993. She was an assistant professor for library and information science at the University of Pittsburgh from 1987 to 1991. Hayden was library services coordinator for the Museum of Science and Industry in Chicago from 1982 to 1987. She began her career with the Chicago Public Library as the young adult services coordinator from 1979 to 1982 and as a library associate and children's librarian from 1973 to 1979.

Hayden was president of the American Library Association from 2003 to 2004. In 1995, she was the first African American to receive Library Journal's Librarian of the Year Award in recognition of her outreach services at the Pratt Library, which included an after-school center for Baltimore teens offering homework assistance and college and career counseling. Hayden received a BA from Roosevelt University and an MA and PhD from the Graduate Library School of the University of Chicago.

Twanna Hodge (MLIS) is the diversity, equity, and inclusion librarian at the University of Florida (UF). Prior to working at UF, Twanna was an academic/research librarian at SUNY Upstate Medical University, information literacy and collection development librarian at the University of the Virgin Islands, and was the first diversity resident librarian at the University of Utah. Twanna earned her MLIS from the University of Washington and her BA in humanities from the University of the Virgin Islands. Born and raised in St. Thomas, US Virgin Islands, she identifies as a Afro-Caribbean, first-generation American and the daughter of immigrants.

Deloice Holliday is tenured library faculty at the Indiana University Libraries Bloomington campus in Bloomington, Indiana. Ms. Holliday received her MLS from Indiana University. She currently serves as the collection manager for African American and African diaspora studies, multicultural outreach librarian, and head of the Neal-Marshall Black Culture Center Library. Ms. Holliday has been a member of the American Library Association, the Association of College and Research Libraries, the Black Caucus of the American Library Association, the Indiana Black Librarians Network, and the Association for the Study of African American Life and History. Ms. Holliday has published book chapters, encyclopedia entries, and articles on diversity and cultural competency in libraries.

Julius C. Jefferson Jr. (MLIS) is currently the 2020–2021 president of the American Library Association (ALA). He has also served on a number of critical ALA committees, including the Finance and Audit Committee, the Budget Analysis and Review Committee, and the Intellectual Freedom Committee, serving as the 2010–2011 chair. Jefferson is also the section head of the Research and Library Services Section in the Foreign Affairs, Defense, and Trade Division at the Congressional Research Service of the Library of Congress. In this role, Jefferson leads research librarians who provide public policy research assistance exclusively to members of Congress, congressional committees, and staffers. He also previously served as the acting chief of research and reference services at the Library of Congress.

In addition to his service to the American Library Association, Jefferson has held a seat on the board of the Freedom to Read Foundation (2012–2016) serving as the 2013–2016 president; served as president of the District of Columbia Library Association (DCLA); and served on the board of the Black Caucus of the American Library Association (BCALA). He coedited *The 21st-Century Black Librarian in America: Issues and Challenges*, the volume that precedes the current text, and is often sought as a speaker on library-related issues such as diversity, leadership, and professional development.

Dr. Aisha Johnson (MLIS, PhD) is an educator and revelator of Southern intellectual history and an advocate for untold stories. She is committed to archival research, the production of minority librarians and archivists for cultural preservation, and redefining the scholar. Much of her research focuses on the development of literacy in the African American community and those philanthropic efforts to develop public libraries in the South. Dr. Johnson currently serves as assistant professor and program director of Master of Library Science at North Carolina Central University. She was honored as the 2020 College of Communication and Information Distinguished Alumni of Florida State University's School of Information.

Michelle E. Jones (MSLS) currently serves as head of reference services and is a professor at Columbus State University in Columbus, Georgia. She earned an MSLS from Clark Atlanta University. Formerly the interlibrary loan librarian, she also has experience teaching a credit-bearing information literacy class in hybrid, face-to-face, and online formats. Jones works heavily with doctoral students in education providing research assistance for dissertation completion. She has authored a guest forum article for *The Informed Librarian* (2020) and a chapter in the forthcoming book *Promoting African American Writers: Library Partnerships for Outreach, Programming, and Literacy* (2021).

Bethany McGowan (MLIS, MS, AHIP) is an assistant professor of information studies and health sciences information specialist at Purdue University. In addition to her MLIS (University of South Carolina) and AHIP certification, she holds a Master of Science in Interaction Design and Information Architecture (University of Baltimore) and a Graduate Certificate in Health Sciences Librarianship (University of Pittsburgh). Professor McGowan's research centers on data and information literacy instruction in extracurricular settings and on understanding the influence of misinformation on information-seeking behavior. Prior to joining Purdue in 2015, Professor McGowan was a health sciences librarian at Howard University (2011–2015) and a

Congressional Fellow at the Library of Congress Congressional Research Service (2010).

LaQuanda T. Onyemeh (MLIS, Med) is a training and consulting partner at ProQuest. LaQuanda's primary responsibility is to educate customers on digital technologies that enhance discovery, sharing, and data management across North America. She is also the proud owner of She Creates Tech LLC, a web design and creative consulting agency specializing in content creation and instructional technology support services for educators, visionaries, and burgeoning entrepreneurs. Prior to her current roles, LaQuanda was employed as a mental health professional for eight years, teacher, and academic librarian. LaQuanda earned a dual Bachelor of Science in Psychology and Sociology from State University of New York, Brockport. She received a Master of Library of Information Studies from the University of North Carolina, Greensboro, and a Master of Education in Educational Technology from Texas A&M University. She is a 2017–2018 ALA Spectrum Scholar, 2018 NASIG's John Riddick Student Grant Recipient, and 2020 past chair of American Library Association NMRT Online Programs Committee. She cofounded WOC+Lib in April 2019.

Satia Orange (MLIS) was the director of OLOS from 1997–2009, and, under Orange's passionate leadership and advocacy, OLOS broadened the association's support and celebration of traditionally underserved library staff and library communities, developed new ALA member units, and increased participation in events and activities, including the initiation of the annual Dr. Martin Luther King Jr. Sunrise Celebration, Joint Conference for Librarians of Color (JCLC), and Bookmobile Day at ALA Annual. Through these initiatives and cooperation from ALA members and affiliates, Orange was able to increase member engagement across ALA. Orange was the driving force behind the inception of the Sunrise Celebration as well as its continued observance as a revered tradition at midwinter. In 2017, Orange was honored with the American Library Association Ethnic and Multicultural Information Exchange Round Table (EMIERT) Distinguished Librarian Award.

Teresa A. Quick (MS Ed) is currently a K–12 school librarian in New Jersey. She is an active member of BCALA serving as meeting recorder for the International Relations Committee. She is currently part of the 2022 JCLC Preconference and Keynote Committee and a member of IFLA, GNRT, and SLA. Teresa was a panelist at the 2019 New York Comic Con #ownvoices panel. Teresa blogs @Ms_Quick_Picks reviewing global children's literature and international librarianship. Teresa is working on her first children's book and pursuing an MSLIS degree.

Cheryl R. Small (EdD) is the central library administrator at Fulton County Library in Atlanta, Georgia. Cheryl is experienced as a public librarian, including an international caveat as academic librarian with the University of the West Indies, Cave Hill Campus, Barbados, and volunteer research librarian with the Barbados Museum and Historical Society, Barbados. She is a graduate of the Harvard Academic Librarian Leadership Institute and holds a doctorate from Pepperdine University in organizational leadership. Cheryl's career and studies have focused on informal learning practices in public libraries, STEM, and digital inclusion. Cheryl is a STEM believer, with literacy at the core of all learning.

Jahala Simuel (MIS, MLS) began her library career in 2004 when she accepted the position of head of reference and adjunct professor (CIS) at Shaw University. She is currently head of access services and medical librarian at the Louis Stokes Health Sciences Library at Howard University. She received her BS degree from Saint Augustine's University and her MIS and MLS from North Carolina Central University. She holds professional memberships with the American Library Association (ALA) and the Medical Library Association (MLA) and serves on various committees in both organizations. Her research interests include health literacy, community outreach, health disparities, and information literacy.

Jamillah Scott-Branch (MLIS) is the assistant director of library services at the North Carolina Central University (NCCU) James E. Shepard Memorial Library. In this role, she oversees research and instructional services, government documents, the music library, and the curriculum materials center. In addition, she supports the director of library services with strategic planning, staff, and budget management and provides support with recruitment, hiring, and performance management. Previously, she held positions as head of research and instructional services at NCCU and technology and media services librarian at Elizabeth City State University, and she has worked for several nonprofit organizations and in retail management. She holds a Master of Library Science from NCCU and a BA in English Literature from Fisk University. Jamillah currently serves as an adjunct faculty member within NCCU's University College.

Kai Smith (MLIS) is the architecture and planning librarian at the Massachusetts Institute of Technology. Before joining MIT libraries, she worked for Cal Poly Pomona, where she liaised with the College of Environmental Design, which included departments such as architecture, landscape architecture, urban and regional planning, and art history, among others. She started as an art practitioner in sculpture, photography, and painting and studied art history. Kai has specialized as an architecture, art, design, and urban planning librarian for over eight years and has experience in a variety of libraries, including academic, museum, government, and public libraries. Past employers include the University of Notre Dame, University of Michigan, City University of New York (CUNY)'s Graduate Center, Housatonic Community College, and the Pequot Library, among others. Kai interned at the Avery Architecture and Fine Arts Library at Columbia University, National Gallery of Art, Whitney Museum, Smithsonian's Biodiversity Heritage Library, American Museum of Natural History, and Barnard College.

Regina Renee Ward (EdM, MLIS) is a former public school teacher and is currently working as the manager of reference and readers' advisory in Pueblo, Colorado. She is a social justice librarian, an educator, and a self-proclaimed library geek. She is passionate about intellectual freedom, books, and the reading experience. Between careers in education and librarianship, Regina Renee served as a Peace Corps volunteer, where she worked abroad to provide equal access to information and resources. She is the treasurer of the Colorado Black Library Association and an affiliate of the Black Caucus of the American Library Association, of which she is an executive board member.